Texas

Dick J. Reavis
Photography by Will van Overbeek

COMPASS AMERICAN GUIDES
An Imprint of Fodor's Travel Publications, Inc.

Texas

Copyright © 1995 Fodor's Travel Publications, Inc.
Maps Copyright © 1995 Fodor's Travel Publications, Inc.

LIBRARY OF CONGRESS CATALOGING-IN-PUBLICATION DATA
Reavis, Dick.
Texas /by Dick J. Reavis: photography by Will van Overbeek.
   p. cm. —(Compass American Guides)
   Includes bibliographical references and index
   ISBN 1-878867-64-4 (paper): $17.95
   1. Texas—Guidebooks. I. Title II. Series: Compass American Guides (Series)
   F 384.3.R43 1994   94-27287
   917.6404'63—dc20   CIP

Although the Publisher and the Author of this book have made every effort to ensure the information was correct at the time of going to press, the Publisher and the Author do not assume and hereby disclaim any liability to any party for any loss or damage caused by errors, omissions, misleading information, or any potential travel disruption due to labor or financial difficulty, whether such errors or omissions result from negligence, accident, or any other cause.

Editors: Kit Duane, Julia Dillon, Jessica Fisher   Designers: Christopher Burt,
Managing Editor: Kit Duane   Candace Compton-Pappas
Photo Editor: Christopher Burt   Map Design: Mark Stroud

Compass American Guides, 6051 Margarido Drive, Oakland, CA 94618
Production Houses: Tulip, Berkeley, CA; Twin Age Ltd., Hong Kong   Printed in China
10 9 8 7 6 5 4 3 2 1

ACKNOWLEDGMENTS

The Publisher gratefully acknowledges the following institutions and individuals for the use of their photographs and/or illustrations on the following pages: **Zbigniew Bzdak** p. 90; **Center for American History, Univ. of Texas, Austin** pp. 23, 24, 30, 32, 39, 63, 72, 73, 138, 166, 173, 182, 187, 233, 237, 252; **Austin History Center, Austin Public Library** pp. 21, 164; **Witte Museum, San Antonio** pp. 177, 188; **Union Pacific Railroad Museum Collection, Omaha** p. 230; **Scurry County Museum, Snyder** p. 250; **East Texas Oil Museum, Kilgore College** p. 109; **Smithsonian Institute, National Museum of American Art** p. 59; **Permian Basin Petroleum Museum, Midland** pp. 49, 68; **Standard Oil (NJ) Collection, Photo Archives, Univ. of Louisville, Ekstrom Library** p. 100; **Rosenberg Library, Galveston** p. 128; **Western History Collections, Univ. of Oklahoma** pp. 186, 241; **Corpus Christi Public Library, Local History Room** p. 199; **Library of Congress** pp. 9, 257; **Texas State Library, Archives Division, Austin** p. 127; **The Texas Collection, Baylor Univ.,Waco** pp. 101, 110; **R.W. Norton Art Gallery, Shreveport** p. 144; **Fort Bend Museum, Richmond, Texas** p. 142; **Catholic Archives of Texas, Austin** p. 195; **Underwood Archives, San Francisco** pp. 46, 125. The Publisher is especially grateful to the following people for their generosity in contributing their valuable experience and scholarship to this guide: Anne Dingus for her expert reading; Chuck Lawliss for his essay "Back in the Saddle"; John McChesney for his piece "Doomsday in Dallas," which appears courtesy of National Public Radio; John Geraci for his piece on Austin; Patti Belichick for the fact pages; Donna Coates and John Slate at the Center for American History, University of Texas at Austin; Candace Coar for proofreading; Sara Deseran, Debi Dunn and Joe Malina for research.

To the original Dick Reavis, my dad, without whose inspiration and hard work this guide wouldn't have been possible.

C O N T E N T S

CHAPTER
DIVISIONS

Maps

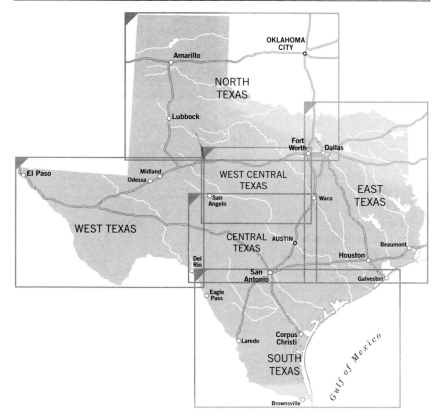

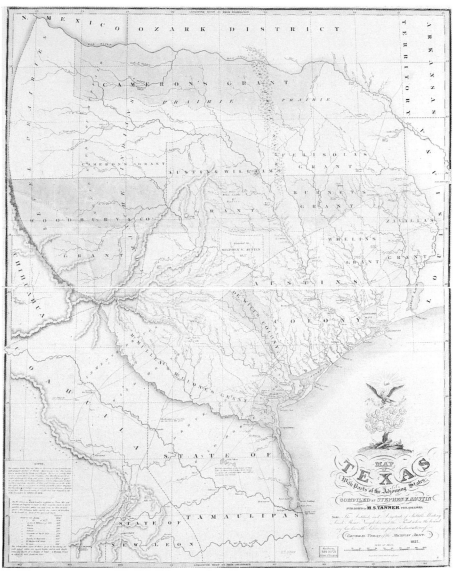

A map compiled by Stephen F. Austin in 1837 depicts the Texas-Mexico border along the Nueces River well north of today's division along the Rio Grande, identified on this map as the Rio Bravo. (Library of Congress)

Literary Extracts

AUTHOR'S ACKNOWLEDGMENTS

Lots of people write and study about Texas, but not many study and write about Texas all the time. In compiling a book like this, one quickly learns who they are, and even if you've known them for years, you come into a more thorough appreciation of their work. In preparing this book, I've learned from several of these masters of Texas: Jan Reid, Gary Cartwright, Anne Dingus, Mike Cochran, Don Graham, Laura Miller, Richard Zelade, Carol Countryman, John Davidson, Pam Diamond, Steven Harrigan, Carlos Guerra, Sandy Sheehy, Bryan Wooley, Susan Chadwick, Paul Burka, and Jan Jarboe among them. I hope that this guide qualifies me to stay in such company.

Will van Overbeek would like to thank Mary Wasiak for her tireless efforts in planning and organizing his photography for this book.

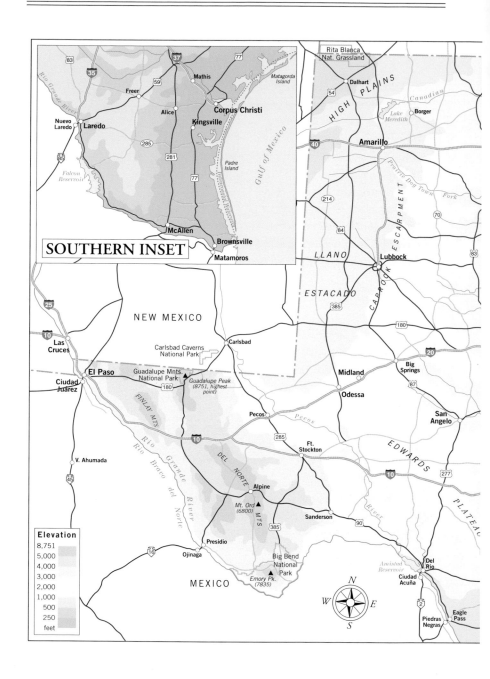

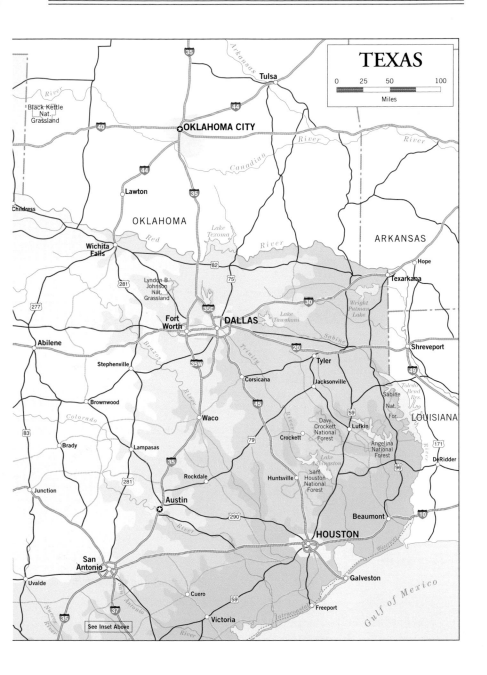

TEXAS

0   25   50   100
Miles

FACTS ABOUT TEXAS

THE LONE STAR STATE

Capital:	Austin
State Flower:	bluebonnet
Became a Republic:	1836
Entered Union:	1845
Joined Confederacy:	1861
Rejoined Union:	1870

The Lone Star design probably derives from a Masonic symbol

*Armadillo, a burrowing, generally nocturnal mammal encased in bony plates. A Texas mascot.

FIVE LARGEST CITIES:

Houston	1,630,600
Dallas	1,006,900
San Antonio	935,900
El Paso	515,400
Austin	465,700

POPULATION (1991): 17,348,200

White	75.2%
Black	11.9%
Hispanic	25.5%*
Asian/Pacific	0.7%
Native American	0.2%

*Population of Hispanic origin is an ethnic grouping and not additive to the population racial groupings

GEOGRAPHY:

Size:	268,601 sq mi (770,885 sq km) 2nd largest state
Highest point:	8,749 feet (2,651 m) Guadalupe Peak
Lowest point:	sea level (Gulf of Mexico)

CLIMATE:

Highest temp. recorded	120° F (49° C) at Seymore on Aug. 12, 1936
Lowest temp. recorded	-23° F (-30° C) at Seminole on Feb. 8, 1933
Wettest place	55" annual rainfall avg. at Bon Weir
Driest place	7.8" annual rainfall avg. at Presidio

*I*n 1901, the Spindletop well came in. During its first year, it produced 3 million barrels of oil

ECONOMY:

Principal industries: manufacturing, tourism, crude oil

Principal crops: cotton, grain, vegetables, pecans, and citrus fruits

Texas leads the nation in the production of livestock, cotton, rice, and crude oil (25% of U.S. production)

Per capita income: $12,904 (32nd highest)

*S*am
Houston

FAMOUS TEXANS:

Alvin Ailey, James Bowie, Carol Burnett, George Bush, Joan Crawford, Dwight D. Eisenhower, Buddy Holly, Sam Houston, Howard R. Hughes, Lyndon B. Johnson, Janis Joplin, Lyle Lovett, Mary Martin, Steve Martin, Audie Murphy, Willie Nelson, Katherine Anne Porter, Sam Rayburn, Nolan Ryan, Sissy Spacek, Tommy Tune

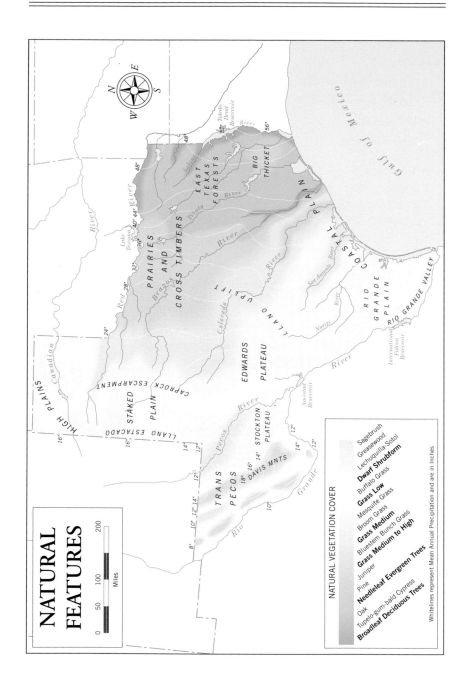

NATURAL FEATURES

Miles
0   50   100   200

NATURAL VEGETATION COVER

Sagebrush
Greasewood
Lechuquilla-Sotol
Dwarf Shrubform
Buffalo Grass
Grass Low
Mesquite Grass
Broom Grass
Grass Medium
Bluestem Bunch Grass
Grass Medium to High
Juniper
Pine
Needleleaf Evergreen Trees
Oak
Tupelo-gum-bald Cypress
Broadleaf Deciduous Trees

Whitelines represent Mean Annual Precipitation and are in Inches

O V E R V I E W

TEXAS IS LIKE THE ELEPHANT THAT THE BLIND MEN EXAMINED. To the traveler who's seen its western extremes, Texas is mountainous desert. The passerby on the High Plains believes that Texas is very much like Kansas, a newly settled land of wheat fields. Pine trees, paper mills, and Confederate flags make East Texas look much like Mississippi, and on its southern boundaries, Texas seems to be a very well-paved version of northern Mexico.

The naturalist regards Texas as a diverse assemblage of desert, wetlands, and plains ecosystems, separated by geological shifts and escarpments. To rock climbers, Texas is a place of desert handholds; for teenagers, it's a cluster of amusement and theme parks. For Generation X, Austin is the Emerald City, and to television viewers worldwide Dallas is the home of oil barons and wives with big hair. Those who live in the endless suburbs of its cities see the state as a free-wheeling, big-spending, exhilarating land of glitz and unpredictable economic indicators.

For cocaine traffickers, Texas is a porous borderland, while the marijuana wholesalers see it as a vast plantation. For the true-crime buff, Texas is the land of Bonnie and Clyde, Machine Gun Kelly, and Lee Harvey Oswald. Hollywood de-picts Texas as Cowboyland, New York writes that Texas is a redoubt of bigots and gun nuts, and Washington gives Texas the greeter's job when Congress names itself Good Neighbor to Mexico.

Since most Texans know only a part of the state, we shrug our shoulders and wonder what Texas really is. With so many vast regions and sometimes contradic-tory images, it can't be any other way. Consensus is never reached even among those natives who are widely traveled and widely read. So we all simplify, generalize, and jump to our own conclusions, making Texas mean something a little bit different to each of us.

The task of defining Texas falls most heavily upon historians, yet many natural events and agricultural developments that continue to shape Texans' lives occurred well before the arrival of Europeans here. Nobody witnessed Texas rise from an uncharted spot of ocean floor, though that distant event was the basis of the state's twentieth-century role as an oil producer. Nor did anyone record the coming of the human species to the turf, nor the important centuries of agricultural experimenta-tion that followed. Herbalists, hunters, agriculturists, and statesmen crossed and made use of this landscape. When Europeans—and recorded history—arrived, more than 50 small tribes were living in Texas, but they were rapidly decimated by the diseases that explorers, colonists, and priests introduced.

■ SPANISH COLONIAL ERA

The state's name tells part of the story. Texas is a latter-day spelling of the Spanish colonial term Tejas, which was a transliteration of a word (*taysha*) used by some groups of Indians from the East Texas Caddo civilization to mean "friend." The Caddo were settled people, keepers of orchards. Those who did not die from disease or depredation during the Spanish colonial period were driven out of Texas in 1859, and today, no remnants of the state's indigenous peoples remain inside the state's boundaries. Two of the three Indian tribes in Texas recognized by the federal government—the Kickapoo and Alabama-Coushatta—immigrated to the region, as the European population did. The third tribe, the Tigua, who today count some 1,200 members, apparently left the area, adopted Christianity in New Mexico, and returned to Texas during the Spanish occupation, in flight from unconverted, rebel brethren. Those tribes known for having ruled over much of the state during the nineteenth century, the Apache and Comanche, also came to Texas on the run. At no point in the state's recorded history was its surface wiped clean of human population and begun anew, but the aboriginal population was very nearly erased.

Spanish attempts to Christianize the Indians and colonize the area were tepid at best. The oldest Texas mission, at Ysleta in El Paso, was founded in 1681 for the Tigua refugees. Scattered settlements arose in East, South, and Central Texas, but none was populous, wildly prosperous, or able to defend itself from hostile designs. The Apache wiped out dozens of them, crops failed when rain didn't come, hurricanes blew them away, plagues brought their populations low. Unlike a few spots in equally forlorn northern Mexico, in Texas no important lodes of gold or silver were found, nothing to inspire feverish immigration or heroic works. But if the Spanish failed to make Texas a populous place, they accomplished much more than the French, who for five years exercised a pretentious and empty claim to sovereignty over the area. French influence in Texas is and was negligible, and where it is evident, owes its strength to Cajuns, immigrants who arrived via Louisiana from Canada, and not to schemes hatched to "benefit the continent."

Mission San Francisco de la Espada near San Antonio was built between
1731 and 1756 during the height of the Spanish colonial period.

■ BASIC DATES IN TEXAS HISTORY ■

1521 Conquistador Hernando Cortes subdues the Aztec empire. Mexico, including Texas, will become a part of the Spanish colonial empire.

1528 A crew of Spaniards are shipwrecked on the Texas coast. Led by Alvar Núñez Cabeza de Vaca, they begin European exploration of the territory.

1681 First permanent settlement established by Spaniards, at Ysleta (near El Paso).

1685 Rene Robert Cavelier Sieur de la Salle and his subordinates, shipwrecked on the Texas Gulf, claim Texas as French territory. Five years later, France cedes its claim to Spain.

1718 San Antonio de Valero mission (the Alamo) is established.

1759 The mission of San Saba de la Santa Cruz is destroyed by the Comanches. The Spanish are humiliated by the defeat—an event that signals their weakening control of the territory.

1819 American adventurers invade Texas, declare independence from Spain, and are suppressed.

1821 Mexico wins independence. Stephen F. Austin brings first Anglo-American colonists to Texas.

1826 Texas Rangers are created by American settlers in Mexican Texas.

1835 Texas Revolution begins at the Battle of Gonzales on October 2.

1836 In the Battle of the Alamo, Americans (including James Bowie and Davy Crockett) are outnumbered by Mexicans 40 to 1, but hold off Gen. Antonio López de Santa Anna for 13 days before being annihilated.

Sam Houston defeats Santa Anna at the Battle of San Jacinto. Texas becomes a republic.

Houston and Austin run for presidency; Houston wins.

1839 Capital moved from Houston to Austin.

1845 Texas admitted to the United States; Mexican War begins.

1848 Mexico cedes the American Southwest, including Texas, to the United States in the Treaty of Guadalupe Hidalgo.

1861 Texas secedes from the United States and joins the Confederacy.

1865 The Union reclaims Texas and abolishes slavery on June 19. (Emancipation Day is now celebrated throughout the state as Juneteenth.)

1866   First oil well drilled in Texas when Lyne Barret in Nacogdoches County devises first rotary drill.

      First cattle drives to northern markets.

1871   Greatest trail drive in history moves 700,000 head of cattle from Texas to Kansas.

1874   State government commissions Texas Rangers to patrol Texas borders.

1901   Oil discovered under the Spindletop dome. First oil boom begins.

1910   Mexican Revolution is declared by exiles in San Antonio. Twenty years of bloodshed ensue; refugees settle in Texas.

1930   East Texas oil field comes in, second oil boom begins. Lasts eight years.

1963   Vice President and Texan Lyndon B. Johnson becomes President when John F. Kennedy is assassinated in Dallas.

1969   First words spoken from the moon are "Mission Control, Houston," July 20.

1973   Arab oil embargo declared, new oil boom begins. Lasts eight years.

1988   George Bush elected U.S. President. Encourages Mexico to join the United States and Canada in signing the North American Free Trade Agreement (NAFTA). Six years later NAFTA becomes effective.

The birthplace of a republic: the first capitol house of Texas was built in the long-gone town of Columbia in 1836. (Austin History Center, Public Library)

■ REPUBLIC OF TEXAS

The Spanish lost what little control they had over Texas in 1821, when their empire lost Mexico, and Mexico, at the time, was too involved in central and southern intrigues to turn attention to its sparsely populated northern areas, including Texas. Had it not been for land hunger in the neighboring United States, the nineteenth century in Texas might have faded away as unnoticed as it opened. But instead, in 1819, a gang of American freebooters, known to historians as the Long Expedition, captured the Spanish settlement at Nacogdoches, in East Texas, and declared the independence of Texas. The uprising failed, but it heralded a momentum that ultimately succeeded. Texas became a place where Anglo, or British-origin, influences dominated, leaving unresolved for future settlement its links to the rest of the hemisphere.

The American and British immigrants who began settling in Texas in 1821 favored Anglo-American jurisprudence, Protestantism, decentralism, and slavery—none of which the Spanish and Mexican governments allowed. Some settlers were content with the Mexican government and others were opposed to extension of slavery and converted to Catholicism in order to own land. The Mexican constitution of 1824 was in tune with the political idealism sweeping the continent—a belief that more egalitarian and democratic societies would take root and European corruption and authoritarianism could be

TEXAS FOREVER!!

The usurper of the South has failed in his efforts to enslave the freemen of Texas.

The wives and daughters of Texas will be saved from the brutality of Mexican soldiers.

Now is the time to emigrate to the Garden of America.

A free passage, and all found, is offered at New Orleans to all applicants. Every settler receives a location of

EIGHT HUNDRED ACRES OF LAND.

On the 23d of February, a force of 1000 Mexicans came in sight of San Antonio, and on the 25th Gen. St. Anna arrived at that place with 2500 more men, and demanded a surrender of the fort held by 150 Texians, and on the refusal, he attempted to storm the fort, twice, with his whole force, but was repelled with the loss of 500 men, and the Americans lost none. Many of his troops, the liberals of Zacatecas, are brought on to Texas in irons and are urged forward with the promise of the women and plunder of Texas.

The Texian forces were marching to relieve St. Antonio, March the 2d. The Government of Texas is supplied with plenty of arms, ammunition, provisions, &c. &c.

A poster in 1836 pleads for help to thwart the advance of Santa Anna's troops on San Antonio. (Center for American History, University of Texas)

(left) Ruins of the old courthouse in Van Horn.

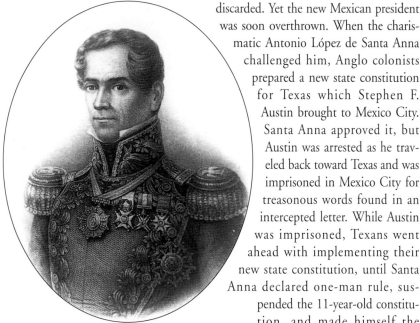

Antonio López de Santa Anna.
(Center for American History, University of Texas)

discarded. Yet the new Mexican president was soon overthrown. When the charismatic Antonio López de Santa Anna challenged him, Anglo colonists prepared a new state constitution for Texas which Stephen F. Austin brought to Mexico City. Santa Anna approved it, but Austin was arrested as he traveled back toward Texas and was imprisoned in Mexico City for treasonous words found in an intercepted letter. While Austin was imprisoned, Texans went ahead with implementing their new state constitution, until Santa Anna declared one-man rule, suspended the 11-year-old constitution, and made himself the dictator of Mexico.

The colony rebelled, and Santa Anna set out from Mexico City to reconquer it. The result, in 1836, was independence, though there is no agreement about whether it came by revolution or invasion. Most Texans regard the men who died at the Alamo and Goliad as revolutionary martyrs, but the flag that Davy Crockett and his crew flew over the Alamo today rests in Mexico City's Museum of Foreign Invasions.

At the town of Independence, Texas became a republic, not because its leaders or people favored the move, but largely because political arrangements in Washington precluded the admission of new slave-holding states. The nine-year history of the Republic of Texas was marked mainly by factional fights and penury, and most of the population was gratified when, in December 1845, Texas was allowed to join the United States. The Republic of Texas and Mexico had never settled a boundary line, and as soon as Texas was admitted, American troops put the issue to a test, by crossing the Nueces River, the line Mexico honored, en route to the

Rio Grande, the boundary claimed by Texas. The Mexican War ensued. In a few short months, the United States conquered its neighbor to the south, extracting nearly half of Mexico's land area as the price of peace.

■ CIVIL WAR

Fewer than one in four families in the state owned slaves in 1860, when the Texas electorate voted to secede from the Union. The decision was controversial; Sam Houston—Father of the Republic and the state governor—opposed it, as presumably the state's 200,000 slaves, a third of the population, would have done. Nonetheless the vote to secede carried by a margin of 76 percent. During the Civil War years, Texas did not, like Georgia or Mississippi, experience military defeat. Except for El Paso, it was still in Confederate hands, and was largely unscathed, when the surrender at Appomattox was signed. The war's last battle was fought near Brownsville, not because Confederate troops in Texas were diehards, but because they had not yet heard that their cause had been lost. The upshot of the Civil War was that, though Texas contributed heavily to Confederate military forces, and though its economy was for a time key to the Confederacy's survival, the prosperous classes in Texas were not ruined, nor were its slaves freed, until after the shooting ended.

■ CATTLE AND OIL

Thanks to cattle, Texas began a new life more quickly than the former Confederate states to its east. No sooner had the war ended than ranchers in Texas began driving herds to new markets in Kansas and Missouri, where they were shipped east for slaughter. The great cattle drives forever fixed the cowboy in the nation's mythology, and fixed him most prominently in Texas. But the myth in Texas was whiter and richer than the reality. If, in the rest of the West, six out of seven cowboys were white, freedmen and Mexicans were arguably the majority among Texas cowboys, although many of the state's great ranches belonged to British financial interests. Railroads, owned by Eastern financiers, some of whom briefly lived in Texas, put the trail drivers out of business within 15 years. There are still cowboys in Texas, but today they account for less than one percent of the state's population, and most of the 18 million people in Texas have never mounted a horse.

By the time that the open range was fenced and the railroads displaced cattle drivers, Texas was entering a new phase of its life as the nation's principal supplier of oil. In 1901, the Spindletop well, which came at a time when steam power was giving way to petroleum fuels, put Texas on the map. The coming of the automobile assured that oil, not ranching, would be the principal source of income in Texas. For the rest of the century, more ranchers remained solvent because of the wells on their property than the cattle running across it.

The oil boom that visited Texas was not merely a one-state affair. It touched Oklahoma and Louisiana as well. Perhaps more importantly for Texas, oil was discovered in Tampico, Mexico, in 1901, and by 1920, Mexico was supplying a fourth of the world's needs. But the big Mexican finds petered out, and in 1938, Mexico expropriated the British and American interests who owned its wells. Under government ownership, production declined, and by 1970, Mexico was importing rather than exporting oil.

The epoch of Texas history that was dominated by oil ended in 1981, as a consequence of both nature and economics. No great new fields have been discovered in Texas since 1930, and existing fields were largely plumbed by the time of the Arab oil embargo of 1973. Most of the activity from the last Texas boom was offshore, and in holes subjected to secondary and tertiary recovery—steaming oil from the walls of wells that previously had been pumped dry, for example. Though there's still oil in Texas, the cost of bringing it out of the ground now averages nearly $20 a barrel, more than twice the cost in 1970, and at a price that is prohibitive in the buyer's market of today.

Among the events that drew the curtain on the Texas oil industry was the announcement, in 1976, of vast new inland and offshore reserves in Mexico. The oil market, dominated since 1970 by Arabs, Soviets, Venezuelans, and Texans, had written off the Mexican boom of the early century as an episode without sequel. But the Mexicans soon displaced the Texans, and political dissolution removed the Soviets from the leaders' list. For 150 years, Mexico had smoldered in resentment at its loss of Texas, but after 1976, it looked—for a time—as if Mexico were buying Texas back. Houston and Midland, the state's oil centers, were flooded with Mexican businessmen and pesos, as Mexico rebuilt its state-owned oil industry. As its own production declined, Texas became the principal provider of equipment and expertise to the Mexican industry, and to the rest of the world: Texas crews operated offshore rigs and supplied refineries from Saudi Arabia to the North Sea to the Yucatán. The resulting glut sent oil prices plummeting, from nearly $35 a

Pump jacks dot the countryside in the remaining oil-producing regions of Texas.

barrel in 1981 to less than $15 in 1986. Exploration and drilling ceased in Texas, and recession set in. In Mexico, which had borrowed even more heavily to finance its boom, a full-blown depression began despite climbing production levels, and Mexican purchasing power fell 60 percent.

One of the remedies sought by both Texas and Mexico for the oil bust was the adoption of the North American Free Trade Agreement. NAFTA, which went into effect in 1994, promised to turn Mexico into a giant workshop for goods to be sold in the U.S. and Canada. It also promised to resurrect Texas as Mexico's shipper and supplier. Texas volunteered to be the doorman for Mexico, and persuaded Congress to open the American house to Mexican-made goods.

The scheme draws on the established success of Mexico's *maquiladora* program, which allowed American manufacturers to use Mexican labor in assembling products for sale in the United States without paying the usual import taxes. Between 1964 and 1994, the *maquila* program brought more industry to border cities on the south bank of the Rio Grande than the towns on its American bank had ever seen. Televisions and automobiles are now manufactured only a stone's throw away from Texas ranches where, even today, electric lines are few and far between. But the prosperity that the *maquilas* heralded for Mexico did not materialize. That country's millions, including those who work for *maquila* plants, continue to live in Third World poverty.

■ CHANGING FACE OF TEXAS

From the end of the Civil War until 1980, Texas relied on agriculture and natural resources to survive, but since 1980, Texas, like the rest of the United States, has itself undergone an economic transformation, having entered an epoch of de-industrialization.

In the midst of this national confusion, some of the coastal and border states—Florida, California, and Texas—have begun to redefine themselves, too, as links in a newly globalized economy: Florida, to South America; California, to East Asia; and Texas, to Mexico. If, in the world now in the making (thanks to NAFTA), Mexico becomes the Western Hemisphere's manufacturing center, Texas will become its commercial, cultural, and political annex. Although Texas is second to California in receiving most of Mexico's legal and illegal immigrants, Texas is Mexico's chief port of entry, chief trading partner, and principal destination of its overseas tourism and investment.

W E S T T E X A S

THE FAR WESTERN END, or Trans-Pecos region, of Texas is the state's most mythical part. Even though few Texans live there, and fewer really know what the place is like, Hollywood has so often used the region as a Texas backdrop that to most movie and TV audiences, the Trans-Pecos *is* Texas. And while the dry desert region is a far cry from the more densely populated areas most Texans inhabit, it does symbolize for many Texans the wide-open, rough-and-ready quality they attribute to their state.

The region is some 30,000 miles (76,800 km) square, about the size of South Carolina or about three times the size of New Hampshire. Yet excluding its only city—El Paso, which sits on its western edge—less than 60,000 people inhabit the place. While measuring the American West, the U.S. Census Bureau determined that an area was "settled" when its population density exceeded six persons per square mile. By those terms, the Trans-Pecos is still frontier. Four of its nine counties—Hudspeth, Culberson, Jeff Davis, and Terrell—have more square miles than people. The area seems a great empty space, an expanse of caliche and rock surrounded by dry mountains.

Even the region's name speaks for that: "Trans-Pecos" might refer to the region lying on either the eastern or western side of the Pecos River, depending on the namer's point of view. Trans-Pecos defines the area on the western side—because there are too few people on that side to name anything.

The Trans-Pecos is as isolated as any area in the United States. Residents of **Presidio,** for example—reputed to be the nation's hottest spot, with summer temperatures often reaching 110° F (45° C)—must drive five hours to the nearest commercial airport at Midland-Odessa. Their daily bread comes from El Paso, another five hours away. People who live in this town of 3,000 drive 90 miles (150 km) to pick up a pizza, 60 miles (100 km) to play a round of golf, and 230 miles (370 km) to attend a district football game. The leading daily in Presidio is the *San Angelo Standard-Times,* whose Sunday edition doesn't reach town until Monday, when the mail arrives.

People who live in tiny **Redford,** 40 miles (65 km) downriver, must drive into Presidio, or 34 miles (55 km) into **Lajitas** (half the size of Redford), over a rough, winding road, to buy postage stamps. The drive over Texas Farm-to-Market Road 170, from Presidio to Lajitas through Redford, is one of the prettier ones in the state. The pavement snakes, climbs, and dives. On one side stand red, rocky canyon walls; on the other fall steep banks leading down to the Rio Grande. On this road, and others in the Trans-Pecos, isolation has its virtues, but can be downright frightening too. Four Trans-Pecos counties have no doctors, and even emergency crews can't reach Redford in less than a half-hour's time.

For a stretch of more than 250 miles (400 km) along the Rio Grande, from the roadless space between Candelaria and McNary on the west, to Langtry on the eastern edge of the Trans-Pecos, settlement south of the river is just as sparse. The long boundary line has only one international bridge, complete with customs house and immigration offices, connecting Presidio with the Mexican town of **Ojinaga,** where medical and dental care is available. Elsewhere along the empty stretch, border crossings are strictly unofficial. At the end of FM 2627, for example, lies a blacktop-covered concrete bridge—but there's nothing on the other side except the mining camp at La Linda, in the Mexican state of Coahuila. Farm-to Market-Road 2627 exists not to take Americans to Mexico, but to get Mexican miners out into Texas, as no roads connect La Linda to any other place in Mexico. Over the rest of the Trans-Pecos border span, footbridges cross the Rio Grande,

High Bridge soars 320 feet (98 m) over the Pecos River.
(Center for American History, University of Texas)

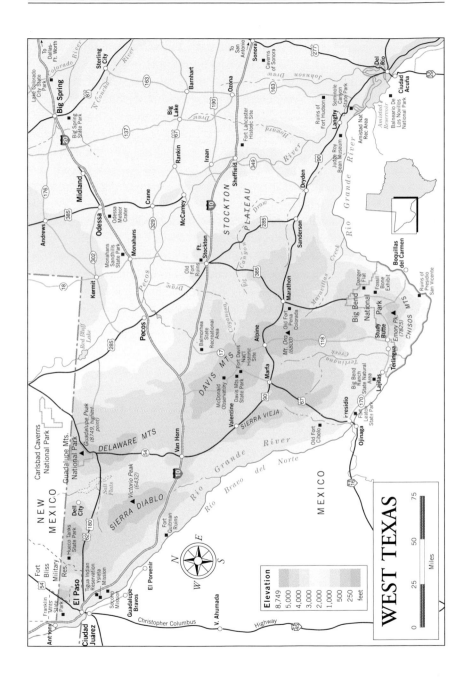

WEST TEXAS

which is only yards wide in this part of the state; and where footbridges haven't been stretched, horses and rowboats carry passengers across.

On the south bank, the villages clustered along the river—Monte Bustillos, Valle Nuevo, Loma Juarez, Santa Elena—number their inhabitants in the dozens. Their denizens earn their livings as shepherds, or by processing the wax of cactus-like candelilla plants and smuggling it into the United States, where it is used in cosmetics. Generally, buses run from these Mexican villages into the interior of Mexico only once a week, or not at all: pickups and horses ply the dirt roads out. To make a telephone call or mail a letter from these hamlets, you've got to go north across the Rio Grande.

Nonetheless, the inhabitants of these remote Mexican villages imitate the outside world. A popular bumper sticker in the Trans-Pecos reads "*Yo* ♥ Benavides." **Benavides** is a town of about 4,000 population, connected to Ojinaga only by dirt roads. Its chief tourist attraction—if it can be said to have one—is cockfighting on Sundays. A Mexican saying holds that, "In the land of the blind, the one-eyed man is king"—and in the Chihuahuan desert, Benavides is a metropolis, despite its dusty appearance.

A photo of a Mexican refugee family along the Texas-Mexico border, circa 1920.
(Center for American History, University of Texas)

A TRIBUTE TO THE SOUTHWEST

*T*he blessed rains, when they come to argue with the dryness, touch the emotions of the people as a religious experience. They are the grace coming before the bounty they promise; they call forth the dormant plants which hasten to adorn the land with flaming colors and to fill it with odors more subtle and powerful than incense. And the high air is then as fine wine.

There is mystery everywhere, of the sun and the shadows on saw-toothed mountains, or mirages on the plain, of distance by day and stars bigger than walnuts, as near as they are far, by night. . . .

[In the words of] H. M. Wormington:

There is something infectious about the magic of the Southwest. Some are immune to it, but there are others who have no resistance and who must spend the rest of their lives dreaming of the incredible sweep of the desert, of great golden mesas with purple shadows, and tremendous stars appearing at dusk in a turquoise sky.

And I one of these.

—Dr. Walter Prescott Webb, "A Tribute to the Southwest," from the inaugural ceremonies of John F. Kennedy and Lyndon B. Johnson, 1961

The great virtue of the Trans-Pecos is that people tired of the urban rat race can go here to get away from it all—and really get away. It's the only place in Texas where drivers don't need rearview mirrors and can hog the road: on routes other than I-10, which runs through the desert between San Antonio and El Paso, a driver will likely meet less than two vehicles per hour. In the Trans-Pecos you can stop your car, shut off the engine, and hear *absolute silence*. No leaves rustle, no birds chirp, nothing disturbs the vast quiet.

Most of the people who live in the Trans-Pecos were born there and wouldn't complicate their lives by going elsewhere. But a fair share of non-natives, both tourists—in Lajitas and the Big Bend area—and urban expatriates, are scattered here and there. Contrasts between the three groups are sometimes significant. Tourists spend surplus income, natives strive to earn it, and expatriates try to ignore it, groaning that they've given up the getting-and-spending lifestyle. Many visitors to this empty region might enjoy a copy of the *New York Times,* or of *USA Today,* but they can't, because national newspapers aren't sold anywhere close by. Most of the area's expatriates came to the Trans-Pecos to get away from the news— and most of the locals, having never seen a copy of either publication, don't know what they're missing. The differences among the area's three types of inhabitants preclude much meaningful contact between them—and as long as it's that way, tourists and expatriates will continue to aid the region's economy, spending money to get to a place where there's little to buy—but much peace and quiet to be had for free.

■ HOLLYWOOD, TEXAS

We can thank Hollywood, and not Texas, for turning the Trans-Pecos into the Texas of myth. Outside Texas, and especially overseas, most people imagine Texas as a vast, open desert encircled by dry, purple mountains and inhabited by desperate, grizzled men and Victorian dance-hall women. Slightly more up-to-date characters fill the screen in *Giant* (1956), *The Last Picture Show* (1971), *Paris, Texas* (1983), and *Fandango* (1985), but none of them much resemble your every-day Texan. (Paris, Texas, it might be noted, is located in northeastern Texas, not in the Trans-Pecos. But the name is catchy, and the movie makes reference to the protagonist's birth in Paris, while showing us his life in the Trans-Pecos and Houston.) Most Texans—who've never visited the Trans-Pecos—view Hollywood's movies with a certain puzzlement: You mean that's where I live? That's how I'm supposed to act?

Purple mountains and desert scenes are so deeply embedded in the public's image of Texas that advertisers and illustrators often choose the saguaro cactus to symbolize the state. But there are not now, nor have there ever been, any saguaro cacti in Texas: it's a species of the Sonoran desert and Arizona (that other setting for the Hollywood Westerns).

Yet while the inaccurate Hollywood portrait of Texas-as-Trans-Pecos makes Texans uneasy, it also encourages some of them to exploit the image abroad. Texans,

MODERN COWBOY

If you visit Big Bend Park and ask for information at park headquarters, you might meet Craig Carter, who seems to be the model for Hollywood's version of Texans. Carter is a blondish, rail-thin young man, with pale eyes and windburned cheeks. Using a vocabulary rich in "ma'ams" and "sirs," he speaks with self-effacing restraint, like Jimmy Stewart. A rope and saddle are his working gear, just as you'd expect. Craig Carter is a born cowboy, all right. Since childhood he's been riding and roping from sun to sun. He's the grandson of a cowboy from this country, and he makes his home near his granddad's place near Big Bend Park. Like the cowboys of lore, Craig didn't go to school a day longer than he had to—in his case, because the nearest high school was 90 miles away. Like older generations of cowboys, Craig got his diploma by correspondence. And like them, he keeps himself amused on lonely nights by the campfire playing guitar and writing songs.

But there's a big difference between Craig and the cowpokes of his granddaddy's day. Carter is a cowboy on a family-operated dude ranch. He tends visitors on horseback as a concessionaire at the Big Bend National Park: ask for him at the park headquarters, or call him at (915) 477-2374. Be forewarned that you are likely to be attended by other members of this family. These days Craig does almost as much singing in Nashville as he does at home, and when he straps on his well-worn spurs, it's likely to be for billboard ads in places like Dallas. Craig is trying to turn his golden cowboy roots into the lead of pop stardom. However, even though it's a far piece to the nearest airport, Carter doesn't think of moving closer to the commercial world where he's seeking fame. The Trans-Pecos is his refuge, just as much as it is for the tourists he serves. "Out here," Carter says, "you may know people 250 or 300 miles away, bankers or whatever, but people know you by your reputation. But in the cities, you're just a number."

EARLY TEXAS IN LONESOME DOVE

Of course, real scouting skills were superfluous in a place as tame as Lonesome Dove, but Call still liked to get out at night, sniff the breeze and let the country talk. The country talked quiet; one human voice could drown it out, particularly if it was a voice as loud as Augustus McCrae's. Augustus was notorious all over Texas for the strength of his voice. On a still night he could be heard at least a mile, even if he was more or less whispering. Call did his best to get out of range of Augustus's voice so that he could relax and pay attention to other sounds. If nothing else, he might get a clue as to what weather was coming—not that there was much mystery about the weather around Lonesome Dove. If a man looked straight up at the stars he was apt to get dizzy, the night was so clear. Clouds were scarcer than cash money, and cash money was scarce enough.

—Larry McMurtry, *Lonesome Dove*, 1985

especially men who don't ordinarily act like John Wayne, do their best to play the part when they travel. Los Angeles, Boston, New York, and Washington are full of Texans who wouldn't wear their cowboy boots back at home, and who never wore them before they left. Hollywood-style typecasting has also made the role of the professional Texan—best-selling author and columnist Molly Ivins, and movie reviewer Joe Bob Briggs are well-known examples—a staple of national culture for at least 50 years. Interesting to note that Ivins is from Houston, and Joe Bob, whose real name is John Bloom, hails from Dallas; few people wear boots in those cities, and nobody wears spurs!

In the Trans-Pecos, though, people do wear spurs. Hollywood uses the region for its Western shoots because it truly is the Old West to this day, even if the desert supports sheep ranches and not the cattle ranches of movie lore. Men on horseback work the ranches, but drawling Jimmy Stewarts and Gary Coopers they aren't. Most of them don't speak English. Ranching as we imagine it came stateside via Mexico from the Spanish, who had in turn learned it from Arabs. In the Trans-Pecos, the tradition hasn't been anglicized yet. A rope has always been called a *lazo*, lasso being the English speaker's corruption.

Country dancing and cowboys have long been enduring images of Texas.

■ EL PASO

With its half-million residents, El Paso is the anchor of the Trans-Pecos and one of the more scenic cities in Texas. Set in a bowl of mountains that also encloses Ciudad Juárez, its sibling across the border, and filled with stucco-facade homes and Santa Fe or mock pueblo architecture, El Paso looks like a tourism poster for modern Mexico.

In some ways El Paso has more in common with cities like Monterrey, Chihuahua, and Hermosillo than with any city to its north or east. The downtown streets appear to be cobbled with squarish black stones, rather than paved with asphalt or cement. As in Mexican cities, this street-surfacing is a contemporary, not a rustic touch: black cement is poured onto the streets and a roller is passed over them, leaving the cobblestone-like imprint. El Paso has in recent years been under federal orders to improve its air quality, which has been rated the worst in the nation. The city can't do much about the situation: its air is the air of its Mexican industrial sister city, Juárez.

If El Paso shares a certain quaintness with other Mexican towns, however, parts of it reveal the impact of the border close by. El Paso's shopping malls are gargantuan, three and four times the size they'd be in a Midwestern city of the same population, because half or more of their customers come from the Mexican side of the border. Middle-aged women hang out in the city's downtown San Jacinto plaza, hawking Marlboros at about 25 percent below the American price. The cigarettes are Mexican-made, and the women, residents of Juárez who cross the river each morning, carry their wares as contraband in handbags.

Despite its Spanish, Mexican, and borderlands influences, El Paso is in other ways sufficiently American, even Midwestern enough, to make some Texocentrics cringe. A series of downtown streets is named after other states, and while other cities in Texas have a street here or there named in honor of Illinois or Oregon, none has shown such a systematic sense of nationhood as El Paso has. The city's sports obsession is the Miners, the basketball team of the University of Texas at El Paso (despite the fact that football is the rest of the state's favorite sport). No other town in Texas—not even Austin, home of the champion Lady Longhorns—cares for basketball as much as El Paso does. The city's economy also sets it apart. El Paso is the home of mining operations, which aren't important elsewhere in the state, and of footwear and garment shops, which were in earlier times located in the eastern part of the state. Perhaps destiny never meant for El Paso to share the Texas experience: alone among cities in Texas, El Paso was occupied by Union troops during the Civil War.

For most purposes, El Paso fits as easily into New Mexico as into Texas. All of Texas is in the Central Time Zone, except for the area around El Paso, which, with New Mexico, is in the Mountain Zone. Elsewhere in Texas, El Paso's Mexican cuisine is known as "New Mexico Mexican food": El Paso is the only Texas city where *sopapillas,* a dessert, are served as a part of local cuisine. In this respect El Paso is part of the Mexican desert tradition, unlike areas to the east on either side of the Rio Grande.

During the 1980s, when Texas regulations forbade intrastate shipping by the United Parcel Service, El Pasoans took their cargo 20 miles (32 km) away, to the New Mexico side of the town of Anthony, which is split by the state line. And from El Paso, it's 266 miles (428 km) north to Albuquerque, New Mexico's capital, but it's 573 miles (922 km) east to Austin, the capital of Texas. Because of this

Union officers take a lunch break near Fort Davis in West Texas during the Civil War. (Center for American History, University of Texas)

hinterland location, there's long been a faction of El Pasoans who advocate seccession from Texas, and attachment to New Mexico. But the idea isn't popular with officialdom on the other side of the state line. Texans are regarded with slight contempt in New Mexico, as well as in Colorado. For example, a bumper sticker on cars in both states reads, "If God Meant for Texans to Ski, He Would Have Made Bullshit White." New Mexico's irritation goes back to the time of the Civil War, and, despite cultural similarities, is kept alive today by demographics: if El Paso were to join New Mexico, it would be the enlarged state's biggest city—and biggest political bloc.

■ EXPLORING EL PASO

■ YSLETA

El Paso is probably the oldest existing settlement in the state. While evidence shows the presence of a prehistoric Pueblo Indian settlement, the first permanent community was founded in 1680. Spanish priests and Christianized Tigua Indians came here after being expelled by the Pueblo Rebellion, the Pueblo Indians' revolt against Catholic authority in present-day New Mexico. The Tigua, themselves of

Interior of Ysleta Mission.

(right) A mariachi band performs at El Paso's La Hacienda restaurant.

EL PASO MAIN ATTRACTIONS

■ U N I Q U E L Y   E L   P A S O

Border Patrol Museum. Exhibits include uniform, canine, and weapon displays. The memorial room commemorates agents killed on duty. Gift shop. *North-South Freeway to 4315 Woodrow Bean Transmountain Road; (915) 759-6060.*

Chamizal National Memorial. This memorial celebrates the 1968 resolution of century-long boundary disputes between Mexico and the United States. Both sides converted their land into national parks. El Paso's side houses a border history museum, theater, and graphic arts gallery. The Mexican side has been developed into acres of botanical gardens and an interesting archaeological museum. *800 South San Marcial Street; (915) 534-6277.*

The Mission Trail. Passes through El Paso's oldest Mexican and Indian districts—neighborhoods filled with notable restaurants, craft shops, and antique stores—and leads to the missions of Ysleta and Socorro, and the presidio of San Elizario. *This 12-mile (19-km) drive begins at the Zaragosa exit off I-10, southeast of downtown El Paso, and ends at FM 1110.*

Tigua Indian Reservation. A living history pueblo. The reservation museum and cultural center hosts a number of demonstrations including ceremonial dancing, weaving, pottery, and bread-baking. The grounds also house two restaurants and Ysleta Mission. *Ysleta del Sur. 119 South Old Pueblo Road., exit I-10 at Zaragosa, 15 miles (24 km) east of downtown; (915) 859-7913.*

■ H I S T O R I C   M U S E U M S   A N D   S I T E S

Concordia Cemetery. Originally divided by ethnicity, religion, and status. Behind one walled-off section are the remains of nineteenth-century Chinese laborers who built railroads in the region. Just outside that wall, in the "Boot Hill" area, lie infamous desperados such as John Wesley Hardin, a Texas thug who claimed to have killed 40 people with his six-shooter. *Just north of I-10 at the Gateway North and U.S. 54 interchange.*

El Paso Museum of History. Life-size dioramas depict the people of El Paso, past and present: Indians, Spanish explorers, cowboys, and cavalrymen. *I-10 East at the Avenue of the Americas, about 15 miles (24 km) from downtown; (915) 858-1928.*

Fort Bliss. Site of the largest air-defense establishment in the nation and headquarters for the U.S. Army Air Defense. The post also houses four military museums. The **Air Defense Artillery Museum** in Building 5000 displays anti-aircraft weapons from around the world. Located in Building 2407 is the **Cavalry Museum,** illustrating the history of the U.S. Cavalry with paintings, photos, and a collection of vehicles used since the Cavalry's founding in 1856. The **Fort Bliss Replica Museum** in building 600 is a reconstruction of the original fort as it stood 1848 to 1948. The **Museum of the Non-commissioned Officer** in Building 1133 traces the changing role of the non-commissioned officer from combat soldier to military bureaucrat. *Main Post, east of U.S. 54 and west of the El Paso International Airport; (915) 568-4505.*

Magoffin Homestead. Completed in 1875 by Joseph Magoffin, son of James Wiley Magoffin, one of El Paso's founders. Filled with ornate Victorian furnishings dating back to the original owner and adobe walls scored to look like stone, this hacienda is a remarkable combination of eastern style and southwestern construction. *1120 Magoffin Avenue; (915) 533-5147.*

Socorro Mission. Originally built in 1681 by now-extinct Piro Indians, the structure was destroyed by the Rio Grande, as was its successor. The present church was built in 1843, but several of the features, particularly the bell tower, are said to be the best representation of Spanish colonial architecture in West Texas. *FM 258 (Socorro Road) at Nevarez, about 25 minutes from downtown; (915) 859-7718.*

Wilderness Park Museum. A 17-acre, indoor-outdoor museum tracing the evolution of the region's climate and recreating the Pueblo Indian life. Outdoor trails lead visitors past replicas of a Pueblo ruin and a pithouse. *2000 Transmountain Road and Gateway South, about 15 minutes from downtown; (915) 755-4332.*

Ysleta Mission. Built by Franciscans and Tigua Indians in 1681, Ysleta is the oldest mission in Texas. The mission is a 1908 restoration erected on the original foundation. *131 South Zaragosa Street, on the Tigua Indian Reservation; (915) 859-7913.*

■ EXPLORING OUTDOORS

Hueco Tanks State Park. The 860-acre park, replete with interesting rock formations and a rich variety of flora and fauna, attracts rock-climbers, bird-watchers, and geologists (as well as everyday picnickers). Traces of ancient visitors are throughout the park, the most impressive evidence being over 2,000 pictographs (rock paintings). Archaelogists believe that humans might have inhabited the area as early as 10,000 years ago and according to Indian lore, this land is the site of Tigua Indian creation. *U.S. 62/180 east about 25 miles (40 km), then six miles (10 km) north on FM 2775; (915) 857-1135.*

Pueblo ancestry, came from Isleta, New Mexico, and with the Franciscans founded the Ysleta Mission and pueblo. Now a part of the city of El Paso, the mission stands in the 100 block of South Old Pueblo Road, about 15 minutes east of downtown, and adjoins the Tigua Indian Reservation. The tribe was so influenced by the Spanish that its internal organization included the archaic title of *caicique,* or chief, a term that the Spanish conquistadores borrowed from the Mayans. (The word is still in use south of El Paso, but its referent is usually derogatory.)

Today the Tigua, like other American Indian tribes, want to bring gambling to Ysleta. Gambling is presently forbidden on both sides of the Rio Grande, and a casino on the reservation would draw a lucrative binational trade. If the state of Texas, which is negotiating the request, doesn't permit the Tigua to operate a casino, the tribe is likely to press a land claim long ago ignored by the state legislature. If satisfied, the claim would give the tribe most of El Paso. Be on the lookout for one-armed bandits in Ysleta.

The mission at Ysleta is one of four historic religious sites in El Paso. Though founded in 1681, the buildings here and at the other venerable church sites date to reconstructions between 1843 and 1908. In San Antonio and Goliad, some colonial structures survive, but Rio Grande flooding in El Paso carried most of the city's Spanish architectural legacy to the Gulf.

Jaime Kroc at Tony Lama's famous boot factory store, one of El Paso's many thriving businesses.
(right) Martin Silva is the war captain of El Paso's Tigua Indians.

■ **ALONG THE BORDER**

El Paso is home to several unique borderlands institutions, among them the **U.S. Border Patrol Museum,** housed in a Spanish Colonial Revival building at 4315 Woodrow Bean Transmountain Road. The town was picked because so many Border Patrol agents, who serve only on the Canadian and Mexican borders, spend a part of their careers in the service's El Paso sector. The green-suited boundary scout's chief job is catching and returning Mexican entrants, who usually enter the state without immigration or tourist visas by stealth, avoiding bridges or other official entry points. Agents will tell you that their duty is a game of cat-and-mouse, in which no one gets hurt—and no would-be immigrant gets delayed very long. Most of the people halted by the Border Patrol are back in the United States within a week of their capture, or often the same day; in current practice, agents issue citations, drive their charges to the border, and watch them walk south. Ironically, returning Mexican immigrants was not the Border Patrol's duty until nearly 10 years after it was created in 1924. The Border Patrol originally came to El Paso to enforce the Oriental exclusion laws—Chinese were illegally entering the city from Mexico. In those days, Mexicans could immigrate by putting a coin in a turnstile at international bridges.

The first time that the Texas Rangers and Mexican Fiscales worked together to "suppress crime along the Rio Grande" was captured in this photo of February 1920. The Border Patrol was formed four years later. (Underwood Archives, San Francisco)

Another border institution in El Paso is **Fort Bliss,** built shortly after the end of the Mexican War, and today a facility for training soldiers to use missiles. Because the Mexican revolutionary Pancho Villa supplied his Army of the North from El Paso, and because troops who participated in the 1916 Pershing Expedition into Mexico came from this region, the base is as important to Mexican as to American history. On the facility are several museums open to the public, including a museum to the cavalry, both in its horseback and motorized incarnations, and a museum to the non-commissioned officer (read: Yes, Sergeant! As you say, Sergeant!). Also on base is the **Air Defense Artillery Museum,** devoted to rockets, with a gift shop that sells defensive missile toys. The base occupies the whole northeastern sector of El Paso, with entrances from U.S. 54.

■ EAST OF EL PASO

It's a long way from El Paso to anywhere, or from anywhere to El Paso. Two roads lead east from the city: U.S. 180/62, to the north, and I-10, the more southerly highway. Along the northern route, usually taken by travelers headed to New Mexico's Carlsbad Caverns, lies the turnoff for **Hueco Tanks State Park,** about six miles (9 km) north of the highway on FM 2775. The park is important to the Tigua Indians, whose lore says that they were created there. Tribesmen say that some of the ancient pictographs found in the park were the work of Tigua, although scholars believe that passing Apache, Comanche, and Kiowa produced most of them. Most visitors to the park, though, come for the rock climbing. The park's 300-foot (91-m) boulders are pocked with small hollows, or "huecos," important in the past because they held rain water, important today as hand- and footholds. The hollows, along with the cracked and uneven surfaces of the park's outcroppings, provide challenges for experienced and novice climbers alike. The best season for climbing is October to May; in summer months the rocks can become too hot to handle.

The nearest town of any size to the west of the park is **Dell City,** about 75 miles (120 km) east of El Paso on U.S. 180/62 and 15 miles (24 km) north of the highway on FM 1576. In spring and summer, passers-by can admire a unique juxtaposition of two landscapes: in the foreground, cotton fields; in the background, mountains. That gold and purple backdrop is **Guadalupe Mountains National Park,** home to Guadalupe Peak and El Capitán. With elevations of 8,749 feet

Guadalupe Peak is the highest point in Texas at 8,749 feet (2,666 m).

(2,666 m) and 8,085 feet (2,464 m) respectively, these are the highest patches of land in Texas. Snowfall is common in the mountains even in springtime, and windsocks affixed to road signs warn of invisible hazards. Camping is permitted, but overnight and auto facilities in the park are scant; it's a place for either the Sunday driver or the serious outdoor buff, not for a family vacation. In winter people visit the park to see snow, in fall to see the changing foliage, and in spring and summer to glimpse the smooth red bark of the madrone tree, which grows wild nowhere else in the state. A word of advice is in order, however: take water when you go. Once you step outside your auto in the Guadalupe Mountains, even in chilly months, you'll soon feel thirsty: these mountains, however green, stand above the driest climate in Texas.

The southern road out of El Paso goes through the Hudspeth County seat **Sierra Blanca,** named for the mountain range to the northeast of town. In 1881, a transcontinental railroad was formed here, when the Texas & Pacific line met the Texas & New Orleans.

Most travelers don't stop until they reach **Van Horn,** and inn-keeping is Van Horn's leading industry. There are 18 motels and 536 rooms in this town of

3,000, or about one room for every six people. (Dallas, an important convention center, has some 40,000 lodging house rooms, about one for every 25 residents.) Some travelers may be surprised to learn that most of Van Horn's inns, like those in many small towns and on by-ways across the nation, belong to (East) Indian immigrants—even the motel that, during a jingoistic, nearly racist local dispute some years ago, changed its name from Best Western Lodge to Best Western American Inn. The new name was a riposte to other operators, who were hanging signs saying "American Owned" outside of their motels!

Van Horn is especially important as a stopping-point for those travelers who are coming from the west, headed south into Big Bend National Park. After Van Horn there's not another town for 75 miles (120 km) along the Big Bend route, U.S. 90. But—though few people notice—there is a post office at a wide spot in the road named Valentine. Come February 14, the place overflows with people from across the country, all wanting a Valentine postmark on their love notes.

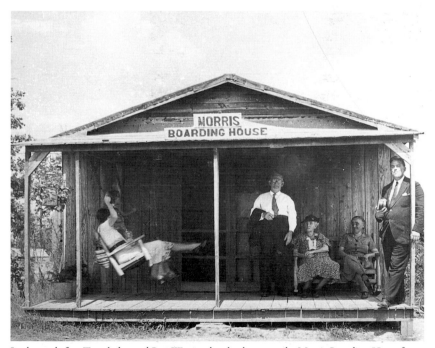

In the era before Travelodge and Best Western hotels, there was the Morris Boarding House for weary travelers. (Eugene Aimes Scrapbook, The Petroleum Museum, Midland)

The next town down the road from Van Horn, **Marfa** was named for a heroine from a Russian novel but is most widely known as the filming site for the 1956 Rock Hudson-Elizabeth Taylor-James Dean epic, *Giant.* Marfa's use as a location for the film says a lot about Hollywood's version of Texas. In the eponymous novel, from which *Giant* was scripted, Edna Ferber combines the stories of a real-life ranching family from the Gulf Coast region and of an oil wildcatter from East Texas—locales that are hundreds of miles and worlds away from Marfa. Neverthe-less, the ruins of the movie set, about 15 miles (24 km) west of town, are still an unofficial tourist attraction, and, in an unusual twist, have themselves become a minor myth in Hollywood: the set was used for filming parts of the 1985 Kevin Costner-Sam Robards film, *Fandango.*

Within the Trans-Pecos, locals know Marfa for lore of a different sort—the **Marfa Lights.** For over a century people have sporadically reported strange and transient lights in the sparsely settled area around Marfa, notably from a viewing site called Mitchell Flats, nine miles east of town. On most nights you'll see cars parked at the viewing site, their occupants scanning the skies above the mountains to the southeast. When seen, the lights appear clearly but briefly, vanishing before any pur-suit can be made. Explanations of them are speculative, and include nighttime

The mysterious Marfa Lights have been observed since the late nineteenth century.
(left) Marfa has been used as a set for many Hollywood films, including Giant.

mirages, St. Elmo's fire, natural gases that have become ignited, and even piezo-electricity—a phenomenon involving polarity and pressure. Though a few Marfa townsfolk steadfastly maintain that the lights are a hoax, for years they've provided a diversion for area teenagers—Mitchell Flats is a kind of lovers' lane—and also serve as an excuse for an annual civic shebang, the Labor Day weekend Marfa Lights Festival.

Most Big Bend travelers breeze through **Alpine,** seat of Brewster, a county larger than Connecticut, and head straight south on TX 118 to the western gates of Big Bend. But Texans are apt to linger awhile in town, because it's home to **Sul Ross University.** Despite an enrollment of only 2,500 students, the school's cowboy poetry meets, rodeo team, and agriculture program—specializing in ranching, of course—are unmatched anywhere else, giving the whole town a reputation for Texas-style coolness.

Rock collectors come into town on their way to the **Woodward Agate Ranch,** about 15 miles (24 km) south off TX 118, where they gather opal, amethyst, and other semi-precious stones from the ground. The ranch charges for finds by their weight, and for the lazy, sells sample rocks already weighed and cleaned.

Study Butte, Terlingua, and **Lajitas** are the settlements nearest Big Bend on the west. All three are revived ghost towns. Study Butte and Terlingua were founded in the early part of the century as outposts for Mexican laborers who worked mercury mines in the area. Their lives weren't anything to envy: "Many of the miners of Terlingua have never been 10 miles from the spot," the authors of the 1940 WPA guide to Texas found. The unsurpassed but venerable 1952 *Handbook of Texas* reports that Lajitas

> . . . is inhabited by Mexicans and Indians who have lived there for centuries. . . . The community took on the aspect of a village in 1915, when United States Army troops were stationed . . . to protect the Big Bend area from Francisco (Pancho) Villa's raids. . . . In 1940 the community . . . had a population of ten.

By the end of World War II, all three communities had ceased to exist.

A more modern version of the history of Lajitas would say that the place was founded in 1979, when a Houston developer built a motel and small-craft airstrip there. The neighboring ghost towns also returned to life under the stimulus of tourist trade. Terlingua sponsors a widely celebrated annual chili cookout, and is a starting point for horseback tours of the Mexican side of the Chihuahuan desert.

Study Butte is home to a company that offers rafting tours of the Rio Grande, through the canyons of Big Bend Park. But business expansion is not necessarily a cause that residents propound. People who live in Study Butte and Terlingua are mainly refugees from the hubbub of urban life. They take shelter in mobile homes placed on plots of divided ranch land, or in unplumbed, sometimes unwired adobe huts that once served the mining camps. Some have independent incomes, some work for the tourist trade—and most of them speak of Lajitas as if it were Babylon. Why, they'll tell you, there's a shopping center there! And a hardware store! The fear, of course, is that commerce will overwhelm their refuge. That day, however much it is dreaded, seems still far off: the total population of resurrected settlements is less than 500.

■ BIG BEND NATIONAL PARK

Big Bend National Park dates from 1944, when the government accumulated public land parcels and smaller tracts donated by Texans interested in the project. The name comes from its setting at the toe of the 100-mile-long (160-km) dip in the Rio Grande, where it turns from a southeasterly course to run northeast. The park's nearly virgin wildland covers 801,000 acres—an area a bit larger than the state of Rhode Island. Parts of it—like 7,825-feet-high (2,385-m) Emory Peak, are nearly perpendicular. Contained within the park, the **Chisos Mountains,** a roughly circular range about 20 miles (32 km) in diameter, are home to hundreds of protected javelina *(ha-vay-lee-na)*—stubby porcines with fierce tusks—coyotes, mule and whitetail deer, gray fox, jackrabbits, skunks, raccoons, and even a few black bear, who are believed to commute to Mexico.

The mountains and the valley greenery close to the Rio Grande are rich birding country: 430 species of fowl, from small desert wrens to golden eagles, gray-breasted jay, hummingbirds, and the Colima Warbler—found within the United States only in its Chisos Mountains nests. The bird most often seen is the paisano, or road runner, a common and fiesty bird that can reach land speeds of 20 mph (32 kph), fueled on moisture it extracts from lizards and snakes.

More than 1,100 species of plant life also inhabit the park, mostly on the desert floor, including creosote, a dozen cactus varieties, and ceniza—a bush that grows to five feet, with gray perennial leaves and purple flowers that blossom anytime it rains. Ceniza ("ashen" in Spanish) is known to most Americans, especially fans of Ohio dentist-turned-novelist Zane Grey, as "purple sage." At higher altitudes you'll find quaking aspen shimmering in light breezes, pine juniper, and wild-flowers in summer and fall.

Visitors can enter the park from Alpine on the west or from Marathon on the east. A motel for visitors is located in Chisos Basin, just below Casa Grande, an imposing stack of rocks 7,325 feet (2,233 m) high; nearby are a restaurant, shops, and a campground. Most of the year the motel requires reservations in advance (see "PRACTICAL INFORMATION"). The rooms offer spectacular sunset views through a pass in the mountains appropriately known as the Window.

Chisos Basin is 10 miles (16 km) from the area's other outpost of civilization, park headquarters, where trail maps and advice on hiking are dispensed. From there, it's 34 miles (55 km) through the wild to the Rio Grande at **Boquillas Canyon Overlook**, where, on the Mexican side, the river has cut its rock sides into a high cliff. The village of **Boquillas del Carmen** is just across, and can be visited without the formalities of immigration and customs checks. From the end of the paved park road, a path leads a few hundred yards down to the river, where a Mexican entrepreneur will guide you in a scramble down to the water and across in a metal fishing boat: a few dollars for the crossing, a few more for the half-mile ride

The resort town of Lajitas (above) is set in Santa Elena Canyon along the Rio Grande (right).

up the slope to Boquillas by burro or pickup. The main attraction of the village is cold beer—not available in the park—on days when Boquillas has electricity, anyway. Authorities in both countries ignore the Boquillas crossings because it's easier to control the roads leading out than to set up a customs house. On the American side, an illegal entrant faces 54 miles (87 km) of exposed, two-lane road to get out of the park, and another 40 (64 km) miles through open country to reach a highway going towards urban civilization. And on the Mexican side, there are no paved roads—and hence, no speedy way out.

■ FROM BIG BEND TO PECOS

The eastern route from Big Bend, U.S. 385 (on its eventual way to Mount Rushmore, South Dakota), leads through **Marathon** near its junction with U.S. 90, the east-west highway that served the Trans-Pecos before interstate highways were built. Marathon is a ranching town, the former stomping grounds of Albert Gage, who owned 385,000 acres and whose headquarters, built in 1927 and recently restored, are now the Gage Hotel. The hotel's 17 period rooms bring the '20s to life—as do the limited bathrooms: only eight of the restored rooms have them, so ask before booking.

Marathon is a good stopping place for a trip westward through Alpine and north to **Fort Davis,** a former army post established in 1846 and named after Jefferson Davis, then President Pierce's Secretary of War, and later, president of the Confederacy. During its 40 years of operation, mainly as an outpost for troops battling the Comanche and Apache, the fort headquartered the Indian-fighting black troops known as buffalo soldiers. Here as well, the army experimented in substituting camels for horses, and the sight of cavalry officers attempting to ride camels must have had its comic aspect.

■ MCDONALD ASTRONOMICAL OBSERVATORY

Today, most travelers head northwest of Fort Davis and into the Davis Mountains to see stars, not wars: in the middle of a winding 30-mile (48-km) highway through the peaks sits the McDonald Astronomical Observatory, 6,791 feet (2,070 m) above sea level on the rounded peak of Mount Locke. The drive on TX 118 to the observatory takes you into an almost Appalachian setting, dominated by pines and red-skinned madrone trees. The University of Texas, which operates the observatory, chose the site because the dry Trans-Pecos region offers cloudless night skies, and the high elevation keeps the telescopes above desert dust and interference from artificial lighting. Visitors to the observatory can look through smaller scopes, but the facility's 107-inch lens—soon to be replaced by a 340-inch telescope—is available to the public only one night a month, by reservation.

Below, back on the desert floor, the terrain seems almost barren; the area receives less than 10 inches of rain a year. Evaporation exceeds precipitation; white dust—the universal of the Chihuahuan desert, of which the Trans-Pecos forms a part—is everywhere. As Texas naturalist and writer Stephen Harrigan notes, in the desert's lowland "hardly anything grows higher than your waist." Creosote bushes, ocotillo, pitaya, lechugilla, and other water-hoarders account for most of the sparse greenery. The desert is also home to creatures elsewhere unknown. Here live kangaroo rats, which never drink water—they manufacture it from seeds—and members of an all-female species of whiptail lizards which clone themselves naturally. Meanwhile, in the mountains, some of which reach 8,000 feet (2,438 m), piñon, juniper, and oak trees survive. At those elevations it rains up to 20 inches (32 cm) a year, and the air is usually 20 degrees F (11° C) cooler.

■ PECOS

The junction of Interstate 10 with TX 118—the road linking McDonald Observatory to U.S. 90—is about 10 miles (16 km) west of the terminus of Interstate 20, which goes eastward through Dallas to Shreveport. From the I-20 split it's about 50 miles (80 km) to the Pecos River, where the region begins. On these riverbanks sits the town of Pecos, known for the succulent cantaloupe grown there by irrigation, and for being the launching pad for wheeler-dealer, and later convict, Billy Sol Estes. The city was established when the Texas and Pacific Railroad put a stop there in 1881, still frontier days in West Texas, a time when to "pecos" a man meant to kill him and throw him in the river. For a glimpse of this era, stop by the **West of the Pecos Museum** at 120 East First at Cedar Street in the old Orient Hotel. In the courtyard out back are horse-drawn buggies and wagons, as well as the grave of gunfighter Clay Allison. If you visit the town in July, you might attend the Pecos Rodeo, a century-old tradition and a fine place to see the classic rodeo events, plus special ones like the wild cow milking contest. Call (915) 445-2406 for dates and information.

■ FORT STOCKTON AREA

About 30 miles (48 km) southwest of Imperial lies the much bigger town of Fort Stockton, where controversy between civic sentiment and commerce has been brewing for 40 years. In at least three Texas cities—San Marcos, Austin, and Fort Stockton—natural springs give residents their most important source of civic pride and identity. The springs at San Marcos have been commercially developed as Aquarena Springs, a showplace of water fauna and swimming skits, while Austin's Barton Springs has been preserved, in a long-running fight with developers, as a swimming hole. But Fort Stockton's **Comanche Springs**, which draws from a branch of the Edwards Aquifer, has gone dry.

The name Comanche Springs is of latter-day origin. Indians used the site for centuries before the Comanche came to the area, and the Spanish explorer Cabeza de Vaca probably drank from the spring in 1534. In the nineteenth century, this was the place where the San Antonio–El Paso Trail crossed the Comanche War Trail, and in 1859 the U.S. Army encamped here to safeguard the San Antonio–San Diego mail route.

Old Fort Stockton, located in the historic downtown section of Fort Stockton, on Williams Street between Fourth and Fifth streets, became home to the Ninth

This George Catlin painting of a Comanche village in 1834 shows women tanning hides and drying meat. (National Museum of American Art, Smithsonian Institution)

(left) McDonald Astronomical Observatory in the Davis Mountains.

Cavalry, an African-American regiment Indians called buffalo soldiers. They arrived in the summer of 1867, found the fort had been destroyed by Confederate troops during the Civil War, and set about to rebuild it. In 1868, the Ninth ran down a band of Apaches who had raided a wagon train near Fort Stockton and were headed across the Rio Grande. In a running battle which left 25 Apaches dead and two troopers wounded, the buffalo soldiers defeated the Indians.

About 1894, Fort Stockton became famous for a meeting of its leading citizens, who drew lots to see who'd kill their sheriff, A. J. Royal, because he'd been terrorizing the town.

As the town grew, the downtown springs became its heart. Its warm waters filled an Olympic-sized pool, around which courtships, athletic contests, and civic festivals came to revolve. Even today, Fort Stockton's annual fete, the **Water Carnival**, is celebrated at the springs.

During the 1950s, farmers a few miles west of Fort Stockton began irrigating. At first, no great changes were noted in town—other than a new prosperity—but as more farms went under irrigation, the flow from the springs tapered off. By the late '50s, it became dry except in winter months, and by 1962 it was dry even during winters, except for short periods following the region's rare rains.

The townspeople have been divided ever since. Some of them want the wells regulated or capped. "Texas is the only western state," notes Kirby Warnock, publisher of the *Big Bend Quarterly,* "that doesn't have groundwater laws. In every other state, they make you meter your wells, and in some of them, you can't pump out more water than the recharge rate brings in. An aquifer is like a sponge, and if one guy sticks a big straw in it, he can dry it up for everybody else."

On the other hand, says Mary Ezell of the *Fort Stockton Pioneer,* the farms have been as important to Fort Stockton's modern survival as the springs were in its past. "A lot of people are criticizing that they should shut down the farms west of town so that we can bring the springs back," Ezell says. "But the farming and oil was going to high hilt in the '50s, and it was fine to worry about the springs—but only so long as somebody had a job."

Economic development points in one direction, civic pride in the other, and today, Fort Stockton's people are caught in a debate. But they're not entirely without water enjoyments, or a living example of what their springs once were. Fort Stockton's residents, and visitors from across Texas, still go to the **Balmorhea State Recreational Area,** 40 miles (64 km) west on I-10, to scuba and swim in a true desert oasis. There the **San Solomon Springs** feed clear, chilly water up into 1.75 acres of surface area—the biggest pool west of I-35, bigger than Comanche Springs ever was. One species of fish that lives in the San Solomon swimming hole's water carries a name honoring Fort Stockton's loss: the Comanche Springs pupfish.

SIX-MAN ON THE PECOS

The Pecos River begins at a lake on the New Mexico line and flows southeasterly to a spot near Langtry, on the Rio Grande, intersecting I-10 and I-20 as it goes. Not much lies along the river's course, with the possible exception of Imperial, a town of about 300, accessible only by Farm-to-Market Road 1053. Imperial is a good place to visit on autumn Friday nights, because its Buena Vista school is home to a six-man football team. And six-man football is a game even for people who don't like the NFL.

"Six-man is basically a track meet with a football out there," explains Chris Simpson, assistant coach at the Buena Vista school.

Six-man football is played on an 80-yard (73-m) field, under rules that have been adapted from the standard 11-man game. In six-man football, the ball must be moved 15 instead of 10 yards to score a first down, field goals score four points, and the quarterback can't run with the ball.

The game is usually played with three men on the line, and three, including the quarterback, in the backfield. "The quarterback usually pitches back to one of the deep backs, and that's the guy who is free to either run or pass," Simpson explains.

"Because the defense is at a great disadvantage," the coach says, "scoring is high, and fans love the scoring. It's rare to see a game where the score for either side is below 30 points."

In fact, scoring is so wild that it's led to a new verb. In six-man football, a team wins once it scores 45 points more than its opponent: hence the verb "forty-five," as in "Dell City forty-fived Fort Hancock in that game last week."

Imperial plays in a district whose other teams include Fort Hancock, Sierra Blanca, and Balmorhea—even Dell City, a four-hour drive away. Attending the games takes time away from the academic schedule, but not many people would give the sport up, perhaps for the best of reasons: six-man football can hardly be considered a spectator sport, for students anyway. "Out of 23 guys in our high school, we probably get 18 out for football. There's nothing else to do out here," Simpson notes. And that's true even if you're female: the six guys on the playing field are supported by four cheerleaders on the sidelines.

■ LANGTRY AND JUDGE ROY BEAN

Just west of the junction of the Pecos River and the Rio Grande (153 miles south-east of Fort Stockton on U.S. 285 and U.S. 90), is Langtry, a dot on U.S. 90 that owes its existence to the colorful, if not exactly deserving, Texas historical celebrity Judge Roy Bean. In 1882, Bean set up a saloon in a tent in the area to serve work-ers who were laying tracks for the Southern Pacific railroad, on its way west toward El Paso. At the time, the nearest county seat was at Fort Stockton, 150 miles (240 km) miles away, and a Texas Ranger recommended that Bean be appointed justice of the peace in order to bring some semblance of law and order to the vast Trans-Pecos region. As befitted his time and place, Bean applied justice uniquely. For ex-ample, acting beyond a JP's authority, he granted divorces to couples that he had married on grounds of correcting errors he'd made. He is said to have fined a corpse $40 for carrying a concealed weapon, and while hearing the case of a man charged with killing a Chinese railway worker, Bean reportedly released the ac-cused on grounds that he could find no law against killing an Asian. His notoriety spread across the nation in 1886 when he staged the world championship Fitzsimmons-Maher heavyweight fight on a sandbar in the Rio Grande after officials in Texas, New Mexico, Arizona, and the Mexican state of Coahuila had banned it. Bean named the town and his Jersey Lily Saloon for Lillie Langtry, the "Jersey

Judge Roy Bean holds court on the porch of the "Hall of Justice," a saloon in Langtry, providing the only law enforcement "west of the Pecos River" at the time of this photo in 1900. (Center for American History, University of Texas)

(left) A friendly game of poker on a West Texas ranch.

Lily"—a British actress whom he admired, but never met. He sometimes held court in the tavern, fining defendants a round of drinks for the house. Bean died in 1903 of natural causes, and is buried at Del Rio alongside his son, Sam, who was knifed to death at a bordello he operated there. Because of the pair's notoriety, their graves went unmarked until 1936, when the Texas Centennial Commission put modest stones on them.

Today Bean's old saloon is preserved as a state historic center. The tourist commission provides literature and oversees the Jersey Lily from a building just in front. There is a nature walk where native plants, including several varieties of cactus, are labeled by their scientific names. If you stop here, be sure to ask for an official road map. They're free, and the state's map is the only guide to Texas with topographical features, Farm-to-Market roads, and population figures on one sheet.

Seminole Canyon State Historical Park, 41 miles (66 km) northwest via U.S. 90, is worth visiting for its pictographs, some of the oldest in North America. Guided tours are usually offered twice daily in Fate Bell Shelter, and the visitor center has exhibits on the pre-Columbian Indians that once inhabited this area.

A WOMAN IN THE PECOS

*I*f she confessed to Pecos that her claim of masculinity had been a hoax, that for years she had worn the garb of a boy, first to please her father, and later to protect herself in that wild country—if she confronted him with the truth, would he not be so disgusted and alienated that he would leave her? It seemed to her that he would. And anything would be better than to be abandoned to the old fears, the lonely nights, the dreaded days—and now to this incomprehensible longing to see Pecos, to hear him, to know he was near, to shiver at a chance contact and to burn for more. No—she could not bear to lose him. . . .

But she was a woman now and this love had come upon her. What could she do to avert calamity? She had suffered through love of mother, love of father, and suffered still. This thing, however, was different. And she realized that now, with the scales dropped from her eyes, she would be uplifted to heaven one moment and plunged into hell the next. Still, if she were a woman she could find strength and cunning to hide that. Else what was it to grow into a woman? If she were clever Pecos might never find her out and never leave her.

—Zane Grey, *West of the Pecos,* 1931

■ EAST OF THE PECOS: WEST-CENTRAL TEXAS

West Texas east of the Pecos cannot easily be separated by geographic features from the parts of the state that are called plains, or North, Central, or South Texas, but people in West-Central Texas consider land use to define the state's regional identities. In this view, flat, cultivated areas are perceived as plains territory; green rolling hills as Central Texas property; and grassy pastures as South Texas. The area closest to Oklahoma, simply, is North Texas. West and West-Central Texas work together as a unit from El Paso to Fort Worth because history authorizes it, and also because there's no pressing reason to dispute the question.

Sheep and goat ranching, cattle, cotton, and oil are still the mainstays of the economy here, and were it not for seasonal flocks of deer and dove hunters, West (and especially West-Central) Texas would have practically no tourism. Its plentiful native stone buildings have not, as in neighboring Central Texas, become boutiques and European-style cafes. West Texas is frontier Texas as much as modernity allows. Throughout its vast mesquite landscape, evidence of the natural struggle for survival is abundant. Coyotes, rattlesnakes, hawks, buzzards, deer, and rabbits range across the land. Even the Texas horned toad, an endangered species, survives in the West.

The chief difference between East and West Texas is that east of the 98th meridian, Texas gets more than 30 inches (76 cm) of rain a year, while less falls to the west. The more-than/less-than 30-inch mark was important, historically, because without twentieth-century irrigation, cotton couldn't prosper where less than 30 inches of rain fell. The Trans-Pecos, on the rainfall divide, stands out as an area that gets even less than 15 inches (38 cm) a year. Most of West Texas gets more, but sometimes, as an old West Texas joke points out, the difference doesn't amount to much: "You could say that we had a good year last year, 22 inches of rain," the joke begins. "But you should have been here on the day it fell!"

West Texas was settled late in part because it was already the turf of nomadic and sometimes fierce Comanche and Apache tribes, whose resistance wasn't quelled until 1880. West of the 98th meridian, once the area was settled, ranching became more important than farming. On farms, wheat was more reliable than cotton: wheat was not the labor-intensive crop cotton was before mechanized harvesting. West Texas was therefore settled by yeomen, mostly Anglos. The region's cowboys were usually black or brown, but were never numerous. West Texas developed as a domain of Anglos with a significant Mexican minority, but few African Americans.

It was a region where economic leveling was almost a fact of life, because nobody with any real stake east of the 98th meridian could find much reason to brave the dust and Indians of the West. All these factors were reflected in the area's people, who even today are known as open, egalitarian, and—because their ancestors fought hand-to-hand skirmishes with Indians—potentially pretty fierce.

The most important highways in West Texas, as in the Trans-Pecos, are Interstate 10, which runs from El Paso to Sonora, and Interstate 20, which runs from the middle of the Trans-Pecos to Fort Worth, the easternmost point of West Texas, and its titular capital. The first sizable settlement along I-20 east of the Pecos is **Monahans,** the administrative town for nearby **Monahans Sandhills State Park,** with 3,800 acres of Saharan-like sand dunes, some of them 70 feet (21 m) high. The sand dunes here are but a fraction of a huge dune area stretching for 200 miles (320 km) into New Mexico.

Once abundant, the horned toad is now an endangered species.

(right) Virgil Baldwin, rebar and horseshoe artist.

OIL BOOMS AND BUSTS

Oil was selling at prices below $5 a barrel before the Arab oil embargo of 1973; during the boom that followed, it sold as high as $34. The Texas slogan of those optimistic days, "85 in '85!" or $85 a barrel by 1985, now has an almost cruel ring. Texas, like Venezuela and Mexico, is still suffering from the oil price bust of 1982. Today, most Texans who derive income from lease holdings or drilling would happily settle for $20 a barrel, a dollar or two above the cost of Texas production. During the boom of the 1970s and early '80s, the number of exploration operations in Texas rose to an all-time high, 4,530 in 1981. The rig count is less than a tenth of that today, and it's still declining. The oil economy as a whole, which accounted for about a quarter of the state's total economic production in 1982, has been reduced by half. Although some 185,000 Texans still earn their livings from oil, the outlook is for a long slump—mitigated, or hinged, only on the uncertainty of natural gas: if clean-burning natural gas becomes a motor fuel, Texas will boom again.

Desdemona was a quiet village until oil was discovered literally under the city streets in 1918. Oil derricks rose haphazardly around town in the ensuing boom. (Webel Collection, The Petroleum Museum, Midland)

■ OIL COUNTRY

East of Monahans the Permian Basin begins. It's a wide, low spot on the map whose landscape is—well, anything but breathtaking. Its austerity is evidenced in the descriptive name of a small town, **Notrees,** whose residents, with help from garden suppliers, have now given their town what it once didn't have. The authors of the WPA guide to Texas observed that in the rough terrain of the Trans-Pecos, "Gray earth is broken by deposits of gleaming white sand, which sometimes rise in low dunes, from the crest of which the wind often flings smoke-like plumes." Locals insist that the landscape has a scenic aspect, and some visitors will likely concur—especially if they're attracted by what's beneath the surface: oil. In the landscape of this area, pump jacks take the place of trees. The Permian Basin has for at least 40 years been the heart of the inland Texas oil industry and, in part as a result, of Texas higher education. Thanks to oil royalty interests from former state lands in the Permian Basin, the University of Texas is, after Harvard, the nation's most richly endowed educational institution.

The oil economy has two sides: drilling, and, once that's done, pumping and well servicing. Drilling is dynamic, creating boom towns and jobs by the hundreds. Pumping and servicing are more routine: good for stability, but not nearly as spectacular, except when prices are high.

Midland and Odessa are the Permian Basin's oil cities. Though they're the same size (about 90,000) and only 20 miles (32 km) apart, they're not much alike, at least in Texas legend. **Midland,** in the eponymous county, is an administrative town of skyscrapers. Until the 1940s, it had no wells, even though 150 oil companies were headquartered there. **Odessa** is a bricked-over, blue-collar boom town. Its population quadrupled to about 10,000 between 1930 and 1940, the decade following the discovery of Permian oil in 1923, and tripled between 1940 and 1950.

Like jealous siblings, Odessa and Midland snipe and compete. Odessa is the site of the University of Texas, Permian Basin campus, much to Midland's chagrin. The college has built a replica of Shakespeare's Globe Theatre and sponsors an annual drama festival. But if Odessa wins the prize for attractions financed by the state, Midland gets the lion's share of privately financed institutions, like the Permian Basin Petroleum Museum, Library, and Hall of Fame. Its wealthy have also lured away from South Texas the **Confederate Air Force Association,** which owns and flies some 140 vintage planes, including a Japanese Zero, a Messerschmitt, and the world's only remaining airworthy B-29 bomber.

Given the differences between Midland and Odessa, it was appropriate that Yalie George Bush settle in Midland in 1947 to win the oil fortune that, he says, later allowed him to enter politics. It's equally fitting that an earthy and notorious bootlegger, Tom "Pinkie" Roden, would choose to set up shop in Odessa.

Roden, who began his worklife as a bellhop in the 1920s during Prohibition, learned that he could make big money supplying booze to hotel guests. Knowing a good thing when he saw one, he soon apprenticed himself to seasoned moonshiners and bootleggers. A natural at the business, he responded to the repeal of Prohibition by opening a liquor store in Big Spring. When most of the towns north of I-20 banned local liquor sales, Roden closed his liquor store and moved his operations 60 miles (97 km) west, to Odessa. From there he could bootleg liquor into "dry" counties.

To make sure that his drivers could evade detection, Roden flew a plane over the vast area, studying back roads from the air. "He loved the intrigue of being chased," his widow told a journalist, and an old friend observed, "Pinkie has trouble driving at night with his headlights on."

Some of the faces of West-Central Texas include Bert Turner (above), a funeral home greeter in Brady until recently, and Lincoln Edwards (right), here observing a cattle auction in Clyde.

Pinkie's county-line stores supplied consumers and local bootleggers from Fort Stockton to Amarillo, from the Oklahoma to the New Mexico line, over the 6,000-square-mile (15,000-sq-km) area of West Texas and the Panhandle. Even today, residents of some West Texas towns drive 50 miles (80 km) or more to buy a beer. In locales like these, they'll likely buy their six-packs at a Pinkie's store.

The town where Roden opened his first store, **Big Spring**, some 40 miles (64 km) east of Midland on I-20, is an old agricultural town, home to a giant Petrofina refinery. The spring from which is takes its name was a watering hole for buffalo, wild mustangs, and antelope, and for cattle and their drivers on the Overland Trail, as well as for the Indians who coursed across the region. The city itself sits in a rocky gorge between two high foothills of the Caprock escarpment, with two rocky plateaus nearby, one designated as a state park.

Just to the north of Big Spring, along U.S. 180, the northern limit of West Texas, is Borden County and its seat, **Gail**, both named for Texas pioneer and inventor Gail Borden. Borden, who never saw the county and town named in his honor, was a Galveston-area editor who advocated the separation of Texas from

A massive dust storm bears down on Midland during the drought year of 1911.
The scene was repeated frequently during the Dust Bowl years of the mid-1930s.
(Center for American History, University of Texas)

Mexico and supported Sam Houston's bid for the presidency of the Texas Republic. Borden is better known to non-Texans as the inventor of a process for condensing milk, and as a supplier of the same to the Union army. In 1851 he patented his famous invention after moving back to New York.

It's 100 miles (160 km) east from Big Spring to the next city, **Abilene.** Founded in 1881 as a railhead and a cattle-loading stop, it became a tough town with a wild and woolly reputation. Ironically, today the town hosts three denominational colleges with a total enrollment of about 9,000: Abilene Christian University, supported by the Church of Christ; Hardin-Simmons University, a Baptist school; and McMurray University, a Methodist institution.

An unidentified Comanche.
(Center for American History, University of Texas)

North of Abilene about 14 miles (23 km) on FM 600, you'll see **Fort Phantom Hill Ruins.** The word "ruins" is no exaggeration; there's not much left of the place, first occupied by U.S. infantry trying to stop Comanche raids in the early 1850s. In 1869, 150 African-American troops from the Ninth Cavalry, marching to Fort Phantom Hill from Fort Concho, were surprised along the route by 500 Comanches and Kiowas. The hand-to-hand engagement was a bitter one, and the Indians were eventually forced to flee.

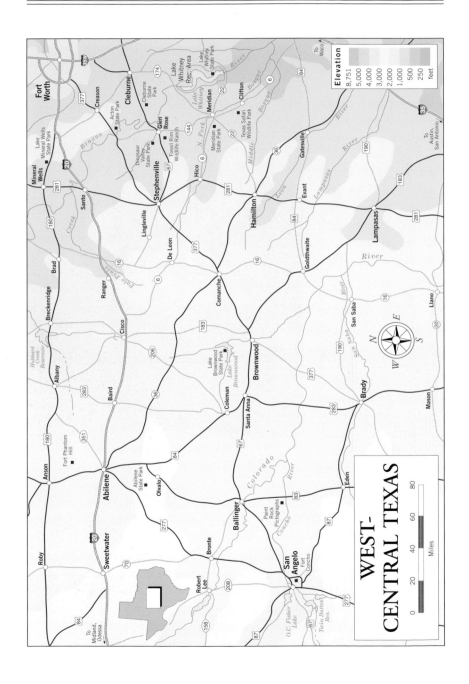

WEST-
CENTRAL TEXAS

■ SAN ANGELO

About midway between I-10, the more northerly route through West Texas, and I-20, the southern conduit, and on a line about midway between Big Spring and Abilene is the city of San Angelo, which besides billing itself as "The Wool and Mohair Capital," is also home to a jewelry item that can't be found anywhere else: the Concho River pink pearl. Concho pearls, produced by tiny mussels, were first noted in the journals of Spanish explorers. But they weren't much more than a rumor until 1969, when, during one of the area's periodic droughts, a couple of local jewelers, Jack Morgan and the late Bart Mann, went wading in the mud of Lake O. C. Fisher, on San Angelo's northwest side.

Over a period of nearly five months, the men brought out 6,000 pink pearls, which they stored in glass jars in their jewelry shop—well, until a local market for them took off. By the mid-1970s, their trade had become so lucrative that divers were looking for pink pearls in neighboring areas in Central Texas. If the hard freeze in 1982–83 injured the bivalve producers, it also added to the luster of Concho pearls: some of those brought in today have a purplish cast that customers

Freshwater pearls have created a new industry for entrepreneurs in the San Angelo area.

like even more than pink. But the supply is dwindling, Morgan reports, largely because divers who elude game wardens are over-harvesting the area's mussel populations. Today, only about 1,000 Concho pearls are found each year. In the span of two decades, the pearls have become rarities.

■ COLEMAN

Coleman, seat of the county by that name, lies about 70 miles (110 km) northeast of San Angelo, and 50 miles (80 km) southwest of Abilene. Today Coleman County is ranching country, and Coleman is a ranching town. Ranching doesn't provide many jobs, however, and only 11,000 people live in Coleman County nowadays. Fifty years ago when dryland cotton farming—and the families of small farmers—were its mainstay, the population exceeded 30,000.

In its earliest days, Coleman was a town on the Western Trail, the most important of the routes over which, between 1871 and 1883, some four million Texas cattle were herded to rail and market connections in Kansas.

■ BROWNWOOD TO LINGLEVILLE

The political and religious character of West Texas is on display in somewhat exaggerated form, 30 miles (48 km) from Coleman at Brownwood, home of the **Douglas MacArthur Academy of Freedom** on the campus of the Baptist-supported **Howard Payne University.** The academy offers courses in subjects like "American Free Enterprise," and its faculty is the beneficiary of endowments like the Othal Brand Chair of Free Enterprise and Public Policy. Though General MacArthur wasn't a Texan and he never visited the Academy, the museums house his Medal of Honor and other war memorabilia. Student-docents provide tours in which they enumerate his accomplishments, using a map of the Pacific studded with blinking colored lights.

Spanning three walls of the Academy's Hall of Christian Civilization is a mural, 32 feet (10 m) high, depicting Biblical history. The academy apparently practices the freedom that it preaches, in regard to art, anyway: the mural depicts some 30 nudes, including two white females and a black male who are bathing, tour guides say, in a pool filled with the blood of Christ.

North of Brownwood, at the juncture of U.S. 183 and I-20, is the little town of **Cisco,** where Conrad Hilton opened his first hotel. Cisco is also one of the few places in Texas where anybody—except lawyers and bureaucrats, anyway—has ever heard of tiny Lingleville.

Lingleville, about 30 miles (48 km) southwest of Cisco, is creating a stink. A village dedicated to the beef industry, Lingleville contains a feedlot where hundreds of bovines are concentrated in a limited space and fattened for slaughter. Areas downwind from feedlots suffer from the scent of too many animals packed together and mountains of manure. In 1991, several residents asked the Texas Air Control Board for relief. The state agency investigated the stink and ordered the defendant, F/R Cattle Co., to apply for a permit that would have required it to reduce the 6,000 or so cattle on its 19-acre lot to less than 1,000. When the state filed an injunction to force compliance, F/R fought back in court. Its attorneys argued that the Air Control Board had no authority to regulate stinks caused by "natural processes." A series of court battles followed, ending in a 1993 Texas Supreme Court verdict endorsing the manure-maker's contention. With the verdict, cattlemen across Texas breathed a sigh of—well, not-very-sweet—relief.

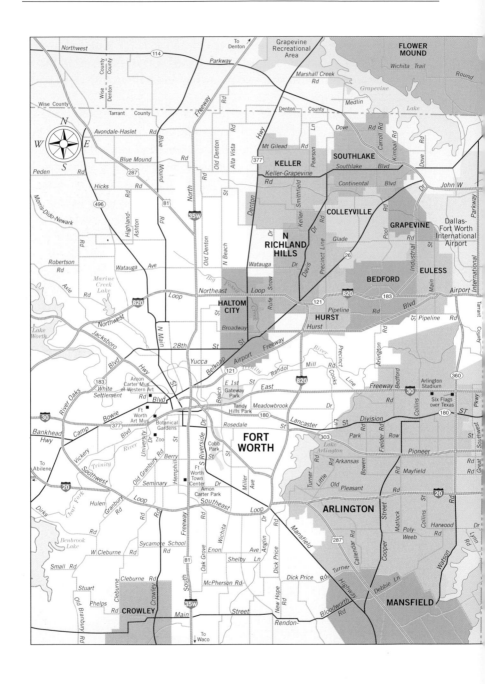

To
Denton

LEWISVILLE

Hebron

Grove Rd

CARROLLTON

Trinity River

Josey

Marsh

County

County

Dallas

Pkwy

Plano Pkwy

Coit

Custer

Jupiter

Expwy

K

Ave

St

W 15th

14th

St

Renner Rd

Rd

121

COPPELL

Garpenter Creek

North Lake

Jackson Rd

77

Ln

Denton

Collin

Dallas County

North

Preston

Collin County

Campbell

RICHARDSON

Arapaho

Big

Springs Rd

Blackburn Rd

Rd

75

Collin County

Naaman School

78

Carpenter Frwy

View

Belt

Line

Ln

Rd

White

Rd

Belt

Central

Line

Plano

Rd

Jupiter

Shiloh

Saturn

Sachse

North Lake Park

35E

FARMERS BRANCH

Ln

LBJ

635

Freeway

Greenville

Audelia

Rd

Rd

Rd

GARLAND

Castle Dr

66

289

Forest

Ln

Ln

Forest Ln

Walnut Hill

Harry

Royal

L.B. Houston Park

Marsh

Midway

Ln

Ln

Biblical Arts Center

North

Rock

Miller

Kingsley

Rd

Rd

Rd

Lake Hubbard

Rd

Walnut Hill

Line

Rd

O'Connor

114

Texas Stadium

183

Hines

12

Lovers Ln

Love Field Municipal Airport

Tollway

Owen Art Center

Mocking-bird

Ave

Abrams

Rd

Ln

White Rock Lake

Centerville

Dr

To Texarkana

30

Belt

IRVING

Freeway

Grauwyler Rd

Elm

Blvd

Fitzhugh

Haskell Ave

Gaston

Garland

White Rock Lake Park

Dallas Arboretum & Botanical Garden

Oates

Line

Rock Island Rd

Shady

Oakdale Rd

Grove Rd

Story

Trinity

Walton

Trinity River Greenbelt Park

DALLAS

Dealey Plaza

Reunion Tower

Ross Ave

Cotton Bowl

Fair Park

Military Rd

Scyene

12

Miller Rd

352

Pkwy

MESQUITE

635

80

Main St

Rd

Belt

12

30

City Hall

St

GRAND PRAIRIE

Carrier St

303

SE 8th

Mountain Creek Lake

Pkwy

Davis

180

Blue Cut

Rd

Illinois

Walker Rd

Westmoreland Rd

Hampton Rd

Blvd

Cedar Crest Blvd

Ave

Zoo

Hawn Frwy

Rochester Park

Lake June

Bruton Rd

2nd

St Augustine

Hickory Tree

BALCII SPRINGS

Rd

Line

To Shreveport

20

Joe Pool Lake

Mountain Creek Lake Park

Ledbetter

Duncanville Rd

Frwy

Red Bird

St

Marsalis

12

Dallas

Ave

Bonnie View Rd

River

Central Ave

Lark Lemmon

342

310

45

Lake Lemmon Park

Freeway

C.F. Hawn Frwy

Frwy

Love

Camp Wisdom Rd

Camp Wisdom Rd

DUNCANVILLE

Clark St

Main

Marvin

Danieldale Rd

Wheatland Rd

Polk St

Dr

20

LBJ

Jefferson Bonnie Rd

Lancaster Rd

Hutchins Rd

Belt Line

Expwy

HUTCHINS

Joe Pool Lake

67

Pleasant Run

Cockrell Hill

DE SOTO

35E

Houston School

Wintergreen

Rd

Cedar Hill State Park

Mansfield Rd

Belt Line

Belt Line

Rd

Hampton

To Waco

LANCASTER

CEDAR HILL

DALLAS-FORT WORTH

0 2 4 8

Miles

D A L L A S   A N D
F   O   R   T   W   O   R   T   H

AT NIGHT FROM THE AIR, Dallas and Fort Worth form one vast expanse of light in the black lake of North-Central Texas. By day they appear strung together by freeways, highrises, and suburbs. Yet they're an odd couple. Dallas belongs to wet, fertile East Texas, to Confederate impulses, and sophisticated finance. Fort Worth is of the Old West—an overgrown cowboy town whose raw edges and rambunctious reputation stand in contrast to the orderly *nouveau riche* hum of its neighbor.

■ DALLAS

With over a million people, Dallas is not only the principal city of northeast Texas, but looms large in the American consciousness as the home of the Cowboys football team, the place where President John F. Kennedy was killed, and the site of J. R. Ewing's ranch, **Southfork,** in a 1980s television serial. Only the assassination site, however, is actually in Dallas. The ranch is outside the town of Parker, 15 miles (25 km) northeast of Dallas; its museum and gift shop are favorites with visitors from southeast Asia and Eastern Europe, where the serial is still showing on prime time.

In real life, "Big D," as Texans have sometimes called it, is primarily an office town, headquarters for regional banks, for national corporations like American Airlines and J. C. Penney, even for the Boy Scouts. Dallas is known for formality, especially in business circles. This is a white-shirt city: no open collars, gold chains, or blue jeans, please. Despite being the birthplace of the so-called gentlemen's topless clubs that dot the American landscape, Dallas, in its usual mode, is a puritanically Protestant town. Liquor isn't for sale across wide swaths of the city, and "power breakfasts"—beginning about 6:30 A.M.—are more common than three-martini lunches. As one writer put it, "The general tone of community life is decidedly on the moral and respectable side."

■ D A L L A S   H I S T O R Y

Dallas was founded on ambition and takes pride in that. There wasn't any need for the city, its natives like to say. Its Trinity River wasn't navigable, and no railroad lines had been laid in 1841, when the first white settler showed up at the present site of the city. But Dallas was promoted from its earliest days with tales of a great river connected to the sea (false) and of fertile black farmland (true). When John B. Billingsley and four brothers came to Dallas with their families in 1842, he recorded in his journal that:

> *We* had heard a great deal about the three forks of the Trinity River and the town of Dallas. This was the center of attraction. It sounded big in far-off states. We had heard of it often, yes, the place, but the town, where was it? Two small log cabins, the logs just as nature formed them . . . chimneys made of sticks and mud and old mother earth serving as floors. . . .This was the town of Dallas, and two families, ten or twelve souls, was its population. . . .

Dallas still has a reputation for boosterism, reflected in street names such as Hyperbolic, Monetary, Nonesuch, and Fabrication. But it was cotton rather than hyperbole that first built Dallas. The 1940 WPA guide to Texas noted that:

> *S*et in the midst of vast cotton fields . . . Dallas is the foremost inland spot cotton market in the United States. . . . It leads the world in the manufacture of cotton gin machinery, due to the inventions in the 1880s of Robert S. Munger, a Dallas man, who made many improvements on the earlier inventions of Eli Whitney. In the United States it ranks first in volume distribution of cottonseed products and its cotton mills produce approximately ten million yards of fabric annually. It ranks second in the United States in the production of wash dresses and in the manufacture and distribution of women's hats.

Because Dallas is a thoroughly commercial city, it is the home of several American firsts. The nation's first convenience store, operated by the Southland Corporation under the name 7-Eleven, was opened at Edgefield and 12th streets, in the city's Oak Cliff neighborhood, on July 11, 1927—or 7/11/27. (7-Eleven Store No. 1 still sits on the same spot, but the original building has been razed.) In 1958, engineer Jack Kilby invented the microchip at the Texas Instruments' plant in Dallas.

Door-to-door cosmetics sales, practically an American tradition, got an important boost in 1963 when a Dallas housewife and widow, Mary Kay Ash, founded her "house party" sales company—an accomplishment enshrined in a museum today. Mary Kay, as the company is called, is probably best known for giving pink Cadillacs to its most effective sales—er, beauty consultants. The operation, now with 325,000 consultants in 23 countries, is listed on the New York Stock Exchange, and its commercial success has been powerful enough to catapult founder Ash to the non-fiction best-seller lists, twice, on the basis of books filled with adages like, "In matters of principle, stand like a rock; in other matters, swim with the current." The **Mary Kay Museum,** off the Regal Row exit of I-35, is a 3,000-square-foot (280-sq-m) exhibit hall containing such items as the household checkbook from which the company was founded, advertising memorabilia, and of course, plenty of pink things.

But if Dallas fosters the entrepreneurial spirit, a few of its citizens—members of the Church of the SubGenius—promote the virtue of Slack. In the 1950s, Dallas C-movie actor J. R. "Bob" Dobbs began teaching a quirky survivalist philosophy of self-development. After heavy use of LSD in the '60s, though, Bob changed his message radically, and his following became an anarchic, counter-culture "church." Today, there are decentralized "clenches," or branches, all over the country. Members use false names—like Buck Naked, a Dallas SubGenius pastor—and hold "Devivals," huge parties/rallies open to the public where church members can rant against work, authority, and "the Conspiracy."

■ K E N N E D Y A S S A S S I N A T I O N S I T E
Dallas never wanted to be remembered as the place where John F. Kennedy was killed, yet 30 years after the event, day in and day out, scores of visitors descend on the one-time Texas School Book Depository and the Triple Overpass, on Commerce Street downtown, to look at the spot where Lee Harvey Oswald is said to have gunned down the President. Most then look onto Dealey Plaza from the grassy knoll, the shooting position favored by conspiracy buffs. The **Sixth Floor,** a publicly operated museum at the former School Book Depository, showcases the Warren Commission theory. Its professionally done displays and video exhibits bring tears to the eyes of those old enough to remember the tragedy. Serious assassination buffs also hunt out more obscure locales of the controversy, like the Texas Theater, where Oswald was arrested, and his former home, both in Dallas' Oak Cliff neighborhood.

Assassination souvenir vendors frequent Dealey Plaza, site of the JFK shooting.

DALLAS MAIN ATTRACTIONS

■ U N I Q U E L Y   D A L L A S

Pioneer Plaza. Seventy bronze steers and cowboys, larger than life, crest an artificial hill on a trail ride through Skyscraper Canyon. *Griffin at Young.*

Six Flags Over Texas. The Texas and Warner Bros. answer to Disneyland and Disney World is this theme park with Batman and Bugs Bunny as hosts. *2201 Road to Six Flags, off I-30; (817) 640-8900.*

The Sixth Floor. The site from which President Kennedy was allegedly assassinated, the sixth floor of the former Texas School Book Depository, has been turned into a permanent exhibit. The life of the former president is chronicled through photographs, artifacts, and films. *Northwest corner of Houston and Elm streets; (214) 653-6666.*

Southfork Ranch. The exterior won worldwide fame as the Ewings' luxury ranch home in the TV show, "Dallas." The ranch is now a museum devoted to the television show. Exhibits feature cast memorabilia, including the gun that shot J. R. *From I-75 north get off at Parker Road, go east six miles (10 km), turn right at FM 2551.*

■ H I S T O R I C   S I T E S

Dallas Arboretum and Botanical Center. Sixty-six acres of floral and vegetable gardens bordering the eastern edge of White Rock Lake. The land actually comprises two estates, the **De Golyer Home** and the **Camp Home.** The De Golyer home was the former hacienda of American geologist Edward De Golyer and now serves as a museum with a fine collection of antiques and eighteenth-century furnishings. *8525 Garland Road; (214) 327-8263.*

Dallas City Hall. The Brutalist-style building designed by I. M. Pei features a sculpture by Henry Moore in the courtyard. *1500 Marilla at Ervay; (214) 744-3600.*

Dallas County Historical Plaza. A compilation of several plazas: **Founder's Plaza** (Main and Record) features a reconstruction of Dallas founder John Neely Bryan's original log cabin; **Dealey Plaza** (Houston and Elm streets) honors both George Bannerman Dealey, early executive of the *Dallas Morning News,* and John F. Kennedy with plaques; **Kennedy Memorial Plaza** (Main and Houston streets) also commemorates the assassinated president with a monument designed by architect Philip Johnson, a Kennedy family friend. Anchoring the eastern edge of the Memorial Plaza is **"Old Red,"** the massive Dallas County Courthouse, constructed in 1891 of dark red sandstone.

■ HISTORY MUSEUMS

Age of Steam Museum. An outdoor collection of trains featuring the world's largest steam locomotive, a 1903 depot, and a passenger train from the 1930s. *Fair Park, Washington and Parry; (214) 421-8754.*

Biblical Arts Center. A non-denominational museum showing art and artifacts with religious themes. One highlight of the permanent collection is the mural *Miracle at Pentecost,* by Torger Thompson. *7500 Park Lane at Boedecker; (214) 691-4661.*

Museum of African-American Culture. Highlights African and African-American art, artifacts, and photography from life in Africa to the present day. *1515 First Avenue; (214) 565-9026.*

Old City Park Museum. The museum was founded in 1966 as a museum of architectural and cultural history. Consisting of 38 historical structures, each one authentically furnished, the park grounds provide a living history of Texas from 1840–1910. The museum has collected private homes, farmhouses, and commercial buildings from all over Texas and restored them to their original condition. Among those on exhibit are a doctor's office and apothecary, Citizen's Bank, and two general stores. *1717 Gano; (214) 421-5141.*

■ ART MUSEUMS

Dallas Museum of Art. An impressive number of American abstract expressionists are the highlights of the permanent collection. The museum also houses Impressionist, modern, pre-Columbian, and African works. One of the period rooms displays eighteenth- and nineteenth-century French furnishings in a recreated Mediterranean villa. Other pleasant exhibits include the outdoor sculpture garden and the children's **Gateway Gallery.** *Ross Avenue and North Harwood Street; (214) 922-1200.*

Meadows Museum of Art. A small but admirable showing of Spanish and Portuguese art, including Goya, Picasso, Murillo, Velázquez, and Miró. The outdoor sculpture garden features mainly contemporary artists such as Noguchi and Henry Moore. *In the Owens Fine Art Center, SMU campus, Bishop and Brinkley; (214) 692-2516.*

Dallas skyline.

■ C E N T R A L   C I T Y

Like many formerly bustling central business districts, downtown Dallas seems to have hit the skids. Neiman-Marcus, the Bloomingdale's of Texas, still operates its flagship store at Main and Ervay, but the city's other grand department stores have hiked to the suburbs. Poor folk have taken over the sidewalks, waiting to change city buses and browsing in the cheap-goods stores. Yet, step onto the down escalator in any office tower, or pass through the glass door at Thanksgiving Square (at the juncture of Pacific Avenue and Bryan and Ervay streets), and you'll find yourself in a different world. More than 200 restaurants and specialty shops are located below ground in a network of tunnels. Underground Dallas is especially the place to be in July and August, when outdoor temperatures reach 100 degrees (38° C). It doesn't rain there, cold winds don't blow in the winter, and the poor rarely venture in.

Nothing tells what Dallas is like better than the history of its latest snapshot spot, **Pioneer Plaza,** a four-acre park adjacent to the downtown Dallas Convention Center at 650 South Griffin Street. "Ten years from now, this is absolutely going to be considered one of the greatest monuments in the entire world," multimillionaire developer Trammel Crow, the park's author, declared to the *New York Times* as the park was being built. Not everybody agreed. "The making of Pioneer Park is a grim story—one of the most blatant examples of good-ol'-boy politics in modern Dallas history," wrote longtime Dallas columnist Laura Miller.

Completed in 1995, the Plaza features an artificial waterfall, an artificial hill, and a bigger-than-life reproduction of a Western cattle drive: bronze statues of 70 steers with three cowboys and their horses. The project's sculptures and improvements sit on city-owned land, but the Dallas Parks Foundation, a private, non-profit group, took care of most of the $4 million price tag.

■ **SPORTS**
The Dallas Cowboys won the Super Bowl in 1993 and 1994 under the leadership of head coach Jimmy Johnson, whose stiff, silvery coif was complemented nicely by his team's silver helmets and the silver boots of the Cowboy's flashy cheerleaders. Johnson took the place of the Cowboys' first coach, the much-admired Tom Landry, who first brought the team to stardom in the 1966–67 season; now Johnson

A party at Neiman-Marcus, the upscale department store which has long been a Dallas institution, finds artist Leroy Neiman (no relation) and Carolyn Farb hamming it up for the camera.

DOOMSDAY IN DALLAS

There are demons loose in cyberspace—green monsters heaving fireballs, pitiless pink chomper demons that will bite the life out of you if you stumble on them in one of the dark corridors of the computer game Doom. Doom has become a digital world phenomenon.

It's hell on Earth and hundreds of thousands, some say millions, of people are rejoicing. Parents worry about it, grown men ponder their addiction to it, and corporate executives have had to ban it from company computers so employees can get some work done. The game centers around the story of an errant marine who ends up on one of the moons of Mars, but Jay Wilbur, Doom's marketing director, says the real story is "If it moves, shoot it."

Actually, the most interesting Doom story is about the handful of young men who created it. Their small cluster of offices is located in the placid Dallas suburb of Mesquite. But they started several years ago in an apartment in Shrevesport, Louisiana, with a shoestring budget. Their first game was called Commander Keen, subtitled Aliens Ate My Baby Sitter. Their company is called ID, and Wilbur says that his company's games are the Freudian id gone wild.

The nine ID employees, all between 23 and 30 years old, are Net Heads—people who hang out on and know their way around the vast network of networks called the Internet. That's where ID sells the game—on the Net. They put a game's first chapter out on the Net as "shareware," meaning that anybody can download the game and play it for free. But if they get hooked, they have to buy the other chapters from ID for $40. By the time Doom came out, ID had already developed a reputation on the Net, and the Doom download was a cyberspace event of the first order.

The principal technological reason Doom has caught fire is the speed with which it allows a player to tear through its three-dimensional world. This is a very fast game, fueled by testosterone and adrenaline in equal parts. Players dash down darkened corridors and race through a hellish landscape, ambushed and assaulted from all sides by fiendishly conceived monsters. Players fight back with a small arsenal of weapons—pistol, machine gun, rocket launcher, and a strange-looking weapon called a plasma rifle, the BFG 9000. According to the Doom creators, this stands for "a Big . . . um . . . Gun."

One of the features that endears Doom to enthusiasts is that you can play it over a network and stalk your colleagues (or their icons at least) through the hallways of hell.

The ID staff gave this reporter a demonstration of what's called a Death Match. Four players sitting at computers in different offices, banging on the walls, pitted against each other.

This quiet little demo match went on for nearly an hour and half, which gives you some idea of why Doom has been banned on a lot of corporate networks. That doesn't bother the Doom makers, though. A couple of Ferraris and a new Dodge Viper in the ID parking lot bear gleaming testimony to their sudden financial success. But according to John Romero, one of the company's founders, ID will stay small, and concentrate everyone's energies on only one game at a time. That way everyone stays happy.

—John McChesney, Technology Reporter for National Public Radio, Dallas, 1994

has been succeeded by Barry Switzer, who with ace quarterback Troy Aikman and star running back Emmett Smith can be seen during the season at **Texas Stadium,** located in Irving, just off TX 183.

College football fans (and there are many in Texas) catch the New Year's Day game at the **Cotton Bowl** in Fair Park, between Grand and Nimitz. In the fall, hordes of UT alums show up at the Cotton Bowl to cheer their alma mater's team, the Longhorns, when it plays rival University of Oklahoma—the Cowboys' coach Switzer's old team!

Dallas itself is home to one pro team, basketball's Mavericks, and in Dallas, pro basketball fans are seriously appreciated. That's because they're in short supply. The Mavericks are known for something the Cowboys aren't: losing more games than any other team in their league. Mavericks fans go to games at **Reunion Arena,** 777 Sports Street in downtown Dallas.

Drawing neither the fame of the Cowboys nor the notoriety of the Mavericks is the city's middle-of-the-pack baseball team, the Texas Rangers, owned by George W. Bush, Texas politician and a son of the former President. One of baseball's longest career players (and formerly a Houston Astro), pitcher Nolan Ryan retired from the Texas Rangers in 1992, after playing 26 years in the majors and setting records for career strikeouts (5,668) and walks (2,755). The team has always been based in the west-of-Dallas suburb of Arlington, which also is home to Six Flags Over Texas, the Warner Bros. rival to California's Disneyland and Florida's Disney World. (Batman and Bugs Bunny are its hosts, instead of Mickey Mouse and Donald Duck.)

In 1994—just in time for the baseball strike—the Rangers christened a new open-air stadium that makes even lukewarm play a pleasure for spectators. In designing the **Ballpark in Arlington,** as the Rangers' showplace is called, its architects drew ideas from the team's former Arlington Stadium, and also from baseball tradition, especially Chicago's Wrigley Field. The result was a ballpark with a red-brick facade, natural grass, and a vaguely Ivy League air. Stadium seats at the ballpark are angled towards the center of play, so that double-header fans don't get sore necks. A part of the center field stands was left open: it's a pedestrian park inside a ballpark. Even jogging trails are provided! Seventy-five concession stands and a center field restaurant that seats 500 were designed into the plan to improve the fare that is almost as much a part of baseball as hits, runs, and errors.

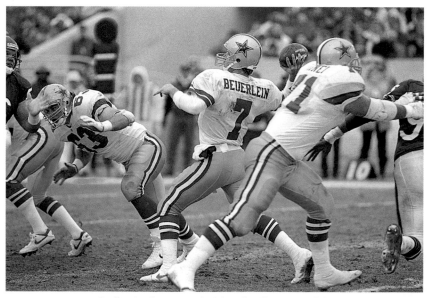

Dallas Cowboys at work. (Photo by Zbigniew Bzdak)

Dallas developer Trammel Crow poses with one of the 70 bronze steers that grace Pioneer Plaza in the heart of Dallas. Controversy has surrounded the development of the plaza, situated adjacent to the city's convention center, where some felt a hotel to serve conventioneers should have been built instead. Furthermore, some residents felt the new Plaza promoted Dallas's image as a cow town instead of the sophisticated financial center it is—a similar outcry having been made when Tex Schramm named the new Dallas football franchise the Cowboys. Eventually, however, Crow prevailed when the city council approved the project so long as the private Dallas Parks Foundation footed the $4 million bill for construction costs. The city council's decision was not without its own controversy as former councilman Jerry Bartos recalled for the Dallas Observer, *"It was done in such a way—nobody, and I'm saying nobody, including me—remembers the process."*

KKDA RADIO

KKDA, 730 on the AM dial, located in Grand Prairie, one of the Mid-Cities, has long been the voice of the Dallas area's poor, non-white, and dissident.

Nearly 90 percent of KKDA's audience is black, and the station proclaims itself as "Soul 73." Though its bent is toward blues classics and an over-40 audience, its disc jockeys play what listeners request by telephone, and sometimes *only* when they make requests: a great deal of air time is devoted to public service of a very direct kind—solving problems that are presently at hand.

Listeners call in to ask for help with their bills, or to report a stolen auto, or to locate a missing relative. Or they'll say that their car has broken down on a freeway: can a mechanic come lend a hand? Its lines are so busy that sometimes callers must wait half an hour to get their minute on the air. Disc jockeys work music into the extra space.

The king of KKDA is "Cousin" Linnie Henderson, a thin, chain-smoking elder who refuses to disclose his age. He's KKDA's voice of patience, calm, and persistence. Henderson opens his shows by greeting the more than 50 towns in the listening area, name by name, a litany that consumes nearly five minutes of time. He answers most callers with a resounding "Hi, ya, hi, ya, hi, ya," and usually refers to female callers as "Sister" or "Dear Sister." For three hours a day, from 3 to 6 P.M., he broadcasts a mixture of Biblical quotes and counseling jargon, playing sin music in the dead spots, and—as often as he can—a gospel tune dedicated to "the sick, shut-in, and bereaved." When the telephones are really ringing, the "Cuz" is likely to let out with folk expressions that are a relic of simpler times, such as, "we're as hot as a pot of neck bones!"

■ FORT WORTH

The capital city of West Texas is Fort Worth, a city of about a half-million, known in everyday parlance by two other names and even an adage. Names: Panther City (from nineteenth-century reports of bobcat sightings), and Cowtown (cattle drivers came through there). Adage: "Dallas is where the East peters out; Fort Worth is where the West begins." The adage takes note of Fort Worth's greatest problem: that it is near to, and shares the world's largest airport with, Dallas—which in Fort Worth is perceived to be a city of snobs. The rivalry between Odessa and Midland is repeated on the edge of West Texas, with Fort Worth taking Odessa's role as blue-collarish town, and Dallas, across the East-West divide, proudly playing Midland, a city of skyscrapers and expensive suits.

Fort Worth is the hub of the Bell Helicopter Company, the Chance-Vaught aircraft company, and several other defense-industry plants, most of them located in its suburbs. The aircraft and auto plants that encircle it have made it a labor union town and sometimes a liberal stronghold, by West Texas standards, anyway. But historically it is better known as an oil and cattle town. Oil wealth especially has endowed it with attractions not usually associated with the name Cowtown, and most of them are located in the city's cultural district, southwest of downtown (see "Fort Worth Attractions"). They include the **Modern Art Museum;** the **Kimbell Art Museum,** a center of both modern and pre-Hispanic exhibitions; the **Amon Carter Museum,** a storehouse of Western art; the **Fort Worth Museum of Science and History,** known for its planetarium; and the **Sid Richardson Collection of Western Art.** The latter is a legacy of a wealthy wildcatter who lived in Fort Worth until his death in 1959, leaving behind a dynasty of grandnephews in the Bass clan: Perry Richardson Bass, Sid Richardson Bass, Edward Perry Bass, Robert Muse Bass, and Lee Marshall Bass, whose cumulative assets total some $7 billion, and make them holders of the second largest fortune in Texas. But to Fort Worth's dismay, the richest man in Texas is H. Ross Perot, of Dallas, whose net worth is estimated at $3.5 billion.

The Tandy Corporation, parent to the Radio Shack transnational chain, is the work of the late Charles Tandy, as is the **Tandy Center,** a showplace on the edges of downtown, connected to its center by a subway line. The **Livestock Exchange and the Stockyards Museum,** located in the Stockyards National Historic District on the north side of downtown, is a reminder of how the town really started, with the arrival of the Texas Pacific Railroad in 1876. The railroad, not overland cattle drives, made the former army outpost into a packing-house location as well. The old stockyards district is today a center of Western-style nightlife. Houston's Gilley's Club, the crossroads of life in the 1981 John Travolta film *Urban Cowboy,* may be closed and gone, but in Fort Worth, all that and more—indoor rodeos and western souvenir shops, for example—still live at Billy Bob's Texas, one of the nearly two dozen nightclubs in the stockyards district, about three miles (4.8 km) northwest of downtown, on North Main at TX 183.

Other cities in Texas (and most Texas towns) are tied to Fort Worth by a unique cultural institution, the **Southwestern Baptist Theological Seminary,** cradle of Southern Baptist preachers. In the early years of the century, Fort Worth's Baptists won a battle with their co-religionists from Dallas over the location of the seminary, which was originally seated at Waco. Today Southwestern produces some 800 preachers a year—newsman Bill Moyers is perhaps its most famous non-clerical graduate—including most of those who assume pulpits in Texas, where Southern Baptists are the largest Protestant denomination. Over the past decade, the denomination has been convulsed by internal strife between "inerrantists"—essentially, people who believe that the Bible is literally true—and "moderates." In most of the battles, the more fundamental inerrancy faction has unseated its rival. As a result (much to Fort Worth's dismay), Southwestern, historically identified with the "moderates," is now subject to the control of a largely inerrantist board, and that's not the best of news for Fort Worth: the inerrantist movement's godfather is W. A. Criswell, pastor of the First Baptist Church—of Dallas!

Billionaire entrepreneur and former presidential candidate H. Ross Perot is based in the Dallas/Fort Worth metroplex.

(right) Dallas minister George Gregory preaches at the Johnson Baptist Church.

FORT WORTH MAIN ATTRACTIONS

■ U N I Q U E L Y   F O R T   W O R T H

Fort Worth Water Gardens. Curiously called a garden, this popular attraction is actually four blocks of concrete, waterfalls, and water sculptures designed by architect Philip Johnson. *Between Houston and Commerce, south of the Convention Center.*

Stockyards National Historic District. Developed in the 1880s, the Fort Worth stockyards grew to be the largest in the world and brought the city enormous prosperity. Exchange Avenue was the district's main artery and is lined with restored nineteenth-century buildings. The most popular is the mission-style edifice at 131 East Exchange Avenue, the **Livestock Exchange,** which was once the center of activity and still holds hog and cattle auctions. Also housed in the Exchange building is the **Stockyards Museum,** depicting the history of Fort Worth and the stockyards. Livening up the present-day district are clusters of restaurants, saloons, art galleries, and western clothing shops. *North Main and Exchange streets; (817) 624-4741.*

Sundance Square. Named for the Sundance Kid, who together with Butch Cassidy hid from the law in downtown Fort Worth. The square covers four city blocks and includes a number of restored turn-of-the-century buildings. Among these is the medieval **Knights of Pythias Hall** at 317 Main Street, the oldest building in the square and the world's first Pythian Temple. Sid Richardson's Collection of Western Art is another of the Square's sights worth seeing. *Main and Second Street.*

Cattleman's Museum. Presents the history of Texas' cattle industry with audio-visual displays, historic photographs, and artifacts. Exhibits also honor ranching pioneers such as Samuel Burk and Charles Goodnight, as well as the lesser known but well-represented, black cowboys—nearly 8,000 black ex-slaves and free men joined the cattle industry after the Civil War. *1301 West Seventh Street; (817) 332-7064.*

■ S C I E N C E   M U S E U M

Fort Worth Museum of Science and Industry. Many of the exhibits are geared to, but not exclusively for, children. Displays range from fossils to computers and topics covered include geography and the history of medicine. Also connected with the museum is the **Noble Planetarium,** offering astronomy and laser shows, and the amazing **Omni Theater,** projecting films on an 80-foot dome. *1501 Montgomery; (817) 732-1631.*

■ ART MUSEUMS

The Amon Museum. A great admirer of the American West, newspaperman, oil mogul, and philanthropist Amon G. Carter established this museum, insisting his beloved Fort Worth was in need of great art. Carter's appreciation for art, specifically western art, flourished with the influence of his friend Will Rogers. Carter opened the museum with his collection of paintings by Frederic Remington and Charles M. Russell. As the museum expanded the collection grew to include works by Georgia O'Keeffe, Winslow Homer, Grant Wood, Laura Gilpin, and Ansel Adams, among others. *Off Camp Bowie Blvd. between Lancaster and Montgomery; (817) 738-1933.*

Kimbell Art Museum. Texas industrialist Kay Kimbell left his art collection and estate to the Kimbell Art Foundation which in turn opened this museum in the early 1970s. The assortment of works by El Greco, Velazquez, Rembrandt, Cézanne, and Picasso occupy spacious, and light-drenched galleries—the award-winning design of Louis Kahn. Theater and musical performances are hosted often by the museum. *3333 Camp Bowie Boulevard; (817) 332-8451.*

Modern Art Museum of Fort Worth. Stunning works by Picasso, Rothko, Pollock, Warhol, and Stella are found here. *1309 Montgomery; (817) 738-9215.*

Sid Richardson Collection of Western Art. Located in the colorful Sundance Square this one-room gallery exhibits the works of Frederic Remington and Charles M. Russell. Sid Richardson favored western art and surrounded himself with the works of these two artists. *309 Main Street; (817) 332-6554.*

■ EXPLORING OUTDOORS

Fort Worth Botanic Gardens and Japanese Garden. Miles of rose bushes and a rich variety of trees. The unique Fragrance Garden is designed especially for the blind. In addition, the gardens include a large and tranquil Japanese Garden and Conservatory filled with tropical plants. *3220 Botanic Garden Drive at University Drive, north of I-30; (817) 871-7686.*

E A S T   T E X A S

TEXAS EAST OF THE 98TH MERIDIAN and north of the 30th parallel—or in simpler terms, east of I-35 and north of I-10—stands out from the rest of the state as a color: it is unremittingly *green*. Only in this part of Texas do dogwood trees bloom and fish swim in a natural lake—Caddo Lake, nearly on the Louisiana line. (Texans can thank the Army Corps of Engineers for the state's other lakes.) The lushness of East Texas is unmistakable to any traveler, even in winter. Of some 207 species of trees native to Texas, 142 grow in East Texas; 79 of them, including the Southern Sugar Maple and Pignut Hickory, are to be found only there. East Texas is so verdant largely because it receives more than 30 inches (75 cm) of rain a year, with the eastern edge receiving nearly twice that amount.

East Texas is the most densely populated area in the state. Its some 50,000 square miles (112,500 sq km) account for only 19 percent of the state's land area, but are home to more than 40 percent of its people, most of whom live in Dallas and Houston. West Texas, by contrast, occupies about a quarter of the state's land area, but accounts for only 17 percent of the total population. Drivers in West Texas can go 90 miles (150 km) without sighting one of the silvery steel water towers that stand about 300 feet (100 m) above every small Texas town. In East Texas, on the other hand, most towns lie within five miles (8 km) of each other. A road map of West Texas has lines. East Texas maps are furrowed.

East Texas is also the favorite habitat of the nine-banded armadillo, an almost comical-looking creature with a head shaped like a rodent's, short legs, a long skinny tail, and a spherical body covered in small bony plates (armadillo means "little armed one" in Spanish). The armadillo originally came to Texas from Mexico, through the dry Rio Grande Valley, and continued on to the lusher climes of East Texas, where the species thrives in greater numbers than it does in West Texas. (Armadillo also thrive in the states that border East Texas—Louisiana, Oklahoma, and Arkansas.) In the past 20 years, the armadillo has become an informal mascot for the state of Texas—perhaps because its armor seems to say, "Don't mess with me." Unfortunately, many cars do, and most travelers only see lifeless armadillo on the side of the road. To see them in the wild you've got to traipse into creekbed areas, and keep your distance: some scientists claim that the little critters transmit leprosy to humans.

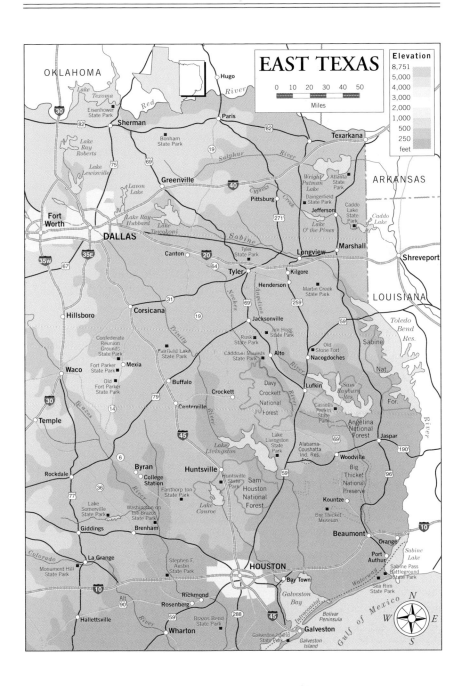

■ COTTON, CATTLE, LUMBER, AND OIL

When journalist John Gunther drove through Texas in 1946, he noted that, "The east is, by and large, cotton country, with tenant farming, a Mississippi Delta culture, mushrooming industries, big towns, poor whites, most of the state's Negroes, and, of course, oil." The key words in his description were "cotton," "industry," and in Texas, what is the same, "oil." In regards to all of these pursuits, East Texas was the pioneer for the state.

All of Texas ultimately became American territory because the eastern and southeastern regions were settled by Americans. Though the Spanish had established several outposts in Texas prior to the nineteenth century, nowhere was it thickly populated until Anglo settlers came to East Texas following the Mexican War of Independence in 1820. The settlers came from Missouri and the Old South in search of new lands to seed in cotton. Since the crop couldn't thrive west of the 30-inch rainfall line without deep-well irrigation, East Texas became the site of the state's first big cotton plantations and the birthplace of commercial agriculture in Texas.

Cotton cultivation began in East Texas during the era of slavery, and continued as a labor-intensive crop. When the twentieth century opened, about three-quarters of the state's acreage lay east of today's I-35, and two-thirds of those who cultivated it were tenant farmers. But the tractors and harvesting machines that became available

to American farmers after World War II made it possible for a single family to cultivate a large plot—up to a half-mile square (1.3 sq km), or 320 acres, sometimes more. In fact, the cost of machinery made big farms almost necessary:

The Great Depression struck hard in the rural communities of East Texas, forcing many families such as this one off their land and onto the road in search of a better life. (Standard Oil-N.J.-Collection, University of Louisville)

The Waco Texas Cotton Palace Pageant in 1927 featured Neptune, flourishing a cotton branch and hoisted onto an archway composed of cotton bales. (The Texas Collection, Baylor University.)

volume had to be high enough to justify a large expense. And while land in East Texas was costly and already divided into small 40-, 80-, and 160-acre tracts, it was cheap and available in large parcels in the western part of the state. Insect infestations were rare in dry West and North Texas, and when deep-well irrigation became common in those regions at the end of World War II, the East Texas cotton economy speedily declined. By the early 1960s, most Texas cotton farming had shifted west of the I-35 line, where most of today's crop is grown. For most of this century, Texas has been the United States' leading cotton producer.

After the Civil War and the emancipation of slaves, two less labor-intensive agricultural activities took the old crop's place in East Texas. According to Texas myth, ranching was always conducted on huge spreads of South and West Texas, but East Texas has long been the industry's literal birthplace, and remains so today:

cattle are born here so that mother cows and their calves can feast on East Texan grasses until the latter can forage for themselves. As yearlings, the calves are shipped to larger spreads in the western part of the state—where the bacteria and insects that flourish in humid climes can't harm them as much.

Before the late 1960s, cattle populations were fairly well dispersed across Texas, with the exception of a few desert counties in the sheep-and-goat country of the Trans-Pecos. Today, the highest concentrations of cattle in Texas are in the eastern and far northern ends of the state: the cattle are born in East Texas, fattened and killed in North Texas.

But unless you leave the highways and drive down one of the million dirt roads in rural East Texas, you might never guess that cattle are there. Like so much else in the region's life, cattle are screened from view by a curtain of pine trees along the highways. And their numbers aren't great in any one pasture, because the cow or cow-calf business is mainly a mom-and-pop operation. Most of these small-time farmers keep between 10 and 100 cattle on their home places.

As cotton fled East Texas, the area's economy turned not only to cattle, but to a natural resource. East Texas was the only naturally wooded part of the state. But between 1890 and 1940, some 16 million acres of virgin pine forests were felled

(above and right) East Texas is both cattle and armadillo country.

▪ Cultural Timeline ▪

1836 Mexican general Santa Anna takes as chattel the Yellow Rose of Texas, a slave named Emily Morgan. The next year Santa Anna is defeated and Texas becomes a republic, and the Yellow Rose is returned to her owner.

Comanches kill settlers at Fort Parker and kidnap a child, Cynthia Ann Parker. She later marries a Comanche chief and gives birth to Quanah Parker, last great chief of the Comanches, who led attacks on frontier settlements until 1875.

1853 Steamboat captain Richard King buys up 75,000 acres along the Rio Grande and begins to raise Texas longhorn cattle on what comes to be the largest ranch in the continental U.S., the King Ranch.

1860s The great cattle drives begin, ushering in the golden age of the Texas cowboy. They continue through 1885.

1868 Scott Joplin is born near Texarkana. One of America's greatest composers, he was a founder of ragtime, which combined elements of popular music and ballads with African, Caribbean, European, and American Southern music. Most famous for "Maple Leaf Rag."

1870s Stetson hats, made by John B. Stetson of Philadelphia, become standard Texas headgear.

1882 Mr. (later Governor) and Mrs. James Stephen Hogg give birth to a daughter they name Ima Hogg, whether out of insensitivity, cruelty, or stupidity is unclear. She becomes the butt of endless jokes.

1885 The first Dr. Pepper drink is concocted in Waco at the Old Corner Drugstore, one year before Coca-Cola is invented.

1903 Rodeo star Bill Pickett first bites a steer on its upper lip during a rodeo, a trick later known as bulldogging.

1927 First 7-Eleven convenience store opens in Dallas. Becomes a fixture of modern American life.

1930s Bob Wills and the Texas Playboys popularize "Texas Swing" on the radio program "Light Crust Doughboys from Burr's Mills." In 1940 their song "San Antonio Rose" becomes a hit; soon afterwards, the band moves to Hollywood to appear in films.

1936 Buddy Holly is born in Lubbock. Goes on to change rock and roll in the '50s, and with his band, the Crickets, becomes a superstar.

1942 Margarita coctail is invented in Juárez, just across the river from El Paso, by bartender Pancho Morales. Six years later it is invented in San Antonio by Mrs. Margarita Sames. A few years later it is invented again by a Los Angeles bartender.

1945 Comedian Steve Martin is born in Waco.

1956 *Giant,* based on Edna Ferber's novel about a Texas ranching family, is filmed in the Marfa-Valentine area. Elizabeth Taylor and James Dean star.

1958 Engineer Jack Kilby invents the microchip at the Texas Instruments plant in Dallas.

1960 Tom Landry of Mission, Texas, becomes coach of the Dallas Cowboys. A well-known pro-football player during the 1950s, he helps the Cowboys win the 1966–67 NFL Eastern Division title.

1963 Mary Kay Ash opens a cosmetics business with $5,000.

1973 Texas native Willie Nelson, musician and actor, makes his first appearance on "Austin City Limits" and hosts his first Fourth of July picnic. In the following years he helps create the "Austin sound."

1985 Publication of *Lonesome Dove* by Texas author Larry Jeff McMurtry. Raised on a ranch near the North Texas town of Archer City, McMurtry is one of the best-known modern Texas writers.

1980s Southfork Ranch, the on-screen home of TV series "Dallas" and millionaire J. R. Ewing, becomes more famous than the King Ranch.

1991 Tommy Tune wins Tony Awards for best director of a musical and best choreography for the musical *The Will Rogers Follies.* Born in Wichita Falls, Tune has won more Tonys in different categories than any other American.

1991 *Slacker,* a movie with a unique style articulating the mood of a new generation, is filmed in Austin.

1993 Dallas Cowboys win the Super Bowl. Win again the next year.

for lumber. Virgin pine now live only in natural preserves, though plantation pines have since returned to the acreage that cotton once claimed.

With its ample supplies of water and trees, East Texas is an ideal location for paper manufacturers, and more paper than lumber comes from the region's plantation pines. In the modern management of these forests, clearcutting is the rule—to the disappointment of the state's ecologists. The sawmills and paper plants that today dominate parts of the region provide employment to the laboring population still remaining in rural East Texas; the rest of the workers began migrating to the cities when defense plants opened during World War II.

East Texas is also where the oil boom began. The first big strike in the state's history came at Corsicana, shortly before the turn of the twentieth century. The 350 wells around Corsicana produced about a half-million barrels of oil per year, and led to construction of the state's first refinery. In 1901, the Spindletop gusher—a single well near Beaumont—came in, and during its first year, it produced more than three million barrels of oil. For months the well produced more oil than anybody could handle. The surplus was stored in holes, or tanks, dug out of the earth. Then in March of that year, the tanks—and it seemed, the whole atmosphere—went up in a roaring blaze. Only afterwards were ways devised to handle Spindletop's flow.

The Texaco, Mobil, and Gulf oil companies arose from the Corsicana and Spindletop discoveries; refineries sprang up at Port Arthur, Beaumont, and Houston to process Spindletop's bounty alone. But even the Corsicana and Spindletop booms didn't make Texas the leader in national petroleum production. The Kilgore, or East Texas, boom did that. In 1930, a well at Kilgore "came in," or produced, and 1,000 wells shortly followed it, all in a 40-by-5-mile (64 x 89-km) patch. The East Texas field produced a total of 100 million barrels of oil during its best years. But by 1970, most of the oil in East Texas was plumbed, and when the rest of the state experienced a rush of oil-related growth in the 1970s and early '80s, the fields in East Texas were almost quiet.

Because East Texas pioneered cotton, lumber, and oil, Dallas and Houston, the biggest cities in Texas, are here. Insofar as Texas is an industrial power, the whole of East Texas can take the credit. Dallas and Houston so quickly developed a life and dynamic of their own that when East Texas is mentioned today, residents of the two cities assume that reference is being made to the rural part of the region, not to the places where they live.

East Texas is where the oil boom began. Roughnecks like James Ley have kept the oil flowing for the past 90 years.

■ WACO

To travel south from Dallas to Waco along I-35 is to cross 100 miles (160 km) of rolling prairie, punctuated only by a few cedar trees and knots of grazing cows. Though situated on the borders of East, West, and Central Texas, Waco is considered a part of East Texas because of its history. Like Dallas, Waco was built on a river and founded early in the 1840s, during the era of the Republic of Texas. The 1952 *Handbook of Texas* notes that, "As Waco's commerce was dependent largely upon the rich plantations of the Brazos Valley, the town suffered severely during the Civil War." And like Dallas, Waco has survived even though the cotton trade is gone, partly because it is the home to insurance companies and mutual aid associations.

Again like Dallas, Waco is home to a Protestant college, **Baylor University,** a property of Southern Baptists (Southern Methodist University is its Dallas counterpart). Founded in 1845 and moved here from Independence in 1886, Baylor is worth visiting for its **Armstrong-Browning Library,** where poetry enthusiasts can enjoy the largest collection of works by Robert and Elizabeth Barrett Browning in the world. The Italian Renaissance Revival building which houses the library features 54 stained glass windows, each depicting a different Browning poem. You can visit Baylor University at Exit 335B off I-35.

Waco has developed a minor tourist trade centered on several other museums as well. The town is home to the soft drink Dr. Pepper, invented at Waco's Old Corner Drug Store in 1885, one year before Coca-Cola. For years, beverages made with it were called "Wacos" in the rest of Texas—and the bottler has established a shrine to the company's history: the **Dr. Pepper Museum,** at 300 South Fifth Street, the company's 1906 bottling plant.

Wild West fans prefer the **Texas Ranger Museum and Hall of Fame,** known for its collection of nineteenth-century pistols and located at **Fort Fisher Park,** on I-35 at the Brazos River. For the athletically inclined, the **Texas Sports Hall of Champions**—formerly the Texas Tennis Museum and Hall of Fame—is also located at Fort Fisher. The **Texas Masonic Grand Lodge,** whose unusual architecture includes two spires that, its architect says, really represent phallic symbols, is one of the oldest standing buildings in Waco's downtown. Located at 715 Columbus, its ground and basement floors are a public museum of Masonic memorabilia, including the devices used in the legendary "black ball" membership selection process. Because the Texas Revolution was arguably the fruit of a Masonic plot, the Grand Lodge doubles as a shrine for Texas history. There—and only there—one is

CAPTAIN M. T. (LONE WOLF) GONZAULLAS
COMPANY "B", TEXAS RANGERS
(Inside, holding butt of Sub-machine
gun in his 1932 Model Chrysler, armor
protected scout car, at Longview,
Texas, 1932.)

Capt. M. T. (Lone Wolf) Gonzaullas of the Texas Rangers Company 'B' displays a submachine gun mounted in his 1932 Chrysler. (East Texas Oil Museum, Kilgore College)

told, for example, that the Lone Star flag was designed by a lodge member, its design based on the star used in Masonic lore as a symbol of friendship.

■ WACO TRAGEDIES

Two great follies—one bizarre, the other plainly tragic—a hundred years apart, bracket the city's modern history. Waco was the central location, in 1896, for the promotion of what was sometimes called the city of Crush, Texas. Named for an executive of the MKT, or Missouri, Kansas & Texas Railroad, Crush never really existed, though for a day it had saloons, eateries, and politicians on the stump. Crush was only a spot in the countryside between Waco and Hillsboro, a destination for one of the excursions that were popular in that era. In September of 1896, some 30 trains brought some 30,000 passengers to Crush to witness The Great Train Wreck. Two steam locomotives, each pulling six freight cars, met in the center of Crush, backed a mile in opposite directions down the track, and came rushing at each other at full speed. Their engineers jumped to the ground before the spectacular impact—but two spectators, one of whom was watching from a tree, were killed by flying parts.

The toll from Waco's second tragedy, which spanned February through April of 1993, was much higher. Waco's Branch Davidians, a sect of Seventh Day Adventists, had for years been prominent citizens, but under the leadership of David Koresh (a.k.a. Vernon Wayne Howell) they'd begun stockpiling arms at their Mt. Carmel encampment about 10 miles (16 km) northeast of the city. When the Bureau of Alcohol, Tobacco, and Firearms got wind of this development, it marshalled some 100 agents to raid the place. A gunfight ensued, in which four ATF agents and five residents of Mt. Carmel were killed. Afterwards, a 51-day siege by the Federal Bureau of Investigation was begun. On April 19, FBI agents attempted to end the standoff by ramming Mt. Carmel with tanks and injecting tear gas inside. The building at Mt. Carmel erupted in flames, killing more than 70 of those inside. Nobody was more surprised and annoyed than the residents of Waco, who felt that the whole affair gave them a black eye—much like Dallas had received, 30 years earlier, when President John F. Kennedy was killed.

The crash at Crush was a staged event featuring the deliberate collision of two speeding locomotives. Unfortunately, two spectators were killed by flying debris. (The Texas Collection, Baylor Univ.)

Texas A&M cadets, known as "Aggies," are famous for their fanatical enthusiasm.

■ TEXAS A&M

The educational center of East Texas is College Station, usually mentioned along with the town next door, Bryan, as **Bryan-College Station.** It lies about 90 miles (145 km) southeast of Waco, and is the home of Texas Agricultural and Mechanical University, or Texas A&M, an institution of 43,000 students.

Even though most Texans prefer the country-boy stereotype of the honest, self-effacing "Aggie," some Texans—especially University of Texas "Longhorns"—tell Aggie jokes, jibes that paint A&M students and alums as dumb hicks. "How many Aggies does it take to change a light bulb?" they might ask. While teasing quips make A&M a part of everyday conversation across the state, Aggies insist that Texans too rarely discuss the school's real virtues. One of those is undeniable: during World War II, Texas A&M provided 9,000 officers to the American military, more than any other college in the nation.

A&M is the oldest of the state colleges in Texas, founded in 1876, five years before its rival, the University of Texas. When it was taking shape in 1875, the school's board of directors offered its presidency to Jefferson Davis, former president of the Confederacy. He declined, but recommended his friend, Thomas S.

Gathright, who got the job. Because the federal Morrill Act of 1862 gave grants to state colleges with emphases on subjects related to agricultural and mechanical arts, A&M was once an agro-tech college, known for producing farmers and engineers. It also provided training in military science, an Aggie tradition, though less important since the college became coeducational in 1966.

The A&M campus, which sits at the southwest juncture of Bryan and College Station, has 225 buildings, many named for the alums who endowed them. Dozens of Aggie buildings carry names familiar in current Texas history—for example, the Clayton Williams, Jr. Alumni Center, endowed by the West Texas oil mogul who was the 1990 Republican gubernatorial nominee.

■ SAN JACINTO DAY

The richest Aggie custom—and there are many—is the annual "muster," held by Aggie alumni worldwide on San Jacinto Day, the Texas holiday celebrating Gen. Sam Houston's victory over Mexico's General Santa Anna in April of 1836. At gatherings of two to two hundred, Aggies answer a roll call, or muster, to celebrate and to honor alums who have died. The tradition goes back to the 1880s when special events were held at the school on this holiday. For several years, San Jacinto Day was celebrated by a re-enactment of the battle. Then Aggie alums took up observance, to renew school ties. The muster was formalized, and stamped forever, on "the Rock"—the island of Corregidor—on April 21, 1942, as Japanese guns battered an American holdout in the Philippines around the clock.

The deputy commander on Corregidor was Maj. Gen. George F. Moore, Class of '08, who had been Commandant of Cadets at A&M from 1937 to 1940. He asked Maj. Tom Dooley, Class of '35, to scout out the Texas Aggies then fighting on the Rock, in hopes that they could gather on April 21. Dooley assembled a list of 25, and got one of the two wire service reporters on the island to send out a story of an Aggie muster, complete with the list of those counted. The story made headlines across America, big headlines in Texas. The embattled Aggies didn't actually gather, Major—later Colonel—Moore explained after the War: "It was impossible to congregate because they could not be spared from their positions." But Dooley's list was circulated around the island, from Aggie to Aggie, in substitution of a real roll call. Corregidor was surrendered a few days later, and the captured Aggies went off to Japanese prisoner-of-war camps.

■ MODERN A&M

At today's A&M, much to the displeasure of some of its hard-core traditionalists, female students are counted with the males at muster, and serve as their peers in the Corps of Cadets. In recent years, A&M has even opened a department of women's studies. Texas A&M has a medical school, nuclear and aerospace engineering studies, and of course, schools of agriculture and veterinary science. The library of former President George Bush is scheduled to open there, and a major campus street already carries his name.

One of the most fervent college competitions in the country is between A&M and the "Teasips," as Aggies call them, students at the University of Texas at Austin. Their rivalry never stops, but reaches a head each Thanksgiving Day, when teams from the two schools meet on the gridiron.

The two Texas universities share one of the largest endowments in the nation, the Permanent University Fund, composed in large part of some 2.4 million acres of land deeded to it a century ago, much of it in the oil-rich Permian Basin area, around Midland-Odessa. Its book value is set at just over $3 billion.

By a legislative act going back a century, UT receives two-thirds of the income from the fund, A&M the remaining third. This has given the Teasips, or Longhorns, as they call themselves, the basis for what they recite as the original Aggie joke: "Do you know why UT gets two-thirds and A&M gets one-third? . . . Because the Aggies got first choice!"

■ HOUSTON

The biggest of the cities in East Texas—the biggest in Texas—is Houston. With its population of over 1,600,000, it is by some counts the fourth largest city in the United States. It's a fast-paced town, sprawled across 500 square miles (1,280 sq km) of territory. Travelers coming into Houston by highway are often startled to find that to keep pace with traffic on the city's freeways, you've got to speed up, not slow down. Getting downtown, or anywhere in Houston, is a challenge for the valiant, as much because of as in spite of its freeway systems. Interstate-10 enters from San Antonio on the west, continuing east to New Orleans. I-45 comes from Dallas in the north, and runs down the Gulf to Galveston, some 45 miles (72 km) south. In addition to its interstates, Houston has a dozen other highway routes, including a city-circling loop more than 40 miles (64 km) in circumference and one of the two toll roads in Texas (the other is in Dallas). Gridlocks are common on I-10 during working hours, and though the city's dependence on freeways gives rise to comparisons with Los Angeles, Houston motorists display a loud impatience that would shame a Californian. Natives of the city will tell you that the only way to drive in Houston is not to drive at all.

The city's alter ego is **Memorial Park,** a two-square-mile (5-sq-km) swatch of greenery, at the juncture of I-10 and Loop 610 West. The park sits astride still-largely-natural Buffalo Bayou, the creek that at its eastern edge becomes the Houston ship channel. The park contains a botanical garden, but its natural flora includes sycamore, ash, and palmetto, in groves and stands that can be seen while coursing the bayou in a rental canoe. Memorial is especially appreciated by downtown-based joggers, who start at Wortham Theatre Center (the city's opera/symphony/theater house), on Texas and Smith streets, and trot westward along Allen Parkway and the bayou, nearly six miles (10 km) to the park. Along the way, runners get the best view in the city of the downtown district's skyscrapers, and of the redbuds, azaleas, and blooming pear trees that beautifiers have planted. The hiking-jogging trail along the bayou is also lined with modernist sculpture, including a work by Henry Moore.

Houston's skyline has become one of the nation's most spectacular.

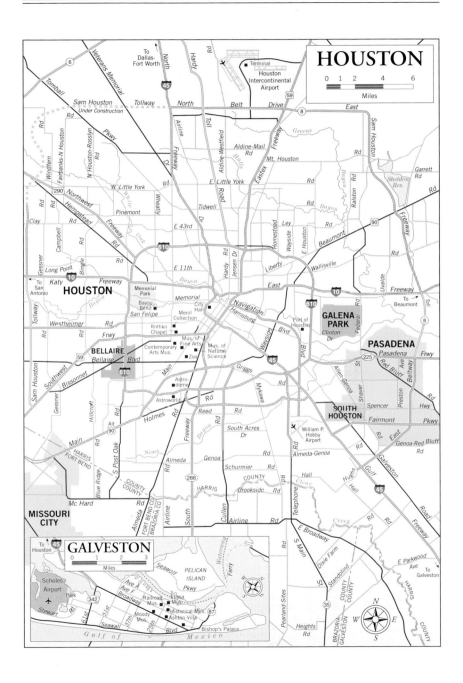

HOUSTON MAIN ATTRACTIONS

■ UNIQUELY HOUSTON

Lyndon B. Johnson Space Center. A training ground for astronauts, design center for building spacecraft, mission control for space flights, and museum. Lunar rocks, photos from Mars, spacesuits, and Mercury and Apollo spacecraft are on display. *25 miles (40 km) southeast of downtown Houston, three miles (4.8 km) east of 1-45 on NASA Road 1; (713) 244-2100.*

The Orange Show. Built by a man devoted to oranges. Jeff McKissack, as a testament to oranges and good health, constructed this folk-art complex of tunnels, murals, and a small museum out of junkyard material and other found objects.
2402 Munger Street; off the Gulf Freeway, Telephone Road, then north to Munger; (713) 926-6368.

■ HISTORIC SITES

San Jacinto Monument. Commemorating the victory of the Texas Revolution, the monument stands on the site where Sam Houston triumphed over Santa Anna in the final battle of 1836. The massive 570-foot spire, the nation's largest masonry edifice, is made of concrete and limestone. An elevator takes visitors to the observation tower on the top of the monument. The **San Jacinto Museum of History,** inside the base of the San Jacinto Monument, traces the history of Texas with rare maps, manuscripts, and artifacts. The **Battleship** *Texas* is the only surviving naval vessel to have been in both World War I and World War II. All three sites are located at: *3800 Park Road on TX 134, in the suburb of La Porte, about a 25-minute drive from downtown Houston; (713) 479-2431.*

■ DECORATIVE ARTS

Menil Collection. An astonishing range of works are exhibited throughout this cypress-wood structure. More than 10,000 pieces are attributed to Dominique de Menil's private collection, including rare Paleolithic, Oceanic, Byzantine, and African objects and a substantial array of surrealist and contemporary works. *1515 Sul Ross; (713) 525-9400.*

■ ART MUSEUMS AND SPACES

Contemporary Arts Museum. Located in the fashionably artsy Montrose neighborhood, this stainless steel structure consists of two galleries, both of which emphasize emerging art. In fact, new shows arrive about every six weeks. This fast-paced schedule ensures that the collections are as strikingly modern as the exterior. *5216 Montrose; (713) 526-3129.*

Museum of Fine Arts. The first museum in the state devoted exclusively to art, and currently one of the most comprehensive art museums in Texas. The extensive collection runs the spectrum from Renaissance works to Impressionism to contemporary paintings, sculpture, and photography. Pre-Columbian, Indian, and African native arts are also well represented. *1001 Bissonnet; (713) 639-7300.*

Rothko Chapel. The de Menils, great art enthusiasts, commissioned a team of architects, including Philip Johnson, to design this octagonal non-denominational chapel and commissioned Mark Rothko to create 14 paintings for the chapel's meditation space. *3900 Yupon Street; (713) 524-9839.*

■ EXPLORING OUTDOORS

Armand Bayou Nature Center. A 1,800-acre preserve with countless trails through woodland, prairie, and marsh. The bayou is also a popular place for boating, both private boats and guided tours. Boat tours are available on weekends. *8600 Bay Area Boulevard; (713) 474-2551.*

Memorial Park. Bordering the Buffalo Bayou, the park is a sycamore and ash oasis—prettily appointed for hiking, jogging, and canoeing. *At the juncture of I-10 and Loop 610 W.; (713) 845-1000.*

■ SCIENCE MUSEUM

Museum of Natural Science. This museum is divided into several mini-museums such as the Harry C. Weiss Hall of Petroleum Science and Technology, the Isaac Arnold Hall of Space Science, and the Museum of Medical Science. From dinosaurs to space travel to rare gems—the exhibits are diverse and fascinating, if not exhaustive. *1 Hermann Circle Drive; (713) 639-4600.*

Despite Houston's efforts to control unchecked urbanization and promote beautification with amenities such as Memorial Park, the city has always gotten its share of bad press. John Gunther wrote that "It is a city where few people think of anything but money. . . . It is also the noisiest city I have ever visited, with a residential section mostly ugly and barren, a city without a single good restaurant, and of hotels with cockroaches." Most Texans who read his book in those days were probably puzzled, and though echoes of what he charged ring true—freeway cities are noisy, after all—Houston has changed so much that today it is probably the best city in Texas in terms of restaurants.

Houston's biggest change came during the oil boom of the 1970s and early 1980s, when a thousand people moved there every week. The help-wanted ads of Sunday editions of Houston's two dailies, the *Houston Chronicle* and *Houston Post*, were being read by thousands of people in the East and Midwest. Rental trailers were stacking up in Houston from all over the country as people moved in. By the mid-1980s, a quarter of Houston's residents had been born outside the state.

During those years the media reported a new trend: the unemployed natives of America's "Rust Belt"—that is, the dying industrial cities of the Northeast and Midwest—were migrating in droves to the "Sunbelt"—the term reporters coined

Houston industrialist Gordon Cain gave his employees stock in Cain Chemical Corporation. When the company was sold to Occidental Chemical, even the janitor made a bundle.

to describe Florida, Texas, the Southwest, and Southern California. This was taken dearly to heart in Houston, which felt the impact of the population shift more than any other city in Texas. Houston became so frantic that every printing company and copy shop in town had a sign outside its door, "Business Cards in 15 Minutes." Half the business cards printed for new enterprises, it seemed, had the word Sunbelt in their names.

But after the oil bust devastated the boom economy, Houston lost some population, and across its suburbs houses were abandoned, their notes unpaid. Nonetheless, oil remains a vital part of the economy, as Houston remains an office town for the petroleum industry—Texaco, American Shell, and Pennzoil are headquartered there. Its suburbs—Pasadena is the most notorious example—are refinery towns.

■ CULTURE AND AMBIENCE
Despite the bust, Houston still thrives, in part thanks to the folks who came in the '80s. The newcomers brought with them an ethnic mix and a savvy cultural expertise that Houston didn't have before. Though essentially a white-black, Southern town like Dallas, in the past 20 years it has also acquired Mexican and Central

Simmons of Captain Benny's Oyster Bar serves up some of his justly famous local delicacies.

American immigrant populations, as well as the state's most numerous Asian minority—now four percent of the city's people. Large communities of American Indians, East Indians, Vietnamese, and Iranians also live here, many of whom arrived to work in oil- and energy-related industries. Another aspect of the city's diversity is its gay community, the largest in Texas, centered in the Montrose district, southwest of downtown. Culturally, the city boasts the excellent Houston Ballet, as well as the Houston Grand Opera.

Houston is also a hospital town; its **Texas Medical Center** became famous for heart transplants by Drs. Denton Cooley and Michael DeBakey, and the **M.D. Anderson Center** is known everywhere for pioneering cancer work. The **Galleria** shopping mall, like Houston's health care industry, draws a steady traffic of Latin American clients.

Economically, Houston was, and still is, a port—the biggest grain depot in the United States. Labor unions have always been stronger in Houston than in Dallas, thanks largely to refineries, mostly organized by the Oil, Chemical and Atomic Workers Union—whose birthplace was Fort Worth. Because it is a union town, claims lawyers across the state petition judges to try their suits in the Houston area. But even if Houston is in many ways a blue-collar town, 24 of its residents (as opposed to 20 from Dallas) found a place on *Texas Monthly*'s 1993 list of the 100 richest people in the state.

One result of Houston's mixed-use and mixed-class character is that the city is not, like Dallas, run by a long-standing oligarchy; everybody gets a turn at leadership or rule. The shifting and somewhat decentralized nature of power in Houston means that control of the city is loose—very loose: Houston is the largest unzoned city in the United States. The best way to run a city, its leaders seem to believe, is as a free enterprise.

Since it's hard to define Houston by its place in the economy, Texans define it by its weather. Houston is not the hottest big city in Texas—Dallas takes that prize—but it may be the most miserable, because its humidity is always high. Its Julys, Augusts, and Septembers are nearly unbearable. When President Bush hosted a summer meeting of the G-7 nations in his favorite town, to spare his prominent guests the hardship of Houston's humidity, he had air conditioners installed—out-of-doors!—along the sidewalk leading to their limousines.

A BRIT'S VIEW OF HOUSTON

*I*n the 1980s, Houston faced its first ever slump. When I went to visit the city towards the end of the decade, I found people much cheerier. Property prices were bouncing back, and a house in River Oaks, quite the poshest part of town, was on the market for 35 million dollars. The realtor who was dealing with it said: 'I do admit that this property might not reach its full asking price. It does not have a fireplace, and for thirty-five million dollars you *expect* a fireplace.' I mentioned this to a Houstonian friend, who did not sound at all surprised. 'Daddy loved a fire,' she said. 'Of course it meant that he had to keep the air-conditioning on full.' Of course. In Houston, nature knows its place.

The city loves its great rococo murders. These are not the squalid muggings of New York, but elaborate marital affairs, Agatha Christie on the Bayou. Some are straightforward. Joan Sandiford shot her husband in the back one night, while he was armed only with a copy of *Time* magazine and a milky drink. Juries are lenient on such peccadilloes, so she got a probated sentence and never went to jail. Also, nobody liked him anyhow, so they held a celebration barbecue when she was released. Sandy Sheehy, who wrote a book about the city's rich, says: 'The thing about Houston is that you can murder your husband, and still get invited to the right parties afterwards.'

—Simon Hoggart, *America*, 1990

■ SIGHTSEEING

Nestled between Houston's freeways are dozens of attractions, scattered all over the map. **Rice University**, sometimes called "The Harvard of the South," with an elite student enrollment of 4,000, is near the city's center point. It is named, not after the grain crop, but to honor business pioneer William Marsh Rice, whose estate provided the money for opening the school in 1912. Rice became a merchant during the days of the Republic of Texas, moved to Mexico during the Civil War, and had gone to New York in 1896, where four years later he was murdered by his valet and his lawyer, both of whom, it seems, were interested in collecting the estate upon which today's university rests.

Just to the west of Rice, off I-45 at the Calhoun exit, lies the main campus of the **University of Houston,** which enrolls almost 50,000 students through its various branches. In recent years, the university has been especially known for its creative writing program, whose faculty has included Rosellen Brown, Daniel Stern, the late Donald Barthelme, and *Paris Review* poetry editor Richard Howard.

Both the NFL's Houston Oilers and the National League's Houston Astros play in the **Astrodome.** Since quarterback Warren Moon's departure in 1993, running back Gary Brown and offensive lineman Bruce Matthews are the Oilers' main men. The 'Dome, as it is often called, located along Loop 610 South, is probably known by more people outside Texas than any other Houston landmark. The mammoth building is testimony to Lone Star ambition and daring. Opened with a game between the Houston Astros and the New York Yankees in 1965 (the Astros lost), it was the world's first air-conditioned sports arena. The annual Houston Livestock Show and Rodeo is staged there, along with hundreds of conventions and expositions. Less famously, the 'Dome was the first place where artificial grass, or Astroturf, was used in professional play, largely because natural grass couldn't survive in its artificial climate.

Since its construction, the Astrodome has been imitated and duplicated—and in some senses, surpassed—by domes in Detroit, Seattle, New Orleans, Atlanta, Dallas, and San Antonio. But having once won a trail-blazing big gamble in the world of sports, Houston's schemers and prophets, its city and county governments, are now again asking what the city can do to amaze the sports-fan world: be on the lookout for a successor to the 'Dome. The NBA's Houston Rockets play their season, meanwhile, at the **Summit,** on U.S. 59 at Edloe in the Greenway Plaza business complex.

■ N A S A

In addition to being the adopted home of former President George Bush, Houston is best known overseas as the home base for the National Aeronautics and Space Administration, or NASA. **Space Center Houston,** a.k.a. Lyndon B. Johnson Space Center, is south off I-45, in the suburban community of Clear Lake. Travelers, be warned: I-45 south of Houston is one of the few freeways in the Houston area where speed limits are routinely enforced. Practically every suburb uses the flow of traffic to fill its coffers. If you drive to NASA, beware.

NASA's home base offers a tour of the high-tech world of space exploration, including a view of the Mission Control Center. The room will be familiar to

Mike McGuire, a model maker at NASA, holds up one of his creations.

television viewers as the dispatching station for all space flights, although it's smaller than it appears through the wide-angle lens of the TV camera. Several tours through the complex allow you not only to see but to touch moon rocks. Other exhibits give visitors a chance to fiddle with space ship controls in a simulator, see a documentary on a screen five stories tall, and look over a 320-foot-long (100-m) Apollo rocket, complete with three-stage boosters. A call to the visitors center at (713) 244-2100 is a good idea before making any excursion: when manned flights are underway, both Mission Control and other parts of the Space Center are off-limits to visitors.

For buffs not content to watch flights from the ground, there's another attraction in the Houston area, one unmatched anywhere in the state. Hooks Memorial Airport in **Spring**, just north of the city on I-45, is home to a company called **Texas Air Aces,** which stages mock dogfights. Air Ace pilots provide their clients with flight suits, helmets, and propeller-driven fighter planes, take them up into the clouds and let them shoot at each other's craft with laser-beam guns. It's an amusement park ride and a video game linked together, with flying and opponents that are real. Would-be aces don't need to know how to fly—the professional Aces take care of that—but do need to be high-flyers: the all-day adventure costs about $700.

Just east of Houston across Buffalo Bayou is the industrial suburb of Deer Park, where Houston's predecessor, Harrisburg, was once located. It was burned in April 1836 by the Mexican general Antonio López de Santa Anna, after which he marched on to Galveston to lose the Battle of San Jacinto (see the essay "Battle of San Jacinto" in this chapter). The battle is commemorated by the **San Jacinto Monument** at the **San Jacinto Battleground Historical Park,** 15 miles (24 km) east of the city by TX 225 and TX 134, just northeast of Deer Park. The 570-foot-tall (173-m) monument is said to be the tallest masonry monument in the world and is patterned on two Washington, D.C., national landmarks: it's designed to look like the Washington Monument atop the Lincoln Monument. The Battle at San Jacinto was decisive for the Texas Revolution, whose victorious, ragtag army was led by Sam Houston, in whose honor the sprawling city is named.

■ GALVESTON

At the bottom or southern end of I-45 lies sandy, flat Galveston Island—27 miles (43 km) long and less than three miles (4.8 km) wide at its broadest point—and the city of Galveston, both named after a Spanish viceroy. If the town remains an important port, it has also become an important tourist destination.

Galveston is the New Orleans of Texas, with its own Mardi Gras celebration, trolley cars, antebellum mansions, and grand hotels. A 40-block area of its stately old brick and wooden homes is only a few minutes' walk from downtown, whose main drag, the Strand, itself anchors a historic district. The **Strand Visitors Center,** at 2016 Strand, provides a map of the route. When you walk it, you'll notice that, as Texas writer Marsha Walker has pointed out, "Galveston is the only city in Texas that thinks that letters of the alphabet, like numerals, are divisible by two"—as in P$^1/_2$ Street!

The Strand is a terminal for the city's trolleys, which run from downtown to the seawall and beach. The city can also be seen from a sidewheeler, the *Colonel,* on two-hour outings in Galveston's green bay. Each December (winters are mild in Galveston) some 75,000 visitors pour into town for a celebration called **Dickens on the Strand,** an evening when locals wrap themselves in bygone fashions to promenade and carouse.

The seawall along Galveston's Strand, seen here in a photograph from the 1930s, was built to protect the city from storm surges caused by hurricanes. (Underwood Photo Archives, San Francisco)

BATTLE OF SAN JACINTO

For nearly six weeks after he arrived at Gonzales on March 11, 1836, Gen. Sam Houston had been backing east towards Louisiana, along with most settlers along the Gulf Coast. The general, his soldiers, and the civilians were trying to escape the fate of the martyrs of the Alamo, all of whom had been slaughtered by Mexican troops.

Houston wasn't the most popular leader in Texas. He was a gangling, rough-hewn man in his forties, who had left Tennessee during a matrimonial scandal, become a Cherokee citizen, and established himself in Texas only the year before. Among the Cherokee, with whom he'd lived as a teenager, he was known both as "The Raven" and "The Big Drunk."

Mexico's elegant General Santa Anna, who had recently rescinded the Mexican constitution and become dictator of the country, was also moving east, stalking the rebelliousTexans.

On April 16, 1836, Santa Anna crossed a bridge on Vince's Bayou with about 950 men, reaching the juncture of the San Jacinto River with a Gulf bay of the same name. Three days later, Houston and his troops crept in, crossing Vince's Bayou and camping about a mile west of the bridge over which they expected their quarry to return. On April 20, they burned the bridge, cutting off any enemy retreat, and on the following afternoon, with about 900 troops, they assaulted Santa Anna's camp. Texas legend has it that when the attack began, the handsome Santa Anna was in his tent, recuperating from a night with Emily Morgan, a comely captured slave, later immortalized in song as "The Yellow Rose of Texas."

Between the two camps stood a ravine whose brush screened the Texans from view until they came within some 300 yards (275 m) of the Mexican barricades. With cannon shot, the Texans breached the barricade—constructed of saddles, brush, and anything else that was handy—and charged into the Mexican ranks, shooting and shouting. In the fray that followed, Houston's horse was felled. He mounted another; it fell, too. Though his ankle was shattered in the mishap, the Texas general mounted a third horse and continued his charge.

Maybe he didn't have time to realize that he was in pain. In 18 minutes, the Mexicans were put to rout. Some of them fled along the bayou, some took refuge in the waters of the bay. The Texans cut down those who tried to escape to the west on dry land—and any others that they could reach. "Take prisoners as the Mexicans was the cry in this, the last act in a bitter civil war. Only darkness halted the slaughter. Houston listed some 650 Mexicans dead. The Texans lost seven dead and 18 wounded.

Among the Mexicans who survived was a curly-headed man with an aquiline nose wearing a private's uniform—and, according to legend, jeweled underwear! He drew suspicion because the other prisoners treated him with deference, and the Texans soon realized it was General Santa Anna in disguise. Not since medieval times, when kings sometimes led armies to battle, had a victor had such a bargaining chip: the general was also president of Mexico.

Santa Anna was returned to Mexico, where he again assumed one-man rule, but the infamy of having lost Texas dogged him, and he proved an inept and corrupt politician. With a good deal of the Mexican treasury in tow, he later wound up in New York.

Santa Anna surrenders to Sam Houston in this painting of the
Battle of San Jacinto which hangs in the State Capitol in Austin.
(Texas State Library, Austin)

Galveston was the principal city in Texas during the nineteenth century and boasted the state's first electric lights, telegraph, and medical college—the latter now a branch of the University of Texas. During the Civil War, the port of Galveston was blockaded—and for a few days, captured—by Union naval forces. It was there that the conquering Union army disembarked, on June 19, 1865, to declare an end to slavery: Juneteenth, as it is called, has since been a holiday in Texas, and cities across America now celebrate it as well.

Following the Civil War, Galveston became the Ellis Island of the Gulf, the point through which European immigrants to the Southwest passed, and where they sometimes settled. One long-lasting effect of its port-of-entry phase was that the population of Galveston includes many more people of Greek, Italian, and Russian Jewish descent than any other city in the state. Another vestige is an unusual civic pride. Even native Galvestonians who have moved elsewhere distinguish themselves by referring to each other as BOI, or "born on the Island."

Much of the fuel for Allied forces was shipped out of Galveston during World War II, and for years its beaches were dirty with oil spilled from ships sunk a few miles out by German U-boats. Even recently, chemicals from nearby refineries and spills from Gulf oil rigs so polluted Galveston Bay that former U.S. senator Lloyd

The Galveston Hurricane of 1900 was America's deadliest natural disaster, killing over 6,000 of the city's 30,000 residents. (Rosenberg Library, Galveston)

Galveston Bay and the Port of Houston make up one of the Gulf's busiest seaports.

Bentsen called it "the only bay in the country with an octane rating." Cleanups have been effective and Galveston Island is sometimes cited as the scene of an environmental victory.

The city's seawall, 10 miles (16 km) long and 17 feet (5 m) above the mean low tide level, was built after what is still called "the Hurricane"—of 1900! It killed 6,000 residents and destroyed all but the stoutest structures. The seawall has become Galveston's version of Atlantic City's Boardwalk or L.A.'s Venice Beach. It's a local hangout for families and friends, criss-crossed by walkers, joggers, and tourists on rented bicycle carts. Between it and the shoreline sit massive chunks of pink Texas granite, the same rock used in the capitol in Austin, used here to dent the force of hurricane tides.

■ PORT ARTHUR TRIANGLE

Port Arthur sits at the southeasternmost point of Texas, some 20 miles (30 km) off of I-10, the highway that frames East Texas on the south. It's the hometown of the late chanteuse Janis Joplin, former Dallas Cowboys coach Jimmy Johnson, and Joe Ligon, the mainstay of gospel's Mighty Clouds of Joy. Vietnamese Catholics have

GALVESTON MAIN ATTRACTIONS

■ U N I Q U E L Y   G A L V E S T O N

The Strand National Historic Landmark District. In the nineteenth century, the Strand was "the Wall Street of the Southwest," a vibrant and beautifully designed commercial center. Today, restored ironfront buildings, many in the Victorian style, stretch for blocks. No longer a banking hub, the buildings are exceptionally well-preserved and house restaurants, small shops, and lofts. Re-create the Strand's colorful history by picking up a walking tour leaflet at the Strand Visitor's Center at 2016 Strand. *The district is about six blocks, 20th to 25th between Water and Mechanic; (409) 765-7834.*

Seawall Boulevard. Over 10 miles (16 km) long and 17 feet (5 m) above low tide. Originally built to protect the island from hurricanes, Seawall is now hot beachfront property (although below the seawall the beach is undesirable for swimmers). The inland side of the wall is lined with hotels, restaurants, gift shops, sport equipment rentals, and beach condos. *Begins near the island's eastern edge and stretches about 10 miles west.*

East End District. This 40-block district, encompassing several of the grandest houses on the island, is listed on the National Register of Historic Places. Most of these mansions were built between 1875 and 1905, when the neighborhood was home to the city's elite. Although most homes are private residences, self-guided walking or driving tours are available at the Strand Visitor's Center. *11th to 19th between Mechanic and Broadway; (409) 765-7834.*

■ H I S T O R I C   M U S E U M S   A N D   H O U S E S

Ashton Villa. The original owners of the villa were admired members of the Victorian social set. Col. James Brown and his family were among the first in the state to erect an Italianate-style house, but others on the island soon followed their lead. Hundreds of gracious mansions scattered throughout the island owe their elaborate design to the trendsetting Brown family. Today, the house museum displays period furnishings and presents an audio-visual program on the hurricane of 1900. *2328 Broadway; (409) 762-3933.*

The Bishop's Palace. This turreted 1886 mansion of limestone, pink and gray granite, and red sandstone was chosen by the American Institute of Architecture as the most striking residence in Texas. The house takes its name from the Bishop of Galveston, who took up residence here in 1923. Still owned by the Catholic Diocese, the mansion is open to the public but also accommodates the current Bishop when he is in town. *1402 Broadway; (409) 762-2475.*

Elissa and Texas Seaport Museum. A restored 1877 iron-hulled barque, said to be the third oldest operating ship in the world. The *Elissa* was in daily service until 1870, and restored during the 1980s. Museum explains nineteenth-century sailing technology. *Pier 21 at 22nd; (409) 763-1877.*

Galveston County Historical Museum. Housed in a 1906 bank building, the museum presents an interesting history of Galveston, including the Karankawa Indians, the county's notorious pirates, and the devastating hurricane of 1900. *2219 Market; (409) 766-2340.*

Moody Mansion and Museum. A 42-room traffic-stopper, the Moody Mansion was built by one of the wealthiest families in the state. The Moody Foundation has beautifully restored the house. Family heirlooms and other period antiques are arranged as if William Moody, Jr. and family were hosting a turn-of-the-century debutante ball. *2628 Broadway; (409) 762-7668.*

The Railroad Museum. The state's largest collection of retired railroad cars—35 of them—idle on the tracks in the art deco Santa Fe terminal, just as it appeared in 1932. Life-size sculptures of passengers, dressed *a la* 1930s, sit and chat in the waiting room and audiovisual displays recount the history of Texas rail. A working H-O scale model of the Port of Galveston is also on display. For a luxury dining experience, try the restaurants in the restored dining cars. *Old Galveston Railway Station, 123 Rosenberg; (409) 765-5700.*

erected a three-story monument downtown to Mary, Queen of Peace, making Port Arthur a holy city of sorts. Not to be outdone, their Buddhist neighbors several years ago salvaged the Procter Street Baptist Church, redressing it with a six-tier pagoda-like facade. Other than these attractions, the traveler sees mainly decline.

Port Arthur and its sister cities, **Beaumont,** 17 miles (27 km) east, and **Orange,** 22 miles (35 km) northeast, form what is today called the Magic Triangle, a petrochemical, shipbuilding, and papermaking complex that was called the Golden Triangle in better days.

CAJUN CRAWFISH

The Port Arthur-Beaumont-Orange area of Texas, known as the Golden or Magic Triangle, is home to the state's Cajun population—and to their delicacy, crawfish, served in restaurants along waterways, bays, and cities just off I-10. Restaurants that serve crawfish are a mixed lot, some rustic and alongside a marshy bayou, and others, like the Texas Crawfish Company just west of Beaumont, polished food emporiums.

Here and there crawfish are also available in inland Texas. The Landry's restaurants, located in Houston, San Antonio, Austin, and Dallas, are an old western Louisiana food firm that specializes in crawfish, and also in alligator, a Louisiana delicacy that's not nearly so celebrated.

Small crustaceans of the lobster family, crawfish abound in shallow, fresh water—the muddier the better. Most are commercially grown on land that has produced a crop of rice. The flooding that grain requires is utilized by farmers for a second crop of crawfish.

Table-sized crawfish are three or four inches long, with mean looking pincers that can nip. It takes a pile of them to make an entree, when shucked, picked, or peeled from their shells. In Cajun country, crawfish boils take the place of the fish fries of the Piney Woods and the backyard barbecues of the rest of Texas. One starts with a big bag of live crawfish, weighing 60 pounds or so. Cognoscenti dump them into a vat of chilled water, a treatment that causes the creatures to excrete. This step cleans or clears the black vein that is usually left in shrimp, to be worried over or swallowed by the diner.

Once washed, crawfish are then placed into a broth of boiling water and spices—mostly peppers, but every formula differs in the details—for four or five minutes. Removed and cooled, they are ready for shelling and feasting. Most restaurants that offer boiled crawfish supply diners with a good stock of newsprint on which to dispose of the pile of shells that a meal leaves. Crawfish meat is also served with rice étoufée—a thick tomato-based sauce with crawfish served on white rice.

The area's phenomenal growth began in 1901, with the gushing of the Spindletop well near Beaumont. During World War I, the Golden Triangle refined and exported more oil than any place on the globe, giving running starts to such oil companies as Texaco and Gulf. But the Triangle peaked soon afterwards, and has since suffered economic decline.

The **Rainbow Bridge,** which connects Port Arthur and Orange, is a monument

Chapel Hill is a typical small East Texas town.

of sorts to the region's stately past. The 1.5-mile (2.4-km) causeway, completed in 1938, arches sharply to 177 feet (54 m) above the Neches River. It was built into the sky to allow passage of the tallest craft operated by the navy before World War II. Few travelers use the bridge today because it is located on TX 73, instead of I-45, the region's modern link.

These days, Beaumont, Port Arthur, and Orange, with their rusting refineries and boarded-over downtowns, are known mostly as the home of Texas' Cajuns (related to Louisiana's old Acadian culture)—and of alligators and mosquitoes, the latter forming visible swarms in summer.

■ PINEY WOODS

Today, cities mark the boundaries of East Texas on I-35 to the west and I-10 to the south, but small towns and farms are the wellspring of the region's life. Out-of-state tourists rarely visit these towns and their surrounding woods, but they should. East Texas boasts some beautiful national forests and preserves, remnants of the once vast Piney Woods region—the most legendary of East Texas attractions. The Piney Woods runs in roughly a straight line from Baytown, on I-10, north to the Arkansas line, and east to Louisiana. The forested region was once much bigger, about 5,500 square miles (14,000 sq km) of virgin forest, but today, you'll need to visit Big Thicket National Preserve to see virgin pines in their natural state.

The region wasn't heavily settled during the era of the Republic of Texas, and was never home to many plantations or slaves. Historians say that the first American wave of settlement in the Piney Woods came during the Civil War, when mountain boys from all over the South took refuge there to escape the Confederate draft. The hunters' legacy is still in evidence today: ask any working man in the Piney Woods what he makes of the state of the world, and he'll tell you that everything began to go downhill when game wardens first arrived on the scene.

Before the turn of the century, when lumbering became big business in East Texas, the region was dominated by longleaf pines, the oldest of which were four feet (1.2 m) in diameter, and some 150 feet (45 m) tall, almost three times as tall as today's commercial pines at harvesting. The ancient pines of the region produced lumber nearly as dense as hardwood and so rich in resin that boards made from them could withstand weathering for generations without paint or protective coverings. The longleaf's tight grain and the relative absence of knotholes made it ideal for furniture and cabinet making, though most of the trees went into ordinary lumber production.

During the first half of the twentieth century, the timber industry felled virgin pines as fast as consumers could buy them. "They didn't even leave one standing, not even on a courthouse lawn"—except in today's Big Thicket National Preserve, notes East Texas lumber buff Wayne Alderman. Mainly because they respect the old trees, Alderman and others have in recent years begun raising "sinkers," or sunken timber, from the Sabine River, once the conduit for felled trees to sawmills in the Beaumont–Port Arthur area. Despite having lain on the river bottom for more than half a century, the old trees still yield good lumber after drying, thanks to their resin content. Carpenters like Alderman then craft the aged wood into furniture. Unfortunately, the supply of sinkers hasn't been plentiful enough to allow a premium pine furniture industry to develop.

■ TRAVELING THROUGH THE PINEY WOODS

Without a stop at a national forest or preserve, the drive between Beaumont and Texarkana can be monotonous. The seasons bring little change to the region, because evergreens are its backdrop; the chief difference you'll notice is that in summer months mists rise from the highways after a rain; in winter, the water runs off, leaving no sign of itself. The only sight for miles on end are the spindly trunks of pine trees edging the road, the damp red soil of the forest floor, and the black asphalt road you're driving, with only slight rises, dips, and curves.

If a car does whip past it'll probably be a Chevy pickup driven by a guy you'd rather not mess with on a lonely road after dark, or else a pickup pulling a cattle trailer, hauling calves from a small farm to market. Or if not that, a two-ton truck pulling a log trailer that leaves in its wake a mist of bark and dirt.

The loggers are headed to saw- and papermills, and as East Texas cognoscenti will tell you, some of them are carrying logs that aren't theirs. Most of the area's small farms have become small pine plantations, owned by heirs who've moved to the city. In their absence, lumber crews sometimes harvest their trees without permission, and without paying for what they take. The price of lumber rose so steadily during the 1980s that today, a good pine tree can bring $100 at a sawmill, a load of them, $1,000 or more. And it makes no sense, of course, for sawmills to ask the pedigree of what they turn into dust and lumber. According to the forestry department at Texas A&M, the take from stolen trees averages about $15 million a year.

■ BIG THICKET NATIONAL PRESERVE

The Piney Woods region survives in its lush natural state as the Big Thicket National Preserve—eight scattered sites, totaling some 130 square miles (340 sq km) of virgin pines, underbrush, and marshland. Though not a national park, Big Thicket exists today thanks to government intervention. During the Great Depression, the federal government purchased parcels of land from timber companies to keep them solvent. Despite the decades of challenges from both oil and timber companies that followed, the U.S. government chose to protect this wilderness, and in 1974, it established the preserve by an act of Congress.

The chief tourism office for Big Thicket operations is at its Turkey Creek unit, eight miles (13 km) north of Kountze. Here, trails cross primeval terrain that supports virgin longleaf and more than 85 other tree species, 60 shrub species, and some 1,000 varieties of flowering plants. Nearly 300 species of birds use the

thicket, some migratory, others in permanent residence: the pileated woodpecker, wood ducks, and the yellow-billed cuckoo among them. Coyotes, bobcats, and armadillo are common in this region, and among locals, hunting feral hogs has become a swamp- and river-bottom pastime. Despite the narrowness of the park, on hiking trails one hears no swish of auto traffic, sees no sign of telephone wires. Only passing airplanes add man-made sounds to the chirp and rustle of the forest.

■ WOODVILLE AND BASS FISHING

Woodville, about 40 miles (64 km) north of Beaumont on U.S. 69, is to bass fishing what Las Vegas is to gambling. **Lake Sam Rayburn,** located between Woodville and Jasper, 14 miles (23 km) away, is the largest inland body of water in Texas, with a 560-mile (900-km) shoreline and some 115,000 acres of water, stocked with black, white, striped, spotted, largemouth, and Florida bass. Boat rigs—cars or pickups with a trailer and a sturdy, showy fiberglass boat in tow—throng the streets of Woodville and Jasper, and coffee shop conversations centers on catches.

So does much of the area's commerce. In 1994, McDonald's restaurants in the two towns sponsored a quarter-million-dollar tournament, giving away $5,000 each hour, plus boats and other prizes, during a three-day contest. And that was only a slice of the pastime—big business in East Texas. Some two million Texans buy fishing licenses each year, some 75 percent of them for East Texas lakes. So widespread is the hobby that every conceivable split in the population—excepting convicts, perhaps—has its own bass-fishing club. The Dallas Police Department has several clubs, as do prison guards and several dozen churches. Nobody knows exactly how many bass fishermen there are, but more than 100,000 Texans subscribe to magazines devoted not merely to bass but to bass-fishing tournaments. None of this comes cheap. "A man doesn't bass fish serious without putting a lot of money into it," observes Jerry Dean, editor of the tournament magazine *Honeyhole.* "A lot of money" in the bass fisherman's vocabulary is the cost of a boat, motor, and trailer—or upwards of $20,000.

The passion that East Texas bass fishermen feel for their sport doesn't necessarily impoverish them, but it enriches their vocabulary. Here, for example, is a bass fishing tip—the kind of gossip passed by serious fisherman—from Rube Glover, who fishes Lake Bob Sandlin, near Mt. Pleasant.

Miniature horses are raised at the monastery of St. Clare near Brenham.

MOONSHINE

A tension between the stronger versions of Protestantism and whiskey shows itself especially in East Texas. Roughly speaking, the area above I-10—the southern border of East Texas—has long been "dry," the area below mostly "wet." The divide reflects religious differences. South Texas was populated largely by Catholic and Mexican immigrants, and Central Texas by Catholic Germans and Czechs. East, West, and North Texas, however, drew most of their population stock from Dixie and the southern mountain states. Most of those settlers were or soon became Baptists, both black and white—and Baptists eschew booze.

Amongst its "dry" siblings, East Texas stood out in a very singular way: it was the place where moonshine was brewed. North Texas and West Texas relied on bootleggers who smuggled legal or "bond" whiskey. But the pine groves and rolling hills of East Texas gave moonshiners places to hide, and as in the rest of Dixie, its spiderwebbed back roads confused federal revenue collectors—and all outsiders.

Moonshine was made in East Texas for several other reasons as well. Abundant rainfall meant that corn, the basis of bourbon, could be grown without irrigation.

Texas Rangers destroy contraband liquor during Prohibition in the 1930s.
(Center for American History, University of Texas)

The isolation of rural East Texas and its piney terrain meant that stills, or distilleries, could be hidden from view, if not always from smell: the fermentation process that precedes distilling is an odorous affair.

The typical moonshiner was a part-time producer, whose still—consisting of a boiler or big kettle connected to a set of coiled tubes, or, sometimes, tubing connected to free-standing auto radiators—occupied no more space than a couple of bureaus, and could easily be hidden in a blind or inside a barn. The moonshiners, like legitimate bourbon-makers, fermented their corn with varying mixtures of malt and grains, then boiled it off into the cooling lines or tubes. When it condensed, it was known as "white lightning"; it was clear in color because it had not been aged in wooden barrels, nor colored with caramel, like commercial bourbons.

Almost any rural resident of East Texas can tell you where "white lightning" can be had, but moonshining isn't taken very seriously anymore. Times have changed. In one year during the late 1960s, federal agents seized a record 703 moonshine stills in Harrison County, in the Longview-Marshall area. But they find less than a dozen stills a year today, and have essentially quit looking. What they look for now are marijuana plantations, which have become the region's largest source of secret income.

Carolina-rigging a lizard is very effective now, too. . . . Find the outer edges of hydrilla in about 12 to 14 feet of water and parallel the outer hydrilla line. I like to use a six-inch pumpkinseed Berkley Power lizard or the little four-inch tequila sunrise Fliptail lizard for this style of fishing. . . . Don't neglect to throw a buzzbait and a Scum Frog in April. With the water getting warmer, bass will get much more aggressive and start exploding on topwaters.

Power lizards? Bass explosions? Only fishermen know for sure.

Woodville is also home to the **Alabama-Coushatta Reservation,** one of two Indian reservations in Texas. (The other, the Tigua, is located near El Paso.) The Alabama and Coushatta tribes came to Texas following their expulsion from the Southern states, shortly before the Anglo Texas colonists arrived in the 1840s. The reservation was created during the Texas republic at the urging of Sam Houston, the young nation's leading advocate of the rights of indigenous peoples—and later, its leading opponent of slavery. Various dancing and crafts exhibitions are staged at the reservation's **Indian Village** for tourists.

■ LUFKIN TO TYLER

Lufkin, 119 miles (192 km) northeast of Houston and 108 miles (174 km) northwest of Beaumont, is the center of the Piney Woods economy. The gargantuan lumber and paper industry radiates out from that city, home to a Champion Industries plant, and also from a satellite town, **Diboll,** headquarters of a Fortune 100 company, Temple-Inland, Inc.

Temple-Inland metamorphosed from a sawmill at Diboll, through 10 years of merger status with Time, Inc., the publishing firm, and through several other stages into a multi-billion dollar paper, lumber, and financial conglomerate.

The forest industry of the Piney Woods goes well beyond Lufkin, running north from Beaumont up to Texarkana. More than 85 percent of the land area of Hardin County, between Lufkin and Beaumont, is devoted to timber; a few adjacent counties have even more acres of plantation pines. During World War II, chemists perfected a way to make quality paper from southern pine, and ever since, paper products, not lumber, have been the East Texas mainstay.

The **Texas Forestry Museum,** on the east edge of Lufkin at 1905 Atkinson Drive, is jointly sponsored by the Texas Forestry Association and the Lufkin Kiwanis Club and provides exhibits of the area's pine industry past. Open daily, the museum houses early sawmill and timbering equipment, a "talking tree" with messages about ecology, and a library of related books and articles.

Love's Lookout in Jacksonville, about 60 miles (96 km) northwest of Lufkin on U.S. 69, offers what East Texans say is hands down the most spectacular view of the region, a 35-mile (60-km) panorama of pine and dogwood trees. The town is also home, each July, to one of the more important rodeos sponsored by the Professional Rodeo Cowboys Association in Texas. Rodeos are an annual event in easily a third of Texas towns. Riders pay entry fees and compete for trophy belt buckles and cash prizes. Bronc riding, calf roping, and bulldogging are events at most rodeos; the most dangerous event, bull riding, is usually reserved for the finale.

The only women's event common in rodeos is the barrel race: riders race against the clock, running their horses in a cloverleaf formation around barrels at opposite ends of the rodeo arena, usually yanking small flags from atop the barrels as they pass. Competition is keen enough that winners are often determined by tenths of a second's time.

Some 30 miles (48 km) north of Jacksonville on U.S. 69 lies the city of **Tyler,** whose airport serves most of the region. As late as 1940, about half of the roses

A rose queen coronation gown on display at the Tyler Rose Museum.

grown commercially in the United States came from the Tyler area. Though competition has reduced the city's share of the industry, it is still celebrated in the 22-acre **Municipal Rose Garden,** on the Front Street fairgrounds just west of downtown, where some 500 rose varieties are cultivated. The city also salutes its horticultural industry in an annual festival on the adjoining fairgrounds, which—and this is truly progress!—have buried beneath them an unfortunate past. Local attorney Weldon Holcomb points out that today's Rose Garden area was formerly a ceremonial camp for the Ku Klux Klan:

> *I* remember my daddy and all the other prominent men of the time wearing Klan robes and marching, practicing at what is now the fair grounds. You have to remember that back then it was high profile. Being in the Ku Klux Klan was like being a member of the Kiwanis Club.

About 10 miles (16 km) northwest of Tyler, just off TX 64—turn right at the Texas Catfish Farm sign—is the site of the massacre at the **Battle of the Neches,** during the years of the Republic of Texas. Around 1820, a group of Cherokee settled in the area. Their relations with the Mexican government were generally friendly, and they aided it in combatting the 1826 Fredonia rebellion at Nacogdoches. At the outbreak

GUARDS ON DUTY

PHOTO BY
A. KLUCKER

As in much of America, the KKK reached its peak of influence in Texas during the 1920s. (Fort Bend Museum, Richmond, Texas)

of the Texas Revolution in 1836, Sam Houston, the republic's first president, nego-tiated a treaty with Cherokee leader John Bowles, guaranteeing the tribe neutrality in the conflict and promising it lands along the Angelina River. In token of the agreement, Houston gave Bowles a sword. But the republic's senate refused to rat-ify the agreement, and Mirabeau B. Lamar, the republic's second president, ap-pointed a commission to expel the Cherokee from Texas. Bowles refused to comply, and on July 16 and 17, 1839, his people were attacked. Some 800 Chero-kee were slaughtered. Legend has it that Bowles was holding the sword Houston had given him horizontally, in a gesture of surrender, when one of the hostile Tex-ans shot him through the head. For years most Texans believed that the bodies of the Indian dead were left exposed to the elements, but oral history projects done in the largely African-American community of Redlands, nearby, indicate that slaves buried the Indians after the Texans withdrew.

■ CANTON AND CORSICANA

Canton, a small town about 40 miles (64 km) northwest of Tyler on TX 64, and some 50 miles (80 km) southeast of Dallas on I-20, bills itself as the home of the na-tion's largest flea market, **First Monday Trade Days,** the first weekend of each month.

Corsicana, about 55 miles (89 km) south of Dallas on I-45—the chief Dallas-to-Houston highway—blends historical buildings from its antebellum period with monuments of the state's first oil boom. Oil was accidentally discovered there in 1894, and within a dozen years nearly 300 wells were operating in a five-by-two-mile (8 x 3 km) strip just east of town, and in 1897, the state's first refinery was built.

But the oil has played out, and today Corsicana is best known for the Original Deluxe Fruitcake produced by the **Collin Street Bakery** since 1896. The Collin Street cakes, not available at supermarkets, are shipped to all 50 states and 196 countries—mainly as Christmas gifts, of course. Visitors to the bakery need not wait for the holidays: Collin Street cakes are sold there throughout the year.

■ HUNTSVILLE

Located about an hour's drive north of Houston on I-45, Huntsville is a city filled with decorative old trees, especially some beautiful and ancient live oaks. The **Sam Houston National Forest** starts on Huntsville's southeast edge, 251 square miles (650 sq km) of pine trees and hardwoods.

ON SAM HOUSTON

*H*e is decidedly the most splendid looking man I ever saw, one of Nature's noble men the most intellectual countenance and the most fascinating address . . . walking up town with his Mexican blanket thrown over his shoulder, with an air of lordly superiority—intellect and nobility stamped on every feature you would declare that he was a man born to govern.

—Harriet Virginia Scott, after a visit to Sam and Margaret Houston in 1845
Painting: Sam Houston. (Courtesy of The R.W. Norton Art Gallery, Shreveport)

Texans and historians know Huntsville as the town where Sam Houston lived and died. The **Houston Memorial Complex** contains Houston's first and long-time home, as well as the more elaborate Steamboat House, where the one-time general, Texas president, governor, and U.S. senator died in 1863. Both are furnished with period furniture, as is Houston's former law office. Houston and his family are buried in **Oakwood Cemetery,** near today's downtown area.

People outside of Texas are likely to associate Huntsville more with **Sam Houston State University** than with its namesake. The school, with 12,700 students, numbers among its alumni CBS news anchor Dan Rather, and is nationally known for its penology program.

It's not surprising that the university has a highly rated prison studies program: Texans usually think of prison when they think of Huntsville, because the state's far-flung penal system, the second-largest in the United States, is headquartered and centered there. A half-dozen prisons ring the city, and the town is almost synonymous with the Big House to Texans all over the state. Countless blues and country-and-western singers wail about being sent to Huntsville. The city's downtown houses the **Texas Prison Museum,** a collection of more than a century of the tools of incarceration: old balls-and-chains, guns used in notorious crimes, and most gruesome of all, "Old Sparky," the state's electric chair from 1924–64.

On the brighter side, Huntsville is also home to the **Texas Berry Farm,** where in late spring and early summer visitors can pick their own blackberries, raspberries, and blueberries, paying for their take by the pound.

■ NACOGDOCHES

Nacogdoches, some 150 miles (240 km) north of Houston on U.S. 59, is the historical center of the Piney Woods. Caddo Indians were clearing and farming the area where Nacogdoches lies for at least 500 years before 1716, when one of the five original Spanish missions in Texas was established on the spot. About 25 miles (40 km) west of Nacogdoches, on TX 21, lies the community called Alto; six miles (10 km) south of Alto, on U.S. 69—near Lufkin—sit **Indian Mounds,** the remains of the Caddoan culture. The two mounds are the nearest thing in Texas to pyramids: one of them was clearly a burial mound, as bodies have been unearthed there; the other appears to have been a temple mound. Those interested in the state's only extant pre-colonial structure can learn more at the visitor's program held at the mounds on weekends.

Halfway between San Antonio and the Louisiana line, Nacogdoches was for a century Spanish Mexico's gateway to the east, a favorite trading stop for Spanish and American travelers and traders. By the early nineteenth century, it had become a focus of revolutionary fervor. In 1819, a group composed mainly of Mississippians invaded Texas. Under the leadership of Dr. James Long, they set up a seat of government at Nacogdoches, declared themselves independent of Spain, and called their rebel state the Republic of Texas. The Long Expedition, as historians call it today, fell apart within a year, a victim of poor financing, poor supply lines, and a Mexican government counter-offensive.

Nacogdoches became the camp of a more notable insurgency in 1826–27. Haden Edwards was an "empresario"—the head of a settlement company—who ran into problems with the Mexican government over land titles held by the American colonists he'd brought in. With 200 followers, he and his brother Ben declared a revolt. They set up the State of Fredonia and named Nacogdoches its capital. Newspapers across the country ran stories about "200 Men Against a Nation." The affair brought diplomats from the United States and Mexico into negotiations, but was

Ready-to-eat pork ribs at a Mt. Zion Missionary Baptist Church barbecue.

(left) "Old Sparky," on exhibit at the Texas Prison Museum in Huntsville, was the state's electric chair from 1924–1964.

settled, as the Long Expedition had been, when government troops quelled the rebels.

In 1832, the Mexican commander of the Nacogdoches area demanded that the East Texans surrender their guns. The settlers refused. They formed their own militia, and defeated the Mexican garrison at the Battle of Nacogdoches. Although the land remained in Mexican control, never again were Mexican troops stationed there.

The Nacogdoches building known as the **Old Stone Fort,** located on the campus of Stephen F. Austin University, is a replica of the 1779 building that witnessed these turbulent events. At its original location (at today's Main and Fredonia streets) the building stood under nine different flags, including those of three aborted revolutions. It was here that both Long and Edwards set up their governments, and here also that the first newspaper in Texas was for a time published. The building was razed in 1902, but a group of preservationists bought the old stones, and in 1936—the Texas Centennial—they reconstructed the historic building. The **Old Stone Fort Museum** stands at Clark and Griffith boulevards, and contains memorabilia of pioneer and Indian life.

At 211 South Lanana Street stands the house where Sam Houston was baptized a Roman Catholic in 1833, complying with the Mexican law requiring landholders to be Catholic. The house is known as the **Sterne-Hoya Home,** and was built in 1828 by Texas revolutionary Adolphus Sterne for his bride.

If Nacogdoches never became the seat of a Texas government with its own flag, as many of its early settlers and plotters had hoped, descendants of the rebels can at least take comfort in knowing that in 1930 Nacogdoches became the birthplace of the unofficial flag of East Texas: the logo of Lone Star Feeds and Fertilizers. Across East Texas, the Lone Star logo, a blue star inside a white circle inside a red triangle, is ubiquitous. Every grocery and gasoline station in East Texas seems to have a sign displaying the logo; ads for beer, soft drink, and auto manufacturers can't rival it. Because "Lone Star" says "Texas," gimme caps bearing the logo have also become popular items of identification with East Texans in exile; that is, East Texans who live in Austin or Tokyo or anywhere else.

Kilgore, about 50 miles (80 km) north of Nacogdoches on U.S. 259, was the urban center of the 1930s East Texas oil boom. The boom brought some 24,000 wells to a 40-by-6-mile (6 x 10-km) patch of the Piney Woods, and some 1,200 oil derricks stood within the city limits of Kilgore, a few of which are producing today. Two dozen wells once sat on one city block still known as "The World's Richest Acre"; one of those structures is preserved as a monument to the era. Entrepreneurs became so frenzied during the boom that a few of them drilled a well through the terrazzo floor of the Kilgore National Bank!

■ LONGVIEW

Longview, about 200 miles (320 km) north of Houston on U.S. 59/259 and about 125 miles (200 km) east of Dallas on I-20, has participated in all the shifts of Texas history, with one exception: like the rest of East Texas, it had nothing to do with, and felt little effect from, the Mexican Revolution of 1910.

Longview was a Caddo village, a site for immigrant Anglo colonizers, a plantation and slavery town, and in the present century, part of the East Texas Oil Field, opened in 1930 by a C. M. "Dad" Joiner at Henderson, 30 miles (48 km) south. Its population tripled to about 20,000 in the decade that followed, as did that of most towns in the region.

At **Bodacious Barbeque,** on U.S. 80 in Longview, a mural depicts the most famous judge in Texas, Roy Bean, sitting on the porch of his West Texas saloon, in judgment of a couple of horse thieves. For nearly 40 years the Pearl Brewing Company of San Antonio used a print of the scene to sell its beer all over Texas. Sure enough, Bodacious Barbeque sells beer too. But as if to conceal what it does, the restaurateurs have altered the original some. There are no boxes of beer on Judge Bean's porch in the Longview mural—only cases of Pepsi Cola.

For 40 years, the Longview Welding Company (also on U.S. 80) has displayed the message: "Hell is Forever/Jesus Wants to Save You/Repent and Be Converted." Glen F. "Faye" Livers, long-time owner of the place, says that the sign has had salutary efforts on his business, but not for the reason you'd expect. "We put it up to reach people for Christ," he explains. "But what it has also done is that it's made us walk what we talk. It's the best disciplinary device that could be. I don't like a hypocrite, and nobody does."

■ JEFFERSON AND CADDO LAKE

Located about 35 miles (55 km) northeast of Longview, Jefferson is the town East Texans visit on weekends to recall the region's romantic past, to shop for antiques, or just to plain get away from it all. Established during the era of the Republic of Texas, the town sits just a few miles west of Caddo Lake, the only natural inland body of water in Texas. Vacationers love to spoon on the lake in rented canoes, and admire views of cypress trees weeping with Spanish moss. According to Indian legend, the lake was formed one night when a Caddo chieftain enraged some powerful shaking spirits. Historians think the myth could refer to the New Madrid earthquake of 1811, which may have created the lake.

Jefferson's population peaked at 30,000 just after the Civil War, when in tonnage terms, it was second only to Galveston as a Texas port. In those days, steamboats working Big Cypress Creek ran on the Mississippi from Jefferson to St. Louis and New Orleans, by way of the Red River's dip into Louisiana. Furniture came to Jefferson from Europe via New Orleans, and the town even boasted the state's first icehouse and brewery. The legacy of its bygone riverport days is preserved by the *Bayou Queen,* a sidewheeler that takes passengers on one-hour trips

The Kilgore Rangerettes, whose motto is "Beauty Knows No Pain."
(right) Big Thicket National Preserve resembles the bayou country of Louisiana.

in **Big Cypress Bayou.** The bayou is easy to find: all the town's downtown streets dead-end there.

By some accounts, Jefferson began its decline when, confident of the continuation of the riverboat trade, its leaders refused to make deals with magnate Jay Gould. Stung by the town's rebuff, he refused to run a railroad line through its limits, and he sent his line through Marshall instead. Posting a curse for posterity, Gould wrote "End of Jefferson" in the guest register of the Excelsior Hotel. But the Excelsior continues, like many of the antebellum mansions of Jefferson's nineteenth-century elite, as a bed-and-breakfast, and despite Gould's curse the town finally got its railroad—albeit small. It's called the **Jefferson & Cypress Bayou,** and its steam engines take visitors on one-hour, five-mile runs along the Bayou's banks.

Other historians date Jefferson's decline to the 1873 dynamiting of an ancient, 170-mile log jam in the Red River. When the jam was cleared, water levels in Caddo Lake and on the Big Cypress dropped, making riverboat travel impossible. Caddo Lake and the adjacent **Cypress Creek** have been the subject of controversy ever since. In 1914, Cypress Creek, mostly a muddy bayou after the clearing, was dammed, creating Caddo Lake anew, and making barge traffic possible where automobiles couldn't pass because of bayou mud. But this success was followed in 1968 by federal approval of a measure to create deep-water channels linking East Texas to the Red River. The channels haven't been dug yet, but the region's business community has geared up to revive the project. East Texas environmentalists, meanwhile, are opposing any step forward. "Water follows the point of least resistance," notes local historian Harold Culver. "If they dredge, the water will move and drain. The lake may dry up. And they'll destroy the habitat." Popular musician Don Henley, who was raised around Caddo Lake, has joined the environmental crusade, which in 1993 won designation as an ecological preserve, a distinction that environmental forces hope will halt the deep-water plan forever.

In the meantime, campers can pitch tents or spend a day canoeing at either **Caddo Lake State Park** or **Lake O' The Pines,** an almost 19,000-acre impoundment of Cypress Creek on the west side of Jefferson. Both lakes offer campsites, cabins, boat ramps, and canoe rentals; facilities at Lake O' The Pines are administered by the Army Corps of Engineers.

Rev. R. W. Shambaugh laying on hands at an evangelical service.

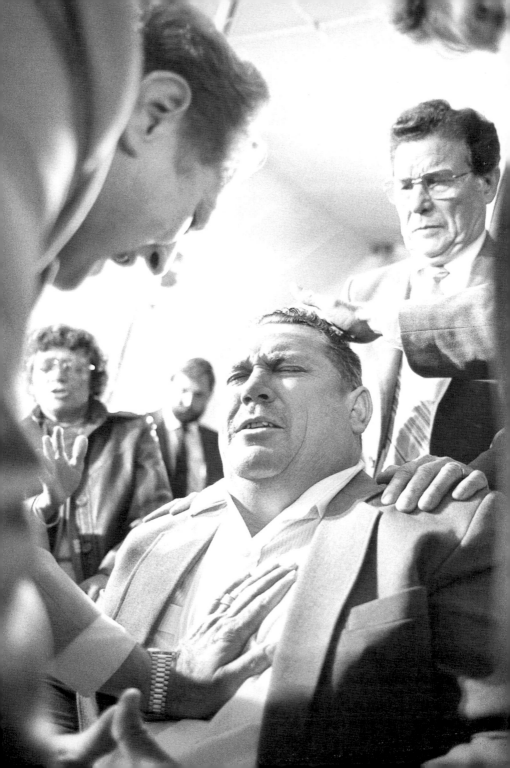

CENTRAL TEXAS

CENTRAL TEXAS, THE STATE'S MOST CELEBRATED REGION—for its natural beauty, its music, its laid-back atmosphere, and its booming economy—isn't a region at all. It's two of them. On the east side of I-35, it's blackland prairie, good cotton country, wet and mild. On the west side of I-35, the land is rougher, whiter and drier, a ranching locale. The terrain is flatter to the east, hilly and wrinkled with rivers to the west; Columbus, east of I-35, is famous for wildflowers, while San Saba, west of I-35, is famous as a pecan center. The halves of Central Texas would be regarded as parts of East and West Texas, if demographics didn't make the region a place apart. But Central Texas is different than the rest of Texas—and in some ways, is the most mythically American region in Texas—because here, European immigrants settled. During the period of the Republic of Texas, Germans—some of them free-thinkers and revolutionists—established colonies mainly to the west of what is now I-35, and during the Reconstruction era, Czech peasants came to the cotton country on the east.

Although their numbers were probably never a majority in the region as a whole—Anglos, Latinos, and African Americans all outnumbered them—the immigrants' villages and towns left a lasting imprint on the region's character. About half of some 20 counties that had been established in Central Texas by the eve of the Civil War voted against secession, because Texans lately of Europe weren't slaveholders. (And perhaps they were influenced by Sam Houston, who opposed slavery.) Almost 60 years later all of Texas north of I-10 favored Prohibition, except Central Texas, which has never banned booze. In Central Texas, the distribution of wealth—and there hasn't been much to distribute—has been more even-handed than in any other Texas region: the oil booms that turned East Texas, and then West Texas, on their respective ears have never been profitable enough to cause more than a momentary giddiness in Central Texas. Portraits of Texans as fire-breathing Protestants, racists, teetotalers, and instant millionaires have simply never been accurate in describing the people of Central Texas.

The region owes its existence to agriculture, and its growth to purely urban virtues. It has become the center of art and education. If they can, academics, musicians, writers, sculptors, and plastic artists move to Central Texas from other areas of the state, which they tend to view as hinterlands. Because it had roots

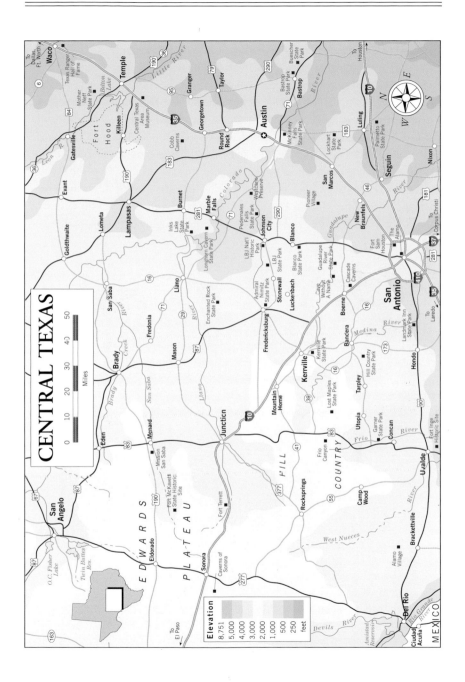

there, and because the University of Texas at Austin—known simply as "UT" or "the University"—has grown to massive size, with 50,000 regular-term students, in recent years high-tech industries have moved to Austin, too. The Austin-Georgetown corridor of I-35 has become the Silicon Valley of the state. An expanding population and increasing prosperity have turned the region's once-harsh Hill Country—roughly, that part of the region that lies west of I-35 and south of the Llano and Colorado rivers—into a vast resort. Dude ranches and entertainment complexes have taken the place of ranches and farms whose owners, a century ago, fought the Comanche Indians and the elements, without ever making much headway. As if Texas were New England, in autumn months tourists drive backroads of today's Hill Country, through hamlets like Tarpley and Utopia, to view the changing of the colors of leaves!

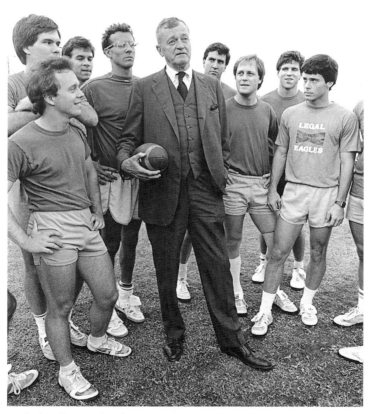

Charles Allen Wright, of Watergate fame, is a law professor at the University of Texas, as well as an intramural coach of the football team the Legal Eagles.

AUSTIN IN 1828

*I*n 1828 a certain José María Sánchez saw the Austin settlement. It was a scattered little town of about two thousand people, and its forms were new in Texas. The Rio Grande frontier had towns built of earth and rock, tinted plaster, and rocky streets laid out at right angles to a square central plaza dominated by a church. They were towns that rose from the river landscape like parts of it. At San Felipe de Austin on the Brazos, Sánchez saw forty or fifty little wooden houses. They were built in the image of the forest and cabin life of the North American frontier, out of logs interlocked at the corners, and chinked with mud plaster. Rock chimneys rose at the end of each house. Many houses had only one room. Those that had two displayed a new mannerism of the American forest primitive style, for the two rooms were separated by an open breezeway under the same roof that covered the rooms. Such a dwelling was called a dog-run house. Later it would know modifications in rock construction and stucco, and remain characteristic of Texas living.

—Paul Horgan, *Great River: The Rio Grande in North American History, vol. 2,* 1954

■ AUSTIN

With its half a million people, Austin is the region's anchor city. The town is situated on rolling hills north and south of a bend in the Colorado River. Though it sometimes calls itself (as does San Antonio) "The River City," Austin's self-image is more tied to a different symbol, **Barton Springs**, a swimming hole in Zilker Park, southwest of downtown, whose artesian waters are a chilly 68° year-round.

Barton Springs was also the site of the first settlement in the area; Spanish priests came here from San Antonio in 1730. They left after a year, though, because the local Tickanwatic Indians remained hostile to the priests and their mission. In 1838, Jake Harrell and a few other traders built cabins and a stockade in what is today downtown Austin, calling their settlement Waterloo. When Mirabeau B. Lamar became president of the Republic of Texas in 1838, he chose the burgeoning town as the republic's capital, even though it was dangerously close to the western frontier. Soon after construction of the capitol began, the town was renamed after colonizer Stephen F. Austin.

The town of Austin became more than a politician's town in 1883, when the University of Texas opened, and again, during World War II, when the Bergstrom Air Field was located there. But as late as 20 years ago, it was largely a sleepy Central Texas town, one whose skyline was dominated by two structures, the state capitol and the 26-story University Tower.

Austin's principal streets are marked with bicycle lanes, and about twice a year cyclists block rush-hour traffic to underscore their demands for more lanes. The city's park system is, compared to other Texas cities, extensive. Just south of downtown, the Colorado River, usually called **Town Lake** within the city, provides nine miles (14.5 km) of jogging/walking/bicycle trails. The **Barton Creek Greenbelt** also offers hiking trails, plus swimming holes when the creek is full—in spring and summer.

Jogging and bicycling are not nearly as quaint as walking—and in car-crazy Texas, walking, outside of malls and commercial districts, is unquestionably quaint. Most people who simply like to stroll, in Austin, wind up at one time or another entering the 22-acre **State Cemetery;** and those who do usually return, time and again. It's close to downtown—between Seventh and Eleventh streets, just a block east of I-35—and it's safe. What more could a city-dweller ask for?

Barton Springs supplies Austin residents with welcome relief from the oppressive summer heat.

AUSTIN

0 .5 1 2 3

Miles

AUSTIN MAIN ATTRACTIONS

■ U N I Q U E L Y   A U S T I N

Congress Avenue and Sixth Street. Listed in the National Register of Historic Places, Congress Avenue has been *"The* Avenue" since the 1800s, and together with Sixth Street (formerly the bawdy Old Pecan Street), this area is still a vibrant downtown. Restored nineteenth- and twentieth-century buildings abound on these streets, and free guided and self-guided walking tours are available through the tourist office at 201 East Second Street; (512) 478-0098. While afternoons in this neighborhood are best spent exploring the district's rich history, the nightlife here reveals the spirit of today's Austin—the many restaurants and music-venues are among the most popular in Texas.

Congress Avenue Bridge. Between March and November, 750,000 Mexican free-tail bats spend their days under the bridge and emerge at night to catch and eat thousands of insects. Watching them is common Austin entertainment. *Town Lake; (512) 327-9721.*

State Capitol. This Renaissance Revival building, the state's third capitol and the nation's largest, was completed in 1888 using native stones: pink granite and limestone. At least two people have been killed by gunplay inside the capitol, whose legislature—though it meets only in odd-numbered years—maintains notoriety by passing dubious laws. Tours begin at the Visitors Desk. *11th Street and Congress Avenue; (512) 463-0063.*

University of Texas. Cass Gilbert, architect of the U.S. Customs House and the Woolworth Building, is responsible for two buildings on campus, Battle Hall and Sutton Hall, but more importantly his preferred style, Spanish Renaissance Revival, set the tone for future building on the campus. Housing a number of fine museums, including the Harry Ransom Humanities Research Center, Lyndon Baines Johnson Museum, Archer M. Huntington Art Gallery, and the Texas Memorial Museum, the UT campus is worth a visit. Guadalupe Street is the campus' main drag, lined with record stores, cafes, and clothing shops. *Bounded by Guadalupe and Red River, Martin Luther King Jr. and 26th; (512) 471-1420.*

■ H I S T O R I C   M U S E U M S   A N D   S I T E S

Governor's Mansion. Austin-made bricks and locally grown pines were used to construct this Greek Revival residence in 1856. Among other period furnishings on display are Sam Houston's bed, Stephen Austin's desk, and Governor Pease's (the first Texas governor to live in the mansion) settee. *1010 Colorado; (512) 463-5516.*

Lyndon B. Johnson Library. A mausoleum of the papers and memorabilia of the former President, including a replica of the Oval Office. Various video and audio presentations extol LBJ's civil rights and anti-poverty efforts. (But don't mention Vietnam.) *On the campus of the University of Texas, 2313 Red River; (512) 482-5136.*

O. Henry Museum. The short story writer whose real name was William Sydney Porter lived in this cottage during his 10 years in Austin, 1885–95, publishing his humorous Austin weekly, the *Rolling Stone,* from its premises. *409 East Fifth Street; (512) 472-1903.*

State Cemetery. A shady, wooded resting place for Stephen F. Austin, founding father of Texas; eight former governors; a variety of literary and historical celebrities; and over a thousand Confederate soldiers. *East Seventh and Comal; (512) 478-8930.*

■ A R T   M U S E U M S

Elisabet Ney Museum. Studio of the nineteenth-century German sculptor and thirty-year resident of Texas. Ney began her career sculpting the most significant figures in Europe, including Humboldt, Schopenhauer, Bismarck, and Garibaldi. By the late 1880s Ney was living in Texas and her subjects were predominately Texans. Today, her studio displays the plaster models for several well-known statues, among them Stephen F. Austin and Sam Houston. *304 East 44th Street; (512) 458-2255.*

Laguna Gloria Art Museum. Former home to Clara Driscoll Sevier, who championed the fight to preserve the Alamo. The Laguna Gloria villa is now a contemporary art museum featuring regional and national artists and photographers, with special attention given to Mexican-related subjects. Located on 28 acres between Mt. Bonnell and Lake Austin, the grounds are beautifully landscaped with native plants. *3809 West 35th Street; (512) 458-8191.*

■ E X P L O R I N G   O U T D O O R S

Barton Creek Greenbelt. A popular spot for jogging, walking, and hiking alongside Barton Creek. There are several swimming holes where people swim and socialize. The creek is mostly dry between August and early March, but quite large in the rainy season. *Starts at Barton Springs and follows the creek west; (512) 477-PARD.*

Mount Bonnell. At 785 feet (239 m), Mount Bonnell offers the best view in Austin, a sweeping panorama of rolling hills and the Colorado River. *Turn right on Mount Bonnell Road, just before West 35th dead-ends.*

To gain perpetual admission at the State Cemetery, however, is a bit trickier. Only those who have been elected to a state office, appointed to a state board, or named in a burial proclamation by a governor or by both houses of the legislature can be buried here. You might be able to predict the results of this stringent policy—but not always. On the highest of the gentle hills in the cemetery lies Stephen F. Austin, the Father of Texas. Longtime residents also include some 1,500 Confederate officers buried in military formation, with identical headstones, as its planners meant for the cemetery to be for Texas what Arlington National Cemetery is for the United States. The maple, cedar, and magnolia trees in the cemetery also shade some interesting admissions to the underground club: historian Walter Prescott Webb, as well as Larry Bales, once the owner of Scholtz Garten—a beer hall frequented by politicians. Most of the headstones in the cemetery are impressive—the biggest stands over the grave of a Reconstruction-era governor—and among them are works by sculptors Elizabet Ney and Pompeo Coppini.

Austin grew tremendously during the late 1970s. Its success arose from two very different sources, both seminal in the turbulence of the preceding decade: defense manufacturers and hippies. During the 1960s, Austin was home to Tracor Industries, a scientific research company that contracted mostly with the Department of Defense. It also became the Haight-Ashbury of the South, and hosted the largest concentration of hippies and anti-war protesters between the East and West coasts. Austin's scientific base grew to include Texas Instruments, Motorola, IBM, Dell Computers, and Apple Computers. Meanwhile, the city's counter-culturalists turned their energies toward music, opening such now-defunct dance halls as the Vulcan Gas Company and Armadillo World Headquarters. In the early 1970s, the hippie musicians who played at those venues were joined by a new crowd, the "countrypolitans"—a.k.a. the "redneck rockers" or "cosmic cowboys"—whose number included Willie Nelson and Waylon Jennings. The result may not have been a distinctly Austin sound, but it did encourage the rise of performance venues and recording studios as important Austin industries. Today the stationery and business cards of some city officials are inscribed with the phrase "Live Music Capital of the World."

Lately, Austin has gained national attention as a city undergoing a renaissance. Increasing numbers of out-of-staters are moving there, attracted to the city's blend of regional flavor and urban sophistication. Some Austinites fear their city is becoming "too much like Dallas"—that is, too fast-paced and focused on money.

SHIRLEY TEMPLE IN LAKEVIEW

*T*he church was the center of all religious and social happenings in Lakeview. There was a Baptist church in town and a Church of Christ, but we were Methodists.

It was nothing romantic—no stained glass, no artifacts, no relics. Not even Sheetrock. Just whitewashed boards all around and a bare elevated pulpit. There was a low railing up in front, and when you joined the church, or when you were called to Jesus, you would walk up the center aisle to that wood railing.

This was a very poor church. The most valuable item that church owned was a Shirley Temple cup. It was smoky blue glassware and had Shirley Temple's face and her signature in white across the front of it. That's what they used to baptize you with. Later on, a man with some woodworking skills joined the church and he made a pedestal and a wooden bowl for that purpose, much more uptown-looking, but for the longest time you were introduced to the Lord by Shirley Temple.

—Ann Richards, *Straight from the Heart,* 1989

Ex-governor, Ann Richards, (right) the second woman to be elected governor in Texas, shown here with another party-goer at the State Capitol in the 1980s.

STATE CAPITOL

The story behind Austin's pink-granite State Capitol, dedicated in 1888, tells much about the ambition of the state's early years.

In 1879, the Texas legislature passed an act authorizing a new capitol. Since the state wasn't flush, the legislature authorized trading some public lands for the building work. The land chosen was three million acres in the sparsely settled High Plains, a spread that ran across 10 counties. The huge spread, traded to a Chicago syndicate, became the XIT ("Ten in Texas"), the largest ranch in Texas until the turn of the century, when it was broken into smaller plots and sold to farmers.

The dimensions that the capitol's Detroit architect gave the Texas seat of government made it, and still make it, the biggest of the state capitols, nearly as big as the United States Capitol—and several feet taller.

Originally, the capitol was to be of native limestone, quarried near Austin, but iron pyrites in this stone caused streaking when weathered. After some debate, the legislature accepted the offer of free granite from Burnet County, about 70 miles away. To reduce costs, it assigned convicts and immigrants to work at the quarry and in stone-cutting. Scandal ensued when the International Association of Granite Cutters protested the use of convict labor and illegal Scottish immigrants.

When it was complete, the pink-granite capitol had 392 rooms, doors nine feet (3 m) tall, supported by eight-pound brass hinges, engraved with a design whose legend says "Texas Capitol." The state's symbol, the Lone Star, was cast into door knobs, and an iron fence installed in 1890 includes some 8,000 stars in its design. In 1935, the capitol was given a new terrazzo floor. Its entryway design includes the state seal and the names of battles from the Texas Revolution.

"The Goddess of Liberty," just before being hoisted atop the State Capitol in 1888. (Austin History Center, Austin Public Library)

TEXAS MUSIC

For Texans, listening to music is as natural as breathing air—be it the Tex-Mex conjunto of Santiago Jimenez' offspring, the whining honky-tonk of Lefty Frizzell, the rockabilly of lost legend Ronnie Dawson, or the metal band around the corner that's playing sped-up Lightnin' Hopkins covers.

Genres blur in Texas, and encompass the Czech music of Frank Baca (who came to Texas from Moravia in 1860), the Western Swing of Bob Wills' Texas Playboys, the blues of Blind Lemon Jefferson, and the techno-rap of MC 900 Ft. Jesus.

So many small towns in Texas are the homes of someone you're heard of: Texarkana (Scott Joplin), Turkey (Bob Wills), Abbott (Willie Nelson), Linden (Aaron "T-Bone" Walker), Sherman (Buck Owens), Mansfield (Ella Mae Morse), Gilmer (Don Henley), Littlefield (Waylon Jennings), Saratoga (George Jones). The music might have well grown up in the big cities—in Dallas, Houston, Fort Worth, Austin—but it was often born and suckled on the outskirts.

Though Austin is perhaps the most well-known Texas music city outside of the state, no one city takes all the credit—especially when you consider that Austin's best-known local heroes (Willie and Waylon and Stevie Ray and Jimmie Vaughan) were all immigrants.

Dallas might well possess the state's richest musical heritage: it was Texas' second-largest city where Robert Johnson, considered the most influential of all twentieth century bluesmen, recorded. Blind Lemon Jefferson and T-Bone Walker, and later, Freddie King and the Vaughan brothers defined at least two generations of blues artists. Jimmie Rodgers and Bob Wills and Lefty Frizzell recorded here; rockabilly legend Gene "Be-Bop-A-Lula" Vincent set up shop. Benny Goodman's guitarist, Charlie Christian, the man who taught the world the importance of the electric guitar, was born in Dallas, and "The Big D Jamboree" lured Elvis Presley and Hank Williams to town in the 1950s. Steve Miller and Boz Scaggs had their first band here, the Marksmen, in the late '50s; the Vaughan boys first heard the Nightcaps performing "Thunderbird."

It was in Dallas that 1960s rockers like the Chessmen, the Briks, the Floyd Dakil Combo; and the Five Americans ushered in Texas garage rock. Ron Chapman's "Sump'n Else Show" exposed teen audiences to Roky Erickson's psychedelia before it had a name. Marvin "Meat Loaf" Aday, Mike Nesmith of the Monkees, and Sam "The Sham" Samudio were born there; and much-heralded newcomers like New Bohemians, the Reverend Horton Heat, Bedhead, Little Jack Melody and His Young Turks, Funland, MC 900 Foot Jesus, and the Toadies honed their craft there. *continues*

Blind Lemon Jefferson. (Center for American History, Univ. of Texas)

There are veterans who say Dallas would have been Nashville had studio owner Jim Beck (who co-wrote the legendary "If You Got the Money" with Lefty Frizzell) not suffocated on cleaning solution in his downtown Dallas studio in the 1950s; and perhaps it would have been a rock and roll center in the 1960s had insurance man John Abdnor, who signed the Five Americans and R&B should-been-great Bobby Patterson, not squandered his resources and efforts on his lunatic son John, Jr.—who scored a hit with "Do It Again—A Little Bit Slower" in the late '60s as Jon and Robin, then wound up in the state penitentiary for killing his girlfriend a decade later.

Houston residents, of course, would dispute the notion that Dallas boasts the richest fruit of the vine. They will point to blues legends Lightnin' Hopkins and Willa Mae "Big Mama" Thornton (the latter of whom wasn't born in Texas, though she began her recording career on Don Robey's Peacock label), singers Victoria Spivey (who spent time with Louis Armstrong) and Sippie Wallace, boogie-rockers ZZ Top (born from the Moving Sidewalks), and modern-day country boys like Clint Black and Rodney Crowell. San Antonio folks will lay claim to Doug Sahm, and Flaco and Santiago Jimenez, Jr.

Fort Worth's got everyone from Tex Ritter to singer-songwriter T-Bone Burnett to blue-eyed soul singer Delbert McClinton, made famous in the '60s by the once-larger-than-life producer Major Bill Smith. Bobby Fuller, whose "I Fought the Law" influenced the Clash during the earliest days of punk, was from El Paso; Janis Joplin hailed from Port Arthur.

There is no here-to-there in Texas music, no simple way to chart what sound began what style; it's all interchangeable, with the Tex-Mex accordion creeping into the Lubbock-bred rock of Joe Ely, just as Elvis' appropriation of black R&B crept into Buddy Holly's brand of country in the early '50s. To define the Lone Star sound is to define music itself; to chart its history, though, is to untangle knots never straightened.

—Robert Wilonsky, 1994

Austin-based Junior Brown with his "Guitsteel."

Austin is also getting crowded, but for the most part, residents are proving resilient as the city grows. Meanwhile, Austin's new life has attracted notice within Texas, and even a little criticism. "If Dallas is New York, and Houston is Chicago, then Austin is California," a common observation says—and in Texas, California is regarded as an exotic, and nearly insane, place.

■ NEW BRAUNFELS' ASSOCIATION OF NOBLEMEN

New Braunfels, about 50 miles (80 km) south of Austin on I-35, is today a tourist and shopping-center town; two outlet malls are located there. But its downtown architecture and civic life show the traces of its birth from a nineteenth-century German organization called the *Adelsverein,* or Association of Noblemen.

The Adelsverein's purpose was to encourage Germans to emigrate from what, in the nobility's view, had become an overpopulated land. The plan was touted to its backers as a way to make money, too. The noblemen who headed the group believed that the value of the unimproved real estate they had secured in Texas would increase as German immigrants disembarked at Gulf ports. The return on the nobility's investment began when prospective immigrants paid fees to join the venture.

The tract that the noblemen had arranged with the republic and Texas promoters to settle lay at a distance from any settlements, in the dry and barren Llano County area, about 70 miles (113 km) northwest of Austin. At the time, the Comanche still held sway there. But since the Association's advance agents didn't venture onto the site, its members, and even its German promoters, didn't know as much. When Prince Carl of Solms-Braunfels came to Texas to manage the Adelsverein's affairs in 1844, he, too, stopped short of the land grant. Instead he bought a spot on the Comal River where springs flowed; New Braunfels is located there today.

Prince Carl's idea was that settlers could use the New Braunfels acreage as a waystation on their trek to the Llano tract. When he left Texas, his replacement, instead of founding a community on the far-away tract, bought a second site, today's **Fredericksburg,** about 75 miles (120 km) west of Austin and named after Prince Frederick of Prussia.

The Adelsverein brought some 7,380 Germans to Texas, most of them between 1845 and 1847. They landed at the old port of Indianola, and while waiting—sometimes months—for oxcarts to take them inland, were stricken by a plague. In fear for their lives, many tried to walk to New Braunfels, and died en route. More than a thousand succumbed to illness in their first few weeks in Texas, and only a few reached the promised Llano land. Although the Adelsverein did not pass out of Texas history until 1853, by 1847 it was bankrupt, and had stranded the emigrants that it had promised to protect. Of the three villages the association established on its Llano County grant, only one, Castell, remains. New Braunfels and Fredericksburg, the old waystations, are the chief legacies in Texas of the German nobility's efforts to colonize the state.

Granger, on TX 95, about 40 miles (65 km) northeast of Austin, is one of the remaining Czech enclaves in Texas. It's a town where "Anglo" means "white, but not Czech," and neighborhood boundaries have long been drawn along ethnic as well as racial lines: African Americans and Mexican Americans live on the northeast side, Anglos on the west, Czechs on the southeast.

Granger sits on the western edge of Williamson County, whose seat is about 20 miles (30 km) west, at **Georgetown,** some 30 miles (50 km) north of Austin on I-35. Some of Georgetown's native limestone buildings date to the town's founding in the early days of Texas statehood, and for years, Austin residents considered an afternoon drive to see Georgetown's architecture and the nearby Salado River a pleasant getaway from looming urbanization. But with its towns becoming bedroom communities for Austin, Williamson County is rapidly changing. None of the county's towns has felt the impact as much as **Round Rock,** whose population has multiplied tenfold since 1970.

Such rapid growth often reveals conflicts of values between newcomers and old-timers. This was made notoriously apparent during the spring of 1994, when Williamson's county commission was presented with the opportunity to attract a computer facility to the Round Rock-Georgetown area, on the condition that it made concessions regarding the county road system. The subsequent county road measure went to a vote—and failed—largely because the county's more conservative elements had geared up for a fight. At issue was a policy of the prospective industry, Apple Computers. The company provides health insurance benefits to its employees' domestic partners—that is, unmarried, longtime cohabitants, including homosexual partners. In casting a decisive vote against concessions to the plant, county commissioner David Hays explained that he did not want to be known as "the man who brought homosexuality to Williamson County."

Gay activists were at once amused at the absurdity of Hays's worry and offended by comments that their lifestyles were indecent or shocking. Local historians just chuckled, knowing that Round Rock had its own claim to a different brand of gender bending. What about transvestism? they asked. Round Rock was the home of Barbette, a trapeze artist famous on both sides of the Atlantic during the 1920s and '30s, and at one time a member of the Alfaretta Sisters high-wire act. The other Sisters were sisters, but Barbette wasn't: she was born Vander Clyde Broadway, who lived in Round Rock before he went on the road at 14. After a fall which left the daring performer paralyzed, Barbette returned to Round Rock to live with his mother for four years.

Meanwhile, in modern Round Rock the battle heated up. Apple had promised to bring some 1,500 clean-industry jobs to Williamson County, and the commission's vote drew calls of protest from across the county—and the state, and the nation. Even the governor got on the phone. About 10 days after the county chieftains nixed Apple, David Hays relented, voting for the industrial concession. And Williamson County, whose population has quadrupled since 1970, prepared itself for a new wave of growth.

Addie Breedlove with some of her antique roses near Independence.

(right) A soft summer sunrise.

◼ HILL COUNTRY AND JOHNSON CITY

About 40 miles (64 km) west of Austin and some 50 miles (80 km) due north of San Antonio is Lyndon Baines Johnson country, proclaimed so by large billboards on highways entering Blanco County. The county seat is **Johnson City**, the late President's hometown. The town wasn't named for Lyndon, but instead for Tom and Sam Ealy Johnson, ancestors who established a settlement there just after the Civil War. Even Johnson City's founding foretells the kind of politicking that would later make Lyndon, the second President from Texas (Dwight D. Eisenhower was born in Denison), both hated and beloved.

Blanco County's first seat was the town of **Blanco**, founded in 1853, and 14 miles (23 km) south of Johnson City. The first courthouse was built at Blanco in 1860, and by the time that the second—currently being restored—was erected in 1885, the town was already under siege by the Johnsons. Within a year after settling Johnson City in 1879, the family succeeded in getting a proposal to move the courthouse submitted to the county's voters. The proposal failed. The Johnsons resurrected it. It failed again. They tried again, it failed again. Finally, in 1891, it was carried by a narrow margin. Persistence and, some suspect, a little vote-tampering got the county seat moved to a town less than a dozen years old.

Young Lyndon grew up in Johnson City in a one-story frame house now operated by the National Park Service, and the town reaped rewards from the power he later acquired. Johnson City's oversized and handsome stone post office was built in 1969 for the former President's retirement years. It included secure and plush upper-floor offices, a private entrance and elevator, and other amenities—which Johnson never used. Today, what was to be his retirement office serves as a base for the National Park Service unit that operates the Johnson City home, as well as Lyndon B. Johnson National Historic Park, the former President's ranch west of town along U.S. 290.

A greater Johnsonian presence than the official memorials is the headquarters for the Pedernales Electric Coop, sometimes billed as the largest electric cooperative in the world. The cooperative, founded with the help of the Roosevelt administration, brought electric power to the then-isolated Hill Country folk, and is generally credited to Johnson's lobbying, first as a congressional aide, and after 1937, as a congressman.

The ex-President's LBJ Ranch, on the Pedernales River about 15 miles (24 km) west of Johnson City, and about the same distance northwest of Blanco near the

President Lyndon Johnson and his wife, Lady Bird, maintained a ranch outside of Johnson City in the Hill Country of Central Texas. (Center for American History, University of Texas)

town of Stonewall, is the site of two historic exhibits at the Johnson Ranch—still occupied by Johnson's widow, Lady Bird. The LBJ ranch house is a comfortable two-story frame house with a Midwestern look. Adjacent to it is the restored birthplace of the President, and the one-room school where he received his first education, at age four, and to which he returned as President to sign the National Education Act. Johnson is buried not far away, beneath a tombstone that carries the Presidential seal.

The location of the ranch is actually just across the western Blanco County line in Gillespie County, which claims as its hero the five-star admiral Chester W. Nimitz, commander of the U.S. Pacific naval forces during World War II. Nimitz made his home in Fredericksburg, county seat of Gillespie.

■ L U C K E N B A C H

About 12 miles (19 km) west of the LBJ ranch, four miles (6 km) south of U.S. 290 on FM 1376, is the hamlet Luckenbach, a forlorn general-store town that, in the late '70s, was as famous as Dallas. Founded by German immigrants in 1850, it has never been much bigger, or smaller, than it is today. In the late '60s, J. R. "Hondo" Crouch and a partner bought Luckenbach, which consisted of a limestone house and general store that doubled as a post office. Shrewd publicists, the two changed it from nowhere into somewhere in less than five years.

Crouch was raised in South Texas, not in Hill Country. During his World War II service as an airman, he married the daughter of an important Hill Country sheep and goat rancher of German descent. After the war, he commenced to lead a fairly standard and respectable life, devoted to the wool and mohair business. But in the '60s, a knack for practical jokes and put-downs of the pretentious seemed to get the better of him. Central to his pranks was a self-cast role as a tobacco-spitting, wood-whittlin' cowboy hick. The persona may have taken off in 1964, when he was depicted in a *Saturday Evening Post* story as a rancher who, when asked by tourists how to get to the LBJ Ranch, acted as if he'd never heard that Texas had a Johnson ranch—or a man in the White House. Later in the decade, when an overpriced Hill Country restaurant became more popular than it seemed to deserve, Crouch went in, sat on the floor of the lobby, and chowed down the supper he pulled from a paper bag—just to say that he'd dined there, he told his friends.

Crouch and his jokester cronies, with cleverly worded press releases, soon turned their town into a stage for extemporaneous guerrilla theater, and also for crowd-drawing events that capitalized on Luckenbach's rustic name. They announced, for example, an annual chili cook-off and a celebration of the "return" of dirt daubers to town. They adopted a motto with an appropriately populist ring: "Everybody is Somebody in Luckenbach!" Ten years earlier, it had seemed that nobody was anybody in Luckenbach.

In 1972, Crouch staged the First Annual Luckenbach World's Fair, headlined by the Austin music scene's dominant figure, Willie Nelson—and 20,000 people came! New Yorker-turned-Texan Jerry Jeff Walker also hung around, as did other rising figures in Austin's music industry. Before long, Hondo and his retinue were appearing as bit players on Western shows, and as a guests on televised programs of chat. In 1976, he and Luckenbach again made the wires by declaring the Non-Buy Centennial, a spoof on the highly commercialized national bicentennial celebration.

About this time two Nashville songwriters heard about Crouch's carryings-on, and though they'd never been there, penned a song, "Luckenbach, Texas." The ditty described Luckenbach as an exemplar of what rural Texas is supposed to be: a place where people can be themselves, without pretense. Waylon Jennings and Willie Nelson, both of whom had moved to Austin, recorded the song in 1977,

Kinky Friedman and Willie Nelson at Willie's Pedernales Country Club outside Austin.

and it hit the top of the country and western charts. Its lyrics brought as many as 4,000 people to Crouch's store on weekends, and the craze went on for years. People went to Luckenbach to dance, drink, clown, and sing, as if they, like Hondo, were freeing themselves from son-in-law lives. As writer John Davidson noted, Luckenbach became "like a happening, a replay of the sixties for the sort of people who had stood by and watched angrily or enviously while students and hippies broke all the rules. Those same people, under the auspices of the quintessential small town, could shed their inhibitions and make up for lost time."

But though the song put Luckenbach on the map, and established its general store as an important outlet for curios, it was released too late to immortalize Crouch in anything but bronze. A bust was placed there in his memory after he died in 1976, at the age of 59. Country music fans and the curious are still stopping by, nearly 20 years after his death, to catch a glimpse of the Texas that was supposed to be.

■ E N C H A N T E D   R O C K
Eighteen miles (29 km) north of Fredericksburg on FM 965 is Enchanted Rock State Natural Area. A round, nearly bald mountain of pink granite, 500 feet (152 m) tall and about a mile (1.6 km) in diameter, Enchanted Rock is—at one billion years of age—one of the oldest *exposed* areas of rock in the United States. The rock is a favorite with rock climbers, hikers, and campers. Sandy Creek winds past it, and the view from the top is magnificent.

Enchanted Rock has long been that way: archaeologists claim that while the rock has hosted periodic encampments for at least 8,000 years, no permanent settlement ever arose. Indians who guarded the rock when whites first arrived in Texas treated it as a shrine, though one that they regarded with a certain horror: on cool nights following hot days, the rock creaks and groans, as if possessed by spirits. In recent years, its mystery has attracted new crowds of the reverent, who gather there from time to time to catch sight of visitors they expect to decamp from some unknown world.

■ K E R R V I L L E
Kerrville, just two miles (3 km) off of I-10, and some 70 miles (113 km) northwest of San Antonio, is perhaps the Hill Country's most typical town. The seat of Kerr County, whose leading industries are tourism and agriculture, Kerrville

pioneered sheep and goat ranching in the state, and today produces cedar posts and firewood for the rest of Texas.

For more than 60 years, the county has been summer camp headquarters for Texas children. Texas whodunit novelist and satirist Kinky Friedman grew up on Echo Hill ranch, a favorite summer stop for Texas youths of Jewish descent. Adults converge on Kerrville in search of health as well as rest. Its dry climate is mild, and in 1921 the U.S. Health Department named it "the healthiest spot in the nation." Today, it's a town favored in winter by deer hunters, and in spring, summer, and fall by dude and tennis ranch vacationers.

The tranquility of today's Kerrville could not have been foreseen by its early settlers, mainly German refugees from the failed revolution of 1848. Almost as soon as the newcomers settled in the Hill Country, the question of state secession came into view. The area's immigrants voted to stay in the Union, and their resistance didn't end when they lost the statewide vote. In 1862, the Confederacy declared Kerr and two adjoining counties in revolt. Sixty-eight of the area's Unionists met on August 1, and headed for Mexico, hoping to escape the Confederate draft.

Hermann Lungkwitz's painting of the Pedernales River in 1875. The river winds through the Hill Country of Central Texas. (The Witte Museum, San Antonio)

About a week later, Confederate troops attacked them near Brackettville, about 50 miles (80 km) north of the Rio Grande. Thirty-four were executed after their capture, 20 reached Mexico safely, and 11 returned home and survived the war, undetected by Confederate authorities among sympathizers in the Hill Country. At the end of the war, the remains of the Unionists killed in what Confederate forces called the Battle of Nueces were buried at Comfort, about 20 miles (32 km) east of Kerrville. Though commemorated in community ceremonies for more than a century, the Hill Country's Union loyalists are not widely known in Texas today, nor regarded as heroes by those who know their fate. Texas, like Dixie, is still struggling to free itself from a past in which villains and martyrs are sometimes confused.

S O U T H   T E X A S

FROM SAN ANTONIO SOUTHWARD, there is no East or West Texas, only the more homogeneous South Texas. Texas State Highway 90 is its northern limit west of San Antonio, Interstate-10 its limit east of the city. From this line south, there are almost no trees except mesquite. The area is a collection of plains—plains of different types, but plains nonetheless. It is a gently rolling landscape, only parts of which, thanks to coastal rains and Rio Grande irrigation, are sometimes green.

■ CULTURE

South Texas is one of the more stable areas of Texas, both in economic and in cultural terms. In the past 20 years, unlike Houston, Dallas, and Central Texas there's been little immigration from other states. Most new residents of South Texas come from Mexico, as always. Nor have large numbers of South Texas natives left their home towns for other regions, even though South Texas is the poorest region of the state. Undoubtedly, this is because the subculture of South Texas arguably exists nowhere else, and leaving the region means leaving home. In South Texas, a high-paying but far-away job simply can't compete with family ties and a familiar ambience.

■ SAN ANTONIO

In 1681, the governor of the Spanish colonial Texas arrived in what is today San Antonio and there encountered a group of friendly Coahuiltecan Indians. Because the meeting occurred on Saint Anthony's Day, Governor Terán named the site San Antonio. Having heard that the Coahuiltecans here were easily ruled, a Franciscan priest established the mission of San Antonio de Valero along the San Antonio River in 1718; the same year, Spanish soldiers founded a presidio there. The civilian settlement of Villa de Bexar was established in 1731 (in part by a group of Canary Islanders, whose San Antonio descendants claim the lineage today), and four other missions soon followed. The religious function of the missions diminished as San Antonio became the center of Spanish Texas, and by 1801, Mission San Antonio (moved upriver to its current site) had become the garrison for a cavalry from Mexico's Alamo de Parras.

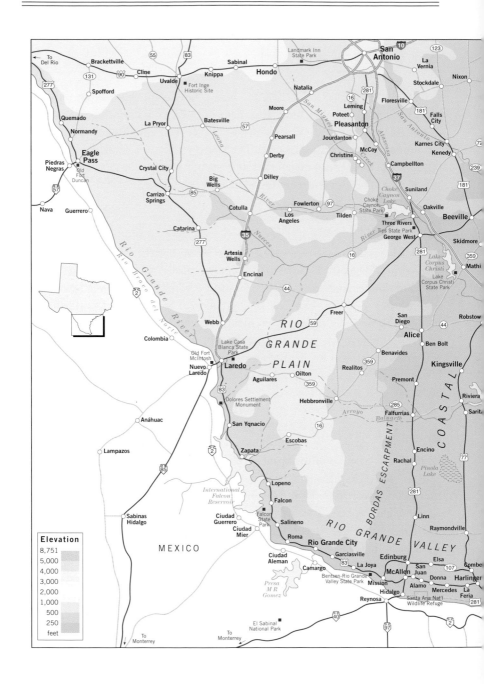

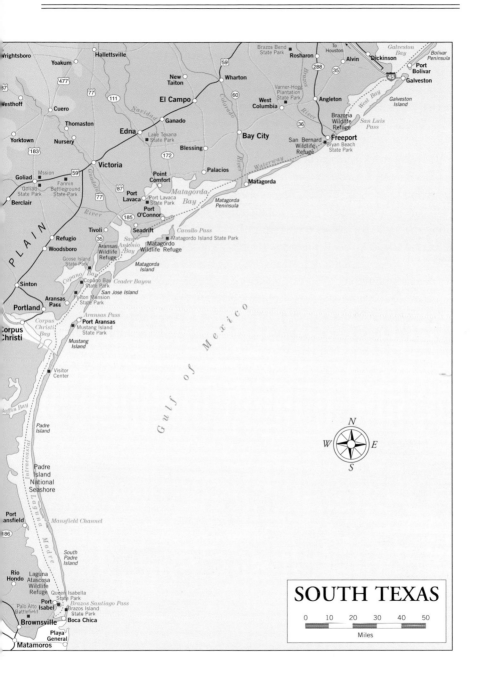

Wrightsboro
Yoakum
Hallettsville
Brazos Bend State Park
Rosharon
To Houston
Alvin
Dickinson
Galveston Bay
Bolivar Peninsula
59
288
35
Port Bolivar
45
37
477
New Taiton
Wharton
Varner-Hogg Plantation State Park
Galveston
Westhoff
Cuero
77
111
El Campo
60
West Columbia
Angleton
Galveston Island
Thomaston
Ganado
Brazoria Wildlife Refuge
San Luis Pass
Yorktown
Nursery
Edna
Lake Texana State Park
36
Bay City
San Bernard Wildlife Refuge
Freeport
Bryan Beach State Park
183
Blessing
172
Victoria
Point Comfort
Palacios
Matagorda
Goliad
Mssion
59
Fannin
Goliad State Park
Battleground State Park
87
Port Lavaca
Port Lavaca State Park
Matagorda Bay
Berclair
77
Port O'Connor
Matagorda Peninsula
185
Tivoli
Seadrift
Cavallo Pass
Refugio
35
Matagordo Island State Park
Aransas Wildlife Refuge
Matagordo Wildlife Refuge
Woodsboro
Goose Island State Park
Matagorda Island
Sinton
Copano Bay State Park
Ceader Bayou
San Jose Island
Aransas Pass
Fulton Mansion State Park
Portland
Aransas Pass
Corpus Christi Bay
Aransas Pass
Port Aransas
Mustang Island State Park
Corpus Christi
Mustang Island
Visitor Center
Padre Island
Gulf of Mexico
Padre Island National Seashore
N
W E
S
Port Mansfield
Mansfield Channel
186
South Padre Island
Rio Hondo
Laguna Atascosa Wildlife Refuge
Queen Isabella State Park
Port Isabel
Brazos Santiago Pass
Palo Alto Battlefield
Brazos Island State Park
Brownsville
Boca Chica
Playa General
Matamoros

SOUTH TEXAS

0   10   20   30   40   50

Miles

The city of San Antonio became a part of Mexico after the Mexican Revolution of 1821, and that same year, Stephen F. Austin received a land grant from the new government to bring 300 Anglo colonists to Texas. By 1836, 3,500 Anglos lived in the city, and when General Santa Anna abolished the 1824 Mexican constitution, these Americans—along with many Hispanic Texans—refused to recognize his presidency, an act of defiance that led to the Battle of the Alamo in 1836.

After Texas won its independence at the Battle of San Jacinto later that year, the next immigrants to arrive in San Antonio were German settlers. After the state's annexation to the United States, Anglos settled the city in greater numbers, and by 1860, San Antonio could claim a population of 8,000. Although growth slowed during the Civil War, when the fighting ended San Antonio became a ranching center, and served as the starting point for major cattle drives to Kansas.

Texas, and San Antonio in particular, has on occasion been the place of refuge for Mexicans protesting their own government's oppression. The principal event in modern Mexican history, the Revolution of 1910, was declared in San Antonio by the exiled Francisco Madero, who later served as Mexico's president from 1911 to 1913. San Antonio gained a small but substantial Asian community long before most Texas cities because, during the revolution, forces led by Francisco "Pancho" Villa were lynching Chinese merchants in northern Mexico. When

San Antonio Plaza in the late 1880s. (Center for American History, University of Texas)

LATINOS AND ANGLOS

The generic term Hispanic needlessly deprives the South Texas reality of its content. Not many people of Puerto Rican, Cuban, South American, or Spanish descent live anywhere in Texas. In fact, more than 95 percent of the Hispanic population is of Mexican extraction, yet nobody but an immigrant would call himself Mexican anymore. South Texas scholars refer to South Texas, for instance, as Anglo/Hispanic, or in an older parlance, as Anglo/Latin. More precise accounts dissolve populations into three categories: Anglo, Mexican American, and Mexican, or, in common discourse, Anglo/Chicano/Mexican.

Chicano was a originally a slang term, derived from the original pronunciation of Mexicano as something like me-she-cano. During the late 1960s and early '70s, the term became identified with the Mexican-American civil rights movement, with the result that, in the conservative '80s, many people turned away from it, calling themselves Mexican American instead. In the most recent turn of terminology, the Spanish word *Latino* is superseding its predecessors. All the terminology takes a twist when it is referring to culture, instead of people. Mexican-American cuisine and alterations in Spanish made in Texas, for example, aren't called Mexican-American, Chicano, or Latino. They're called Tex-Mex or "tejano" instead.

As for Anglos, in Texas people of African, Middle Eastern, German, or Czech descent are usually counted as among this group. Although the word is supposed to mean Americans of British descent, few Americans are pure anything anymore.

American general John J. Pershing launched his futile south-of-the-border hunt for Villa in 1917, he brought the endangered Chinese back to San Antonio with him, and they stayed.

With close to a million citizens, San Antonio today is the capital city of South Texas. Its character reveals itself in a single anecdote: on the south side of its downtown, near what is today called the La Villita section (a restored Mexican village), once ran a street whose Anglo creator wanted to name it Damn If I Know. Since he lived in San Antonio, he spelled that appellation Damifino, as if it were a name from the Spanish language. When pronounced "Dah-mee-fee-no," nobody knew the difference! The street no longer exists, and even local historians aren't sure if it ever did, but the legend says a lot about how San Antonio works. San Antonio is one Texas town where Mexico's cultural influence remains unusually strong. For instance, the mayor may claim to be San Antonio's most powerful resident, but his or her stature will always rivaled by that of the Mexican consul—an important business figure because of the city's role in cross-border trade. U.S. money orders sent home by Mexicans living in the United States re-enter the U.S. economy through San Antonio banks, for example.

The consul is also an important ceremonial figure because two Mexican holidays, Cinco de Mayo (5th of May) and Dieciséis de Septiembre (16th of September)—Mexican independence days—play as big a role in civic life as does the Fourth of July. On these days, the consul makes speeches to civic clubs, rides floats in parades all over town, and is serenaded by mariachis. But the consul isn't a key figure in San Antonio's biggest spectacle, Fiesta Week, whose climax is the Battle of Flowers parade, usually around April 21. The consul doesn't play a leading role—because the celebration commemorates the independence of Texas from Mexico.

Festivities after Mariachi Mass in the ruins of the convent at Mission San José in San Antonio.

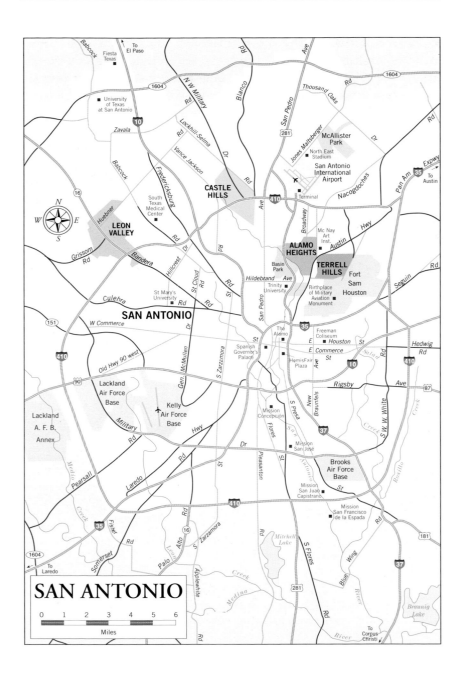

SAN ANTONIO

0   1   2   3   4   5   6

Miles

■ SAN ANTONIO ECONOMY

In 1992, Presidents George Bush and Carlos Salinas chose to sign the North American Free Trade Agreement, or NAFTA, in San Antonio, not only because people along the border favored the treaty, but also because the city's strategic location was the choice of the Mexican president. Mexicans flock to San Antonio because it offers all of the material comforts and advantages of the United States, yet they don't need to speak English to enjoy them. Even on the city's largely Anglo North Side, most concerns transact business in both English and Spanish.

San Antonio's economy depends a great deal on the military: one army and five air force bases are located there. The army base, **Fort Sam Houston,** was established in 1876, and is among other things a center for military medical training and care. The city's active-duty military population of about 85,000 is supplemented by some 70,000 active civilian base employees, and by 75,000 retired military and civilian base employees. In addition, when they retire from active duty elsewhere, many soldiers return to San Antonio because the city offers them a mild climate and access to military hospitals, commissaries, and clubs. Some might come back to be closer to their wives' families, as many soldiers marry while stationed in

Colonel Teddy Roosevelt's Rough Riders are seen here being organized at San Antonio's old Fair Grounds in 1898. (Western History Collections, University of Oklahoma Library)

The San Antonio Gun Club poses for a membership portrait in the early 1900s.
(Center for American History, University of Texas)

the city. Among the nicknames San Antonio has acquired over the years is "Mother-in-Law of the Army."

If the military plays a key role in San Antonio's economy, it is equally buoyed by tourism. In general, the city draws three types of tourists: Texans who come to shop and sightsee; conventioneers; and visitors from across northern Mexico, especially during Christmas and Holy Week. Those northern Mexicans who can afford the expense often buy San Antonio vacation homes, send their children to the city's private schools and universities, consult its doctors—and quite often, retire and die in San Antonio.

■ AMBIENCE

San Antonio is often compared to New Orleans and San Francisco because, like those cities, its history, architecture, and culture are unique in the United States.

Founded in 1718, it was the capital of the Texas territory during the Spanish colonial era. Five eighteenth-century missions, on the south side of town, and the Spanish Governor's Palace, on the western border of downtown, survive from that distant era, all of them open for public inspection. The city's architecture has not been smothered by the anonymous modernity that marks Dallas and Houston, largely because San Antonio was almost unaffected by the oil boom of the 1970s and '80s. San Antonio traffic is laid back, polite, unhurried. The most impressive edifice in its downtown district—only a couple of modern hotels rival it for size—is the 31-story **Tower Life Building**. Built in 1932, it's a plain brick building with a copper dome, not a skyscraper sheathed in reflective glass. The best view of the city is from the 750-foot (229-m) **Tower of the Americas** on the downtown's southern edge. Constructed for a 1968 international exposition called **HemisFair**, the Tower houses a revolving restaurant, making it a major attraction for diners and viewers alike.

A few blocks from HemisFair Park is the **Alamodome**, located at I-37 and Market, where the NBA Spurs shoot hoops. San Antonians are great fans of the home team, especially of center David Robinson, who played on the 1992 Olympic "Dream Team" and continues to pull high numbers for the Spurs.

Seth Eastman's painting of Mission San Jose. (The Witte Museum)

The San Antonio River snakes through the city for 15 miles (25 km), while advancing a mere six miles (10 km), north to south, in city blocks. The Indians called the river "drunken old man going home at night," because of its many curves. Unlike Waco's Brazos or the Trinity in Southeast Texas, the San Antonio was not a navigable river. Instead, it provided water and entertainment, as well as confusion in the city's street layout, which seems to follow few grids or patterns. During the Great Depression, the WPA built sidewalks along the river's banks. Those in the downtown district are now lined with restaurants, nightclubs, and specialty shops, creating what promoters call "The River Walk." With lots of live music venues, souvenir shops, and crowds promenading back and forth, the area is an analog to New Orleans' French Quarter, with a Mexican rather than a Gallic flavor. Getting to the River Walk is like finding a subway. Look for entrances, because the river runs about 20 feet (6 m) below street level at most points downtown. Finding it, however, isn't difficult: there are 35 entrances along the River Walk's 2.8-mile (4.5-km) course downtown, most of them at streetcorner bridges on the business district's south side.

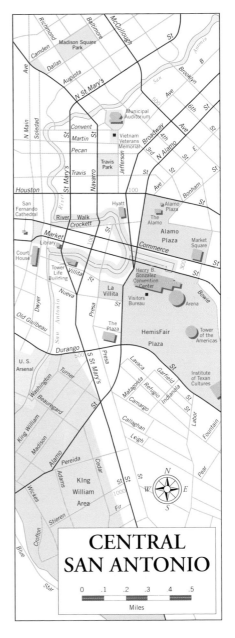

CENTRAL SAN ANTONIO

SAN ANTONIO MAIN ATTRACTIONS

■ UNIQUELY SAN ANTONIO

The Alamo. The stone mission became a fortress in 1836, and ever after, the shrine of Texas Independence. The original 1718 building was restored and remodeled by its operators, the Daughters of the Republic of Texas. Recent additions to the compound include a souvenir shop, the DRT Research Library, and the Long Barracks Museum. The DRT offers guided tours, and the Long Barracks Museum presents a slide show on the Alamo's history as a mission, and another on the famous battle. *Alamo Plaza at Alamo and Houston streets; (210) 225-1391.*

El Mercado. Market Square. A festive bazaar where tiny stalls are crammed with Mexican crafts, food, and housewares, offering reasonable prices on everything from silver and ceramics to tortilla presses and colored glassware. *Market Square West, bounded by I-35, Santa Rosa, West Commerce, and Dolorosa; (210) 299-8600.*

La Villita National Historic District. A former slum, La Villita is the result of concerned San Antonians' effort to preserve their city's history. Today the neighborhood, inhabited by many Mexican and Central American artists, has a Bohemian flavor and is quite charming. Restored buildings of humble limestone and clapboard are now occupied by restaurants, gift shops, and art galleries. *Bounded by San Antonio River, Nuevo, South Alamo, and South Presa streets. (210) 299-8610.*

River Walk. (Paseo Del Rio.) A pleasant cobblestone and flagstone path along the San Antonio River, surrounded by trees and lush greenery. The paths and pretty stone stairways were built by WPA crews in the 1930s. Extending for about two and half miles, the River Walk is lined with sidewalk cafes, bars, hotels, boutiques, a shopping mall, and roaming mariachi bands. *Extends from the Municipal Auditorium on the north end to the King William district at the south.*

■ MISSIONS

San Antonio was home to five missions during the Spanish colonial period, including the Alamo, though that fort's military significance eclipsed its religious role. The other four, somewhat younger missions, are located along the San Antonio River in today's South San Antonio. Though operated by the National Park Service, all four are still active as parishes. They are listed here in order of their proximity to downtown.

Concepción. Stone construction, dating back to the mid-eighteenth century, with some original frescoes on the twin towers. Many believe that this is the oldest unrestored Catholic church in the country that is still in use. *807 Mission Road; (210) 229-5732.*

San Francisco de la Espada. Built between 1731 and 1756. The most rural of the missions, known for its *acequias,* or stone irrigation canals. Little remains of the original structure but the interior, renovated in the 1800s, is lovely and well-preserved and the courtyard contains ruins of the original mission walls. *10040 Espada; (210) 627-2021.*

San José. In the ornate Churrigueresque style, erected circa 1782, this is the prize of the missions. Its Rose Window is a postcard favorite. Mariachi Mass at noon on Sundays. San Antonio's elite frequently stage weddings and other festivities here. *6539 San Jose; (210) 229-4770.*

San Juan Capistrano. More simply designed than the others. Actually, this mission is a former granary to which a bell tower and Moorish arches were added. The *convento* now serves as a small museum featuring mission archeology. *9101 Graf; (210) 229-4770.*

■ **HISTORIC MUSEUMS**

Institute of Texan Cultures. A remarkable museum complete with interpreters and interactive displays. From Spanish colonists to Indian tribes to Dutch dairy farmers, the institute represents every nationality and cultural group that has shaped Texas history and culture. *South Durango at Bowie; (210) 558-2300.*

■ **ART MUSEUMS**

San Antonio Museum of Art. Set in a highly original location, this museum resides in the turn-of-the-century Lone Star brewery. Built in 1903, the brewery closed during Prohibition. In 1981, imaginative designers converted the space into a museum, and the result is stunning. Galleries exhibit pre-Columbian and modern Mexican folk art, eighteenth- and nineteenth-century American painting and sculptures, and early Texas furnishings. *200 West Jones; (210) 829-7262.*

McNay Art Museum. Originally the home of Kansas oil heiress Marion Koogler McNay, the lovely Spanish-style structure and courtyard were converted into a museum by Mrs. McNay. Aside from works by El Greco and Diego Rivera, the museum also features Postimpressionists including Gauguin, Dufy, Cézanne, Picasso, and Van Gogh. *6000 North New Braunfels; (210) 824-5368.*

Old-timers in San Antonio remember the River Walk as an almost neglected area, where for most of the year one could stroll in complete peace, hearing only one sound: the clicking of linotypes on the other side of printshop windows. In spring months, one sometimes heard a more alarming sound—shotgun fire, as police and parks personnel, in annual pest control campaigns, blew blackbirds out of trees on the banks and filled the river with little corpses.

Today, for better or worse, all of that is gone. Along the river are a half-dozen hotels and eateries to suit every taste, serving everything from hamburgers to quail. At the route's northern end is **Southwest Craft Center** at 300 Augusta, formerly the Ursuline Academy and Convent and today a store where ceramic and jewelry items are made and sold. The convent, founded in 1851, was in operation for more than 100 years. On its grounds is a clock tower that is blank on its north side, local legend says, because the Reconstruction-era nuns who commissioned the work didn't want to give Yankee soldiers the time of day.

Further south, at the corner of Soledad and Travis, stands the **Milam Building,** which in 1928 became the nation's first fully air-conditioned skyscraper. A little more than two blocks after the river turns east, strollers encounter the **Hertzberg Circus Museum** at 210 West Market, stocked mainly with photos, posters, and costumes from under the Big Tents. In the northeast corner of the twisting River Walk, in the Hyatt Regency Hotel at 123 Losoya, is a restaurant and club called the **Landing,** known to many National Public Radio listeners as the origination point for semi-weekly broadcasts of Dixieland music performed by the **Jim Cullum Jazz Band.** In between all of these locations, interspersed with eateries and nightclubs, you'll find plenty of shops selling miniature globes in which snow falls on models of the Alamo, as it does but once a decade.

■ A L A M O

The leading tourist attraction in San Antonio, and in Texas for that matter, is the Alamo, located on the downtown's eastern side—take Houston or Crockett street east, and you'll come close enough to see the plaza surrounding it. It is operated by the Daughters of the Republic of Texas, who saved it from ruin around the turn of the century. The Alamo is Texas' most sacred shrine. Each year some three million visitors tour the remodeled site, which enjoys an almost mythic status in Texas. The Alamo, formerly the Spanish Franciscan Mission San Antonio de Valero, was

The most famous landmark in Texas, the Alamo.

built of adobe and stone at its original location in 1718. The mission was moved upriver in the 1720s, and the chapel was erected in 1744. After serving as a Mexican garrison in the late eighteenth century, it had fallen into disuse by 1836, when it was occupied by Texas revolutionaries. And it was there that in early 1836, some 180 of them made a 13-day stand against an army of four to five thousand, led by the self-appointed Mexican president and commander-in-chief, Antonio López de Santa Anna.

Santa Anna was sweeping across Texas in an effort to wipe out the Mexican territory's nascent independence movement when he entered San Antonio on February 23, 1836. The town had been in rebel hands since the previous December. The rebels took refuge in the Alamo and, when Santa Anna sent a messenger demanding the mission's surrender, they answered with a cannon shot.

Santa Anna laid siege, planning to take no prisoners. As he tightened his net, couriers rode in and out of the Alamo, racing past the besiegers, carrying appeals for help. Most notable among them was James Bonham, who returned to the Alamo on March 4, disregarding warnings that he would pay with his life. He traded it for immortality in Texas.

High on the list of defenders were Tennessean Davy Crockett and the other volunteers he had brought from that state; volunteer James Bowie, a former slave runner who'd prospered in Texas; and William Barret Travis, an attorney and veteran of other risings, who held the rank of lieutenant colonel in the rebel army. According to the plan that the defenders drew, Travis, 27, was to share command with Bowie, 41, who was chief of the volunteers. But Bowie fell ill with typhoid, and command devolved upon Travis.

On March 1, the only reinforcements the men at Alamo received—some 32 riders from the town of Gonzales—joined the 150 men inside. Four days later, Santa Anna threw his army at the mission. It was beaten back. At about 5 A.M. the following day, March 6, the Mexican general launched a second assault, which reached the walls of the mission, only to be repulsed again. The retreat left a scattered trail of corpses, but the Mexicans had weakened the defenders and thinned their number, too. Mexican officers spotted points where the Alamo's defense was vulnerable, and after several hours, their battalions regrouped and assaulted again. The Texas defenders fought from the walls, and after these were breached, fought at close quarters, hand-to-hand, until all—or all but a handful—were dead.

Accounts of casualties vary, but Francisco Ruiz, the city's Mexican mayor, who

DEFENDING THE ALAMO

*T*he Texan marksmanship, the speed, continuity and fury of their fire, were frightful. Soldiers fell by the score. But the number of their comrades was great, and gaps were closed, and presently there was a great swarm so near the bases of the walls, that the artillery above could not be traversed downward to bear on them. Suddenly a breach was made on the north side, and another on the south, and soldiers poured in to capture the Álamo plaza. The defenders fell back to the convent and its patio, and to the roofless church. The army turned their own cannon on them, and squad after squad advanced to take room after room in the convent cells, killing all whom they trapped in each. The Mexican bayonets whistled and darted in the early sunlight that rayed into the convent patio. The ground was strewn with dead attackers and defenders. But still the army strove and, when all was silent in the outer courts and rooms, threw its remaining power against the church, which was the last stronghold of the Texans. The main doors were forced, and everywhere—in the nave, the baptistry, the transepts, the sacristy, with their heaps of long-fallen stone and weedy mounds of earth, under the light morning sky within the open walls—the victory was won man by man until after an hour not one defender was seen alive anywhere in the profaned and mouldered mission.

—Paul Horgan, *Great River: The Rio Grande in North American History*, 1954

One of the earliest known photographs of the Alamo, taken in 1871, when it was serving as a storage facility. (Catholic Archives of Texas, Austin)

*Lunchtime at San Antonio's popular Mexican restaurant La Fogata
with owner Jesse Calvillo and friend Marla.*

directed the cleanup, put the number of Mexican dead at 1,600. Santa Anna's force was decimated, and his timetable to overrun insurgent Texas was wrecked. Among the Texans spared from the carnage was Suzanna Dickenson, the wife of a killed defender, her baby, a servant, and another child. Mexican troops escorted them to Gonzales, where they helped to raise new forces for the rebellion that would, within weeks, claim a decisive victory at San Jacinto.

Today, the Alamo has become a battleground again. San Antonio's Mexican-American intelligentsia has raised a furor over the area in front of it. Beyond the Alamo's front door there's a sidewalk, then a small street, then the flagstone Plaza, then a full street, Alamo Street. The whole area, recent historical research has shown, was a cemetery for Indians in the days when the Alamo was a mission. In honor of the dead, Fiesta Week parades no longer pass through the area, and a move is on—hard fought on both sides—to close Alamo Street to traffic.

■ LA VILLITA AND MARKET SQUARE
While in downtown San Antonio, tourists also visit La Villita, a group of restored turn-of-the-century buildings bounded by the river, and South Alamo, Nueva, and

Fuzzy Plunkett at San Antonio's Buckhorn Museum.

South Presa streets. La Villita—accessible from the River Walk, or Durango Street—
is a good place for a quiet stroll. Its limestone huts are now craft shops, many of
which offer Mexican and Central American handiwork, and there's little congestion.

Visitors also enjoy visiting **Market Square**, a restoration of an old market plaza,
known as Mariachi Plaza, and its surrounding buildings, some of them built as
early as 1840. Located west of the downtown area at Commerce and San Saba,
just off I-35, Market Square is the place to take the kids to buy a piñata, machine-
made serapes, and other industrially made "craft" goods. Housed in a renovated
1920s-era building is the **Centro de Artes del Mercado**, an arts center featuring
music and dance performances, art galleries, and meeting halls. For casual entertainment in summertime, stroll through the square around lunchtime to catch
music and dance, held in the center of the square. Appropriately, overlooking the
square is a statue of St. Cecilia, the patron saint of musicians.

■ CORPUS CHRISTI

Three cities form a triangle in South Texas: San Antonio, at the apex; Corpus
Christi, the southeastern base; and Laredo, at the southwestern corner. Interstate
35 connects San Antonio to Laredo, and I-37 connects it to Corpus Christi, a
port, refinery, and naval operations town. Laredo and Corpus Christi are connected by a highway network, but their most celebrated link is the Texas Mexican
Railway, established in 1881 to carry coal from Laredo-area mines to the port. It is
still in service for freight runs today, and from time to time promoters have con-
vinced the railway to make weekend passenger runs between the two cities.

Corpus (Texans usually dispense with the second part of its name) owes its rise to
a boundary dispute. When Texas became a republic in 1836, it claimed the Rio
Grande as its southern border, but was unable to back its claim with force. Mexico
claimed that the Nueces River, which runs roughly the same course as I-37, was the
appropriate international line. Corpus was established at the point where the Nueces
reaches the Gulf. It was a de facto border town with an avenue to the sea—a natural
headquarters for smugglers. Though the area of South Texas that lies north and east
of Corpus was a cradle of the Republic of Texas, not until the Mexican War of 1846
was Corpus brought into Texas and the United States. Accession created a boom:
the town became a supply port for U.S. troops headed into Mexico.

Corpus is one of the calmer cities in Texas, not known for booms, busts, or national events. Its population has shown only slight growth over the past two

decades, and lots of locals would like to see it stay that way. "Politicians always hope for growth, so that they can pay off the debts in 20 years that they've made today," says Corpus defense attorney Douglas Tinker. "But as for me, I hope the city doesn't grow too much."

Downtown Corpus Christi grew up facing its beaches, but following a 1919 hurricane, most new construction headed inland, to a 40-foot bluff overlooking the bay. Today in Corpus people talk of "downtown" and "uptown," in reference to the split-level business district. The district's waterfront, laid out along the spectacular Shoreline Drive, is arguably the most attractive on the Texas coast, with a two-mile seawall that's an exemplar of adorned utility: it was designed by sculptor Gutzon Borglum, who sculpted the four monumental presidential heads of Mount Rushmore.

Three projections, called after their shapes T-heads and L-heads, protrude from the coastline into the Gulf. Pleasure craft and bay shrimp boats dock on the T- and L-heads, boatless fishermen from the piers. Their restaurants and bait shops draw a leisurely trade—no crowds or lines here. Locals go to the docking-points to buy shrimp fresh from the bay.

An old print illustrates the army encampment near Corpus Christi in October 1845. (Local History Collection, Corpus Christi Public Library)

An aircraft carrier, the USS *Lexington,* one of five warships stationed in Corpus, was purchased by the city when the ship was decommissioned in 1990. The ship now sits in the bay, in plain sight of the city's downtown. It has become a magnet for tourists, a locale for big parties—even a camping ground for the Boy Scouts.

As elsewhere in Texas, the beaches in Corpus are relatively free of encumbrances, perfect for strolling, or—where it's permitted—even a beachfront drive. Most beach bums find Gulf beaches of secondary quality: the sand is coarser than on the finest beaches; the water is green, not Pacific blue, and lukewarm and opaque, not cool and transparent; and the crests of waves in the Gulf are diminutive when compared with those on the open sea. But the beaches are great escapes from congestion and noise, and only one precaution is necessary: in the water or on the beach, stay away from jellyfish. There are plenty of them, and two of the Texas varieties can sting, even when they seem to be dead. The stings aren't usually serious— about like those of wasps—but they can ruin an outing.

Access to Texas beaches is free, and you can stay as long as you'd like. It's illegal, under Texas law, for any private party to own property at the shoreline: the state of Texas owns it all. There are, therefore, no beach cottages in Texas, and hotels that

Shrimper and his boat in the fishing port of Rockport just north of Corpus Christi.

Tropical storms pound the coastline of Texas a few times every year.

serve the swimming and surfing trade—and concession stands—are all located about 100 yards (91 m) away from the water. One drawback of the state-ownership-and-maintenance policy is that few Texas beaches are manicured; natural shrubs, weeds, and sometimes detritus stand out in the sand. Back of the shorelines, in Texas, there's only treeless coastal plain, most of it planted in maize or cotton. Texas beaches are better for family than for romantic outings, and though there's plenty of activity, better for sunning than for scuba diving and swimming.

■ LAREDO

Laredo, at the terminus of I-35, is the principal land port for goods going into or coming out of Mexico. It is also the classic Texas border town. Stone and adobe are its oldest building materials, and its finest buildings are in the Porfirian or late nineteenth-century style of Mexico. Its newest and most prosperous residential sections are found on its northern and eastern edges, while commercial areas lie between the newer sections and downtown, which, like I-35, runs right up to the

Rio Grande. The city is characterized by wide, one-way thoroughfares, on which traffic moves at a leisurely pace. It's not easy to get lost in Laredo, as most streets run in a grid, north to south, east to west.

Founded by the Spanish in 1755, Laredo was not a part of Texas until the Mexican War—and according to a popular view, it isn't quite a part of the United States yet. Nor is Nuevo Laredo, the city on the south side of the Rio Grande, wholeheartedly a part of Mexico, even though it was founded by refugees when Laredo became part of the United States. Most residents, on both sides, have mixed feelings about the whole idea of nationality.

Laredo's immersion in Mexican life is evident in its downtown business district, which does not cater to the American trade. Instead it serves the flow of Mexicans who enter on foot over what is called "the old bridge" over the Rio Grande, one of 20 that are unique features of the Texas-Mexico border—and one of three in the Laredo area. Signs in downtown stores in Laredo are more often in Spanish than in English; cashiers ordinarily speak some English, but like their customers, most live on the south side of the Rio Grande. Pesos are used as often as dollars in Laredo's downtown. Announcements posting the exchange rate are as common as time-and-temperature signs elsewhere, and when the rate is volatile, are watched with greater concern.

Because the downtown districts of Laredo and its Mexican twin, Nuevo Laredo, abut each other along the Rio Grande, Mexican push-cart vendors operate on both sides of the divide. In Laredo—and in Nuevo Laredo, along the Texas border—one sees men on three-wheeled bicycle carts, flattening pasteboard boxes as they stop along their routes. They're collecting cast-off boxes for recycling, an old practice in Mexico. Because Mexican customs agents carefully examine products that are still in their boxes, Mexican shoppers in Laredo typically un-box and un-wrap their goods before returning home, hoping to pass off new merchandise as used. The streets of Laredo, were it not for the box collectors, would be knee-deep in cardboard.

Local residents and Mexican motorists do their shopping in the city's suburban-style shopping malls. They're unusually well stocked, and one of the benefits of the Mexicanization of retail commerce is that specialty merchandise is available in Laredo that would not ordinarily reach a town of its size (a population of only 123,000). Laredo's Wal-Mart store is the largest in the United States, and an HEB store, part of a grocery chain, is the largest in its universe.

ALARMA!

The presence in Laredo of the main offices of a Mexican magazine tells much of what the city is about. The magazine, a weekly pulp, is sold widely across the Southwestern United States and throughout Mexico. Written in Spanish, it focuses on crime and gore. "He tried to outrun the train and lost his legs!" cries one headline, next to a photo showing an anguished man on a stretcher. "With One Shot, the Police Kill a Delinquent," reads a headline on the opposite page.

The magazine is filled with letters from the lovelorn, gossip about movie stars and pols, and crossword puzzles whose centerpieces are photos of bikini-clad women. Herbalists and romance counselors advertise in its pages.

The weekly would be a Mexican equivalent to the American supermarket tabloids the *National Enquirer* and the *Globe*, were it not a publication in masquerade. It is editorially a successor to *Alarma!*, once Mexico's biggest-selling weekly magazine. It was founded when the publication of *Alarma!* was suspended by the Mexican government in the mid-1980s, charged with pornography. The charge was ludicrous: *Alarma!* was *carn*ography—chock-full of photos of corpses—not pornography, which sells on the streets of Mexico much as in the United States. *Alarma!* was something else: the cash cow of Publicaciones Llergo, whose more sedate weekly, *Impacto*, was a sort of Mexican *Saturday Evening Post*. *Impacto* during that era had begun to champion the causes of the Mexican government's opposition. There were no constitutional grounds for closing *Impacto*, but the suspension of *Alarma!*, coupled with a simultaneous and murky corporate ownership dispute in the courts, had the same effect. Policemen occupied *Impacto*'s offices, installed a new editor, and the magazine resumed its praise of those on high.

Living in Laredo at the time was a businessman who had come to the United States to establish a distributorship for Publicaciones Llergo. After the government raids on *Alarma!* and *Impacto*, he found himself without a job. But he knew the writers at *Alarma!*, mainly police reporters on regional dailies in Mexico, and he thought that by producing a look-alike scandal magazine in Texas and exporting it, he could save the paper's place in the Mexican market. His strategy worked. Though today *Alarma!* is back in print, it now has a competitor from Laredo. The name of the upstart is *El Arma!*

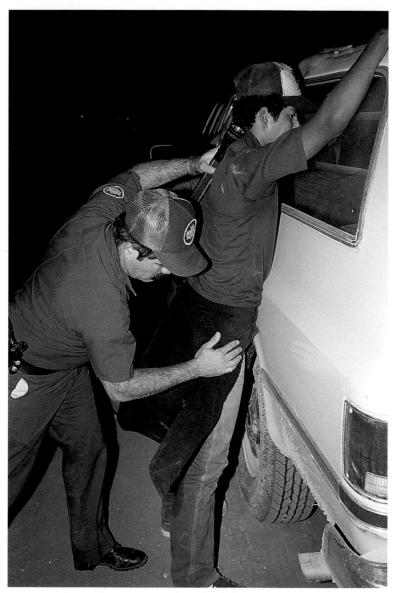

A Border Patrol agent apprehends an illegal alien on the border near Laredo.

THAT LAWLESS BORDER

Inland Texans regard border towns as lawless, and the perception is accurate, but the lawlessness of the border is not of a frightening kind. Instead, it's nod-and-wink lawlessness, something that makes sense out of the nonsensical.

Differing laws and regulations in Mexico and the United States have given rise, in Laredo and other border towns, to a whole set of sometimes legal, sometimes illegal trans-border institutions. Though the problem has eased a bit, thanks to the NAFTA agreement, Mexican customs officials have traditionally been more than officious, and all import/export regulations, of all countries, are long on special interests and short on rationale.

For example, in Mexico imported T-shirts are taxed at one rate, and shirts at a higher rate. T-shirts with collars are taxed as shirts, not as T-shirts. The importation of auto parts, tires, certain machine parts, and electronic goods has at times been subject to prohibitive tariffs—and the result has been widespread smuggling. Though NAFTA has hurt the trade a bit, Laredo and most other Texas border towns have for years been home to airplane companies that make fortunes for their owners and pilots flying such "white contraband" into clandestine Mexican airstrips. A well-known electronics store in Laredo for years sold television sets cheaper than any other American outlet—to customers who paid $75 to $150 for delivery in Mexico: the operation made its profit from ownership of an airborne smuggling ring.

As international mail service to Mexico is undependable, American mail drops have arisen to serve a Mexican clientele. American body shop operators and dentists face a tough go on the border, because their Mexican counterparts do comparable work for incomparably lower fees. Disposable diapers, loaves of bread, and many industrial goods are cheaper on the north side of the border than on the south; people trek across Laredo's international bridges to find the lowest price. When gasoline or beer prices are cheaper in Mexico, the traffic goes south; when they're cheaper in the United States, the traffic goes north. When Mexicans enter the United States by car, even for a day, they're required to have American auto insurance, and Laredo's streets are lined with companies whose only business is selling day-rate policies.

Officialdom is less efficient, less intrusive, and more easily bribed on the south side of the Rio Grande, meaning it sometimes takes less than 10 minutes to cross the border in a car going south. The return trip can take an hour, and some border dwellers, especially Mexican businessmen who live in Laredo, keep bicycles and motorcycles so that they can weave between cars on the international bridges, cutting the waiting time that motorists face. Customs agents are the villains of the border's subculture, smugglers often its heroes.

■ VIEWS OF THE BORDER

A casual visitor to Laredo can witness the panorama of border life most easily by renting a room with a balcony at the city's **La Posada Hotel,** a modern facility built into an old schoolhouse on the banks of the Rio Grande, only yards from the "old bridge" downtown. Customs offices of the two governments sit at opposite ends of the bridge. By day, one can see the traffic parade, creeping north towards American customs inspection, speeding south across the bridge for the cursory Mexican procedure. Northbound trucks form interminable lines, waiting for their special inspection, which takes place beneath the hotel, at river level. By night, the guests can watch Border Patrol agents return groups of illegal aliens to Mexico by accompanying them to the turnstiles on the north side of the bridge. On most nights, a careful observer can also witness the reverse: Mexicans swimming or paddling in inner tubes, surreptitiously crossing the United States between the "new" and "old" downtown bridges.

■ FARMING

U.S. 77, which crosses I-10 at Schulenberg, traces a line nearly straight south for about 90 miles (145 km), until it reaches TX 239. From there it parallels the coastline, about 25 miles (40 km) inland, until it reaches the Rio Grande at Brownsville. As U.S. 77 makes its descent, it divides rural South Texas into a farming and ranching region, the **Coastal Prairie,** and a drier area, the **Rio Grande Plain,** where only ranching is possible. Rainfall and dirt make the difference: the area east of the line is wet and black. To the west the terrain is mostly caliche—leached white soil—where mesquite and brush thrive.

In the Rio Grande Plain, where irrigation and lucky patches of soil make it possible, farming is celebrated in an unusual way. For example, on the west side of the city hall in **Crystal City,** about 130 miles (210 km) southwest of San Antonio, stands a statue of the cartoon character Popeye, built about 60 years ago to celebrate the city's status as spinach-growing capital of the nation. Crystal City's monument to produce is rivaled by those in several Rio Grande Plain towns. Some 50 miles (80 km) west, in **Dilley,** just off I-35, there's a monument to the watermelon. **Poteet,** 40 miles (65 km) south of San Antonio on TX 16, has a giant tribute to the strawberry; and **Floresville,** about 30 miles (43 km) southwest of San Antonio on U.S. 181, immortalizes the peanut. On the courthouse lawn at **Seguin,** about 35

VALLEY AGRICULTURE

Onions, lettuce, carrots, broccoli, greens, cucumbers, tomatoes, cabbage, and most of the aloe vera consumed in the United States flourish in the Rio Grande Valley's 330-day growing season, and make agriculture the most important part of the region's economy. The Valley is also a greenhouse for ornamental plants and trees; the palms at Orlando's Disney World come from Texas, not Florida. In Valley towns, locals cultivate poinsettias in their gardens, and even stage a Christmas-time celebration in the flower's honor. The region blossoms with bougainvillea, hibiscus, oleander, and other bright foliage along the roadways, in yards, and even at business places. But the prize of Valley horticulture is not decorative plants. It's grapefruit and oranges instead.

From about the turn of the century onwards, newcomers to Texas, impressed by its comparatively mild climate, tried to establish a Florida-like citrus industry here, in locales as far north as Port Arthur, nearly 500 miles (800 km) north of the Valley. One by one, their groves succumbed to winter freezes. But the attempt held out long enough in the Valley for an industry to take root.

The Valley's citrus industry produced, and still does produce, oranges. But Texas oranges aren't as pretty as their Florida and California competitors, and tend to be harder-skinned. Most Valley oranges wind up as orange juice. Valley grapefruit, on the other hand, are champions of their kind, largely because their yellow peels blush pink and their meat is red. "Redder is better. Redder is sweeter. We taste with our eyes as much as we do with our tongues," explains Richard Hensz, father of the three most popular Texas species, the Ruby Red, the Star Ruby, and the Rio Ruby.

But the Valley's citrus industry is probably on its way to retirement. Freezes in 1983 and 1989 decimated its groves, leaving the area with less than half of its trees. The survivors were reduced to childhood proportions, losing much of their branch length. And like California earthquakes, killing freezes will be back again, every five to 10 years. In 1993–94, the Valley harvest should have represented full restoration of the groves that withered in 1988–89. But it was less than half as big as the pre-frost harvest. In this age of a globalized economy, the barons of Valley citrus planted new groves after the freeze of '89 further south—in Belize and Honduras.

miles (56 km) west of San Antonio on I-10, there's a painted concrete memorial to the pecan. Though a collection of photos of these monuments might make South Texas look like a winter garden—some towns do call themselves that—perhaps for realism's sake, **Freer**, about 100 miles (160 km) south of San Antonio on I-35, has added an element of rogue realism: its monument is to the rattlesnake.

Bay City, about 70 miles (113 km) southwest of Houston, is a fairly typical Coastal Prairie town. It's a center for rice cultivation, ranching, and some petroleum production, and the town is connected by a deep-water channel to an intercoastal canal, 15 miles away (24 km) in the Gulf. Like most Texas towns, Bay City may seem unremarkable in most respects, but beneath its workaday surface lies a piece of agricultural history—in this case, the genealogy of certain bovines. In 1906, the estate of Bay City pioneer and rancher Abel H. "Shanghai" Pierce sent a buyer to India to purchase Brahman cattle. The humpbacked breed, known for its ability to withstand heat and literally shrug off ticks, had been known in the state through circus exhibits and one earlier commercial importation, but wasn't widely raised because it produced inferior beef. The Pierce ranch buyer shipped 51 head from India. They were quarantined in New York harbor, where 18 died. The survivors came to Bay City, where they became the base of crossbreeding experiments that eventually led to the Santa Gertrudis breed, a cross with the Shorthorn variety that is today the stalwart of coastal ranches from Texas to the Southern Cone of South America.

■ GOLIAD

As one of the three oldest towns in Texas, Goliad, about 90 miles (145 km) southeast of San Antonio and some 80 miles (130 km) north of Corpus Christi, can claim some compelling history. Under different names, it has been known to Western civilization since 1749, when the Spanish founded a mission on the site, including a convent and a fort, or presidio, to guard it. The Spanish selection of the Goliad site followed on the heels of an older settlement by Aranama Indians, one of the dozens of ethnic groups extinguished when Texas was colonized. The fort at Goliad, called La Bahía, provided troops that fought and defeated British regiments in Louisiana and Mississippi during the American Revolution, indirectly aiding its victory.

Rio Grande Valley canteloupes are readied for shipping.

In 1810, Mexico began its own struggle for independence with an abortive uprising led by Father Miguel Hidalgo of Dolores, in today's Hidalgo state. His rising was followed by what historians call the Gutiérrez-Magee expedition, an invasion from Louisiana by troops mostly of American extraction. Their aim was to make Texas part of the United States. The Gutiérrez-Magee expedition reached La Bahía and took over its fort in November 1812. Its invaders withstood a siege, routed their enemy, and in February, marched out and took San Antonio, where they held out until August, when they were crushed. Though Mexican historians generally regard the Gutiérrez-Magee expedition as an act of freebooters, after independence from Spain was won the congress of the state of Coahuila, which ruled over Texas, granted La Bahía municipal status, and, as if to praise it in code, gave the settlement a patriotic name: Goliad is an anagram for Hidalgo (though to get the point of it, you've got to remember that the letter H is silent in Spanish)!

RUNAWAY SCRAPE

In early 1836, following the Battle at The Alamo and the massacre at Goliad by Mexican general Santa Anna's troops, settlers in Central and East Texas began fleeing eastward in a retreat known as the Runaway Scrape. Before mid-April, East Texas as far as Nacogdoches and San Augustine was empty. Here, a settler writes of what he saw during his own retreat:

*T*he desolation of the country through which we passed beggars description. Houses were standing open, the beds unmade, the breakfast things still on the table, pans of milk moulding in the dairies. There were cribs full of corn, smokehouses full of bacon, yards full of chickens that ran after us for food, nests of eggs in every fence corner, young corn and garden truck rejoicing in the rain, cattle cropping the luxuriant grass, hogs fat and lazy, wallowing in the mud, all abandoned. Forlorn dogs roamed around the deserted homes, their doleful howls adding to the general sense of desolation. Hungry cats ran mewing to meet us, rubbing their sides against our legs in token of welcome. . . . There were broken down wagons and household goods scattered all along the road. Stores with quite valuable stocks of goods stood open, the goods on the shelves, no attempt having been made to remove them.

—Diary of Noah Smithwick, 1836

But the little town is best known for an act of heroism that occurred 20 years later. Col. James Fannin of the Texas independence movement was quartered at Goliad in February 1836 with some 500 troops, the largest revolutionary force in Texas, when Lt. Col. William Barret Travis, facing almost certain death at the Alamo, pleaded for support. Fannin set out to join the besieged Alamo garrison, but when he encountered travel difficulties, he turned his troops around. On March 19, some two weeks after the Alamo fell, he and his men left for the coast. En route they encountered and fought Mexican troops for a day, then surrendered. The captives were returned to the presidio at Goliad, and on March 27, Palm Sunday, some 400 of them were executed. A large monument some two miles (3 km) south of Goliad on U.S. 183, and about a mile south of the restored mission, marks the spot where the remains of the Texas martyrs were buried in a mass grave, shortly after independence was won at San Jacinto—by Texans whose battle cry was "Remember the Alamo! Remember Goliad!"

■ KING RANCH

Any map of Texas shows a blank spot, nearly 70 miles (115 km) long and about 30 miles (48 km) wide, running along the Gulf, from a point that starts about 20 miles (32 km) south of Corpus Christi. This seemingly empty area, through which U.S. 77 passes, takes in almost all of two counties, and parts of four. One of the counties, Kenedy, has only 460 residents, yet the county covers some 1,945 square miles (5,037 sq km) of territory, about one and a half times the size of Rhode Island, and only slightly smaller than Delaware.

The legendary King Ranch—model for the Benedict ranch in the 1956 movie *Giant*—1.2 million acres in size, accounts for most of the blank spot. It owes its existence to nineteenth-century conditions in Texas, and to a nineteenth-century figure, the Texas equivalent of the robber barons of his day.

Richard King was the son of Irish immigrants. Born in New York in 1824, he left home at the age of 11 to work as a cabin boy on an Atlantic Coast freighter. That job led to another, on a coastal river ship. Twenty years later, he became friends with another river boat sailor, Mifflin Kenedy, whom he would rejoin three years later in Texas, when Kenedy was supplying the U.S. Army for its invasion of Mexico. In 1850, the two became partners, and for the next 20 years, they operated river boats along the lower Rio Grande.

Two years after forming his partnership with Kenedy, King paid a Mexican family $300 for a ranch that had been created by a Spanish land grant of some 75,000 acres—nearly 120 square miles (200 sq km)—on the Santa Gertrudis creek, about 100 miles north (160 km) of the border. He also tracked down other Mexicans with Texas land grants who no longer cherished their holdings in what had become a part of the United States. In 1858, the rancher-shipper and his wife built a house on the Santa Gertrudis grant, at a site picked by an army visitor with an engineer's eye, Lt. Col. Robert E. Lee.

While establishing himself in ranching, King kept his hand in the shipping business he owned with Kenedy. The two prospered wildly during the Civil War, when the Confederate government contracted with them to supply European buyers with cotton, and the Rio Grande and Texas Gulf coast became the main arteries of Southern trade. After the war, the two shippers divided their holdings.

OIL COMING IN

Leslie Benedict found herself in the fantastic position of a wife who tries to convince her husband that a few million dollars cannot injure him.
"You'll go on with your own work just the same. Better. It won't affect the actual ranch. You'll be free of their complaints now. . . ."
"The whole country's going to stink of oil. Do you know what else Pinky said! He and Vashti are talking of building in town—Viento or Hermosa—moving to town and the family only coming out to the ranch week ends and holidays. Like some damned Long Island setup."

So now the stink of oil hung heavy in the Texas air. It penetrated the houses the gardens the motorcars the trains passing through towns and cities. It hung over the plains the desert the range; the Mexican shacks the Negro cabins. It haunted Reata. Giant rigs straddled the Gulf of Mexico waters. Platoons of metal and wood marched like Martians down the coast across the plateaus through the brush country. Only when you were soaring in an airplane fifteen thousand feet above the oil-soaked earth were your nostrils free of it. Azabache oil money poured into Reata.

—Edna Ferber, *Giant*, 1952

Like many Texas ranchers, Mr. H. R. Wright hit oil on his ranch near Dilley.

King died in 1885 in San Antonio. His youngest daughter, Alice Gertrudis King, married his executor, attorney Robert Kleberg, and descendants of the marriage operate the ranch today. Oil saved the South Texas empire from bankruptcy during the Great Depression, and by 1951, 649 wells had been drilled on its lands. The ranch prospered and expanded anew. The old Santa Gertrudis grant became headquarters for spreads in Cuba, Australia, Brazil, Argentina, Venezuela, and Spain. It meanwhile became a horse-breeding ranch: the first name in the registry of the American Quarter Horse Association is that of a King Ranch stud, and the two-millionth entry was that of a King Ranch filly. In 1946, the ranch also produced Assault, a thoroughbred that won racing's Triple Crown. It also left its name on the map of Texas. King, Kenedy, and Jim Wells counties, and the towns of Alice, Sarita, and Kingsville, are all named after players in the formation of the ranching dynasty.

■ ALICE AND LBJ

The most historic of the King Ranch towns is Alice, some 40 miles (65 km) inland from Corpus Christi. The town is far enough south to grow tall palms along streets lined as well with deciduous trees. Alice is a ranching center, a hub of the oil/gas service business—and a town that would like to forget the historical event for which it is best known.

Alice, the seat of Jim Wells County, is the town that fudged Lyndon Baines Johnson into the U.S. Senate in 1948. Johnson had seemingly lost a Democratic Party primary runoff to former governor Coke Stevenson. But between the closing of the polls, the counting of ballots on Saturday night, and the canvassing of the election at mid-week, a revised tabulation for Voting Box 13, in Alice, added 203 new ballots, 202 of them marked for Johnson. Oddly enough, all 203 of the last-minute voters had cast their ballots in alphabetical order! With this boost and a similar, equally suspicious addition in neighboring Duval county, Johnson emerged with a 187-vote margin out of about a million ballots cast statewide. Undeterred by the nickname he earned from the election, "Landslide Lyndon," he forged on to become the nation's 36th President.

DON PEDRITO OF FALFURRIAS

Some 40 miles (65 k) south of Alice on U.S. 281 lies Falfurrias, location of the principal shrine to one of the more mysterious and enduring figures in South Texas history, Don Pedrito Jaramillo, who died in 1907. He was a thin, white-bearded man, with a haunting, Yoda-like face that still stares out from family altars across South Texas— usually in a pose in which the Don is seated in a chair, a newspaper in his hand. In 1881, when he came from Mexico to the Los Olmos Ranch, just east of what would in two years become the town of Falfurrias, only one doctor lived in rural South Texas, and much of the Catholic ministry was in the hands of horseback itinerants. Pedro Jaramillo filled the gap as only a *curandero,* or cure-maker, could have.

Curanderismo, still widely practiced today, is ordinarily a mixture of mysticism, indigenous herbalism, and lay Catholic ritual. Don Pedrito, as he was affectionately called, was a master practitioner. Living *curanderos* say that, through them, he prescribes for their patients even today. His methods were unusually simple, even by standards of his mysterious craft, and in keeping with its traditions, Don Pedrito never accepted anything more than nominal sums as his fees.

His life is known mainly from the legends that are re-told in South Texas. According to one of them, Don Pedrito recommended that a woman afflicted with migraine headaches have her head cut off and thrown to hogs. She was infuriated, and after her bout of rage, the legend says, never again suffered a migraine. In another tale, a Falfurrias grocer bemoaned to Don Pedrito an oversupply of canned tomatoes. For the next two weeks, the story says, the healer told his clients that in order to be cured, they needed to bathe in canned tomatoes. On a trip there in 1894, the *San Antonio Express* reported that he cured the city's street commissioner of neuralgia by ordering the patient to pull three hairs from his head. Whenever he worked a cure, Jaramillo told his clients, "Your faith has made you whole."

Believers say that Don Pedrito had parapsychological powers, and he left behind a couple of letters indicating that he practiced what is known as "automatic writing," transcribing messages that he believed came directly from God. Yet nothing about his life indicates that he ever saw himself as anything other than an orthodox Catholic layman. He bought the bell that hangs in the Falfurrias parish church today.

Don Pedrito is buried where he lived, about two miles (3 km) east of Falfurrias. His grave has become a pilgrimage site for followers seeking his aid.

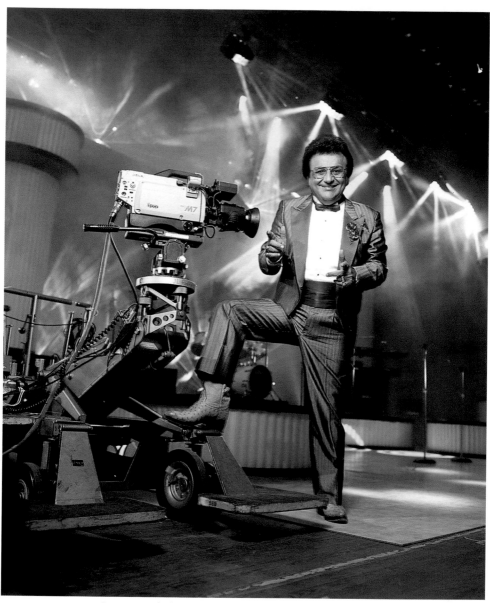

International television personality Johnny Canales broadcasts his
Tex-Mex music show from the Rio Grande Valley.

■ THREE RIVERS

About 50 miles (80 km) north of Alice on U.S. 281, or 75 miles (120 km) south of San Antonio by I-37—just a couple of miles off the freeway, on the west—lies Three Rivers, which in 1948 became the birthplace of the Mexican-American civil rights movement in Texas. Mexican-American veterans of World War II had in March 1948 met in Corpus Christi to charter the American GI Forum, an organization devoted to protecting their military benefits. The organization was drawn into action later that year when the remains of Felix Longoria, an infantryman killed in Luzon three years earlier, were returned to his home in Three Rivers. According to his widow, Beatrice, the local funeral home at first agreed to allow a wake on its premises, then reneged, saying that "the whites wouldn't like it." The GI Forum contacted recently elected Senator Lyndon B. Johnson, who arranged for Longoria to be reburied with honors at Washington's Arlington National Cemetery. The incident put the nascent veterans' group on the map, exposed the problems that Mexican-Americans faced, and gave Senator Johnson a reputation as a crusader for minority rights.

■ RIO GRANDE VALLEY

The Rio Grande Valley at the southern tip of Texas is a collection of some 40 towns—some standing shoulder-to-shoulder—in two Texas counties, Hidalgo and Cameron. The area, and not its separate towns, is billed on some highway markers; and in the minds of most Texans the Valley—as they call it—is one place, sprawled across city limits signs.

But it's not a valley. It's a subtropical alluvial plain, about 60 miles (97 km) wide and 10 miles (16 km) deep, surrounded by flatlands, not mountains. The name was given to the region by the promoters who lured Midwestern farmers—by the trainloads—to locate there in the early part of the twentieth century. The Valley is a river delta, an area of soils made rich by the flow of the Rio Grande, irrigated by waters that are banked at Falcon Reservoir, just west of the region. The Falcon Dam, in turn, is fed regularly by releases of water from the even larger Amistad Dam, some 220 miles (350 km) upriver at Del Rio.

The town of **Harlingen** is the site of the Valley's chief airport. The airport was once also the home of the Confederate Air Force, now based in Midland. But plane buffs need not be dismayed; a newer installation, the **Texas Air Museum**, opened shortly before the CAF moved away, at **Rio Hondo,** 18 miles (29 km) to the northeast. Several buildings at the place house 25 vintage restorations, including a Soviet YAK and two German Focke Wulf 190s, the bane of U.S. and British bombers in World War II. In an arrangement with the Norwegian government, the non-profit foundation that operates the museum has rebuilt the two FW 190s in its stock, both of which were downed in waters off Norway. The pair are among four surviving fighters. Also on display at the museum is a German Fieseler Storch, a utility craft that could land on a runway as short as 61 feet (19 m).

The Harlingen airport is the usual stop for visitors to **South Padre Island,** about 40 miles (64 km) southeast, on the Gulf, a town that's not to be defined by its population count. As its promotion brochures say, "Tourism is the only industry on South Padre Island," and the place has very few permanent residents. What it has instead are some 20 hotels and motels, with a total of 1,500 rooms, and some 60 condominiums with 3,500 additional sleeping rooms, usually rented for a minimum of two to three days.

The island is reached by a 2.6-mile (4-km) causeway, the state's longest, from Port Isabel. A relatively new resort, it was once a refuge of Karankawa Indians and of pirates. Early attempts to promote its 34 miles (55 km) of beach were stymied because developers could not obtain hurricane coverage until legislative acts forced insurers to offer it during the 1970s. The area has not been devastated by a hurricane since.

Lodging houses in South Padre are classified as Gulf, inner-island, and bayside—bayside being those that face the Laguna Madre, the narrow stretch of water between the island and the mainland. Swimmers and surfers want Gulf digs, but bayside lodgings are preferred by fishermen who come to the area, especially those who, despite several kinds of restrictions and prohibitions, aim to catch red drum, whose habitat is the Laguna waters.

■ SOBs OF SOUTH PADRE

South Padre is also an important weekend refuge for prosperous families from northern Mexico, many of whom own condominiums there; for wintering Texans; and for college students, especially during Spring Break, similar to the week-long event that made Florida's Fort Lauderdale infamous. The island is the base of a couple of Spring Break celebrities who call themselves the "Sons of the Beach," or

BARBECUE

Barbecue, also known as barbeque and Bar-B-Q, is a noticeable part of the Texas culinary landscape. Most towns, large and small, claim at least one place that serves "The Best Barbecue in Texas," a number even greater than those claiming the championship title to another Texas delicacy, chicken-fried steak.

In Texas, barbecue—especially beef barbecue—goes back to the days of the open range, when cowhands would frequently butcher a steer—legendarily, one bearing a brand other than their own—and cook its choice parts for hours over an open-pit wood fire. Barbecues came to be social events, the rancher's equivalent of cocktail parties.

Because it takes hours to smoke, preparing barbecue to order isn't possible: only cutting it is. Barbecue therefore is, for Texas, the original fast food, served within seconds, on demand. Because it is speedy, barbecue is a favorite lunch-time meal for office workers.

Other states may make similar claims, but in Texas, where two barbecue cuisines compete, one is truly different. East Texas barbecue, like that of North and South Carolina, is slathered with sometimes spicy tomato-based sauces: it's good, but it's not uniquely Texan. Central Texas and West Texas barbecue—sometimes served with a watery sauce, but rarely basted—is the state's special contribution to the art. The distinct flavor of Central/West Texas barbecue comes from the oak, in some places mesquite, woods used to smoke the meat. In East Texas, people fiddle with formulas for the perfect barbecue sauce; in Central and West Texas, they tinker with mixtures of wood.

On weekends in Central Texas, barbecue is ubiquitous. Part-timers bring out grills made from oil drums, to smoke and sell barbecue at almost every crossroads. Barbecue cook-offs are a part of every civic festival, and barbecue is sold on every festival's midway. When Central and West Texans go to a state park or lake for an outing, they don't go to picnic. They go to barbecue.

The preferred cut for Central and West Texas barbecue is brisket, usually lean. As a genre, barbecue joints—nobody ever calls them restaurants—are fundamental, not fancy. An authentic joint is easily recognizable. Look at its ceiling: if it's clean, the place is probably a fake. If it's smudged and greasy from years of rising smoke, you're in the right place.

continues

Barbecue joints usually price their meals by the weight of meat that the client orders, with extra charges for side dishes like pinto beans, potato salad, or cole slaw; few of them offer any other side dishes. White bread or saltine crackers, pickles, and onions are usually thrown in for free. Many joints are open only for the noon meal. By tradition, there are no waiters or waitresses. Barbecue is served cafeteria style.

The most authentic of the barbecue joints in Central and West Texas started as butchershops; Kreuz Market in Lockhart, South Side Market in Elgin, and City Meat Market in Luling fit this category. Those that still are markets usually also sell pickled hogs' feet, blood sausage, bratwurst, and head cheese—a conglomeration of the spare parts of beef or pork, pickled in gelatin.

The Mikeska "Barbecue Brothers" each operate separate barbecue restaurants in different parts of the state.

South Padre Island attracts hordes of college students during spring break.

"SOBs." "Amazin" Walter McDonald and his partner, "Sandy Feet" Lucinda Wierenga, were formerly a news photographer and school teacher, respectively. They gave up their more traditional lifestyles to become professional sand-castle builders. For about 10 years, they've earned a living by building Disney-esque sand castles and sculptures for Spring Break parties, and as outdoor ads for South Padre condos and hotels. They've even carried their art indoors, building displays for shopping malls. Their sand castles have real steps, towers nearly 10 feet (3 m) high, arches, and other spectacular curls and sweeps that amateur builders can't touch. Of course, there's a bit of fudging here and there: they spray some spans of their castles with a mixture of glue and water, to make sure their artwork holds. During one Spring Break they built a 10,000-foot-long (3,050-m) sculpture which made the *Guinness Book of World Records.* Each April, when the students leave South Padre, the two turn to their off-season work—teaching lessons in sand-castle construction. Over the years, the SOBs have promoted a pledge that has become the creed of South Padre: "I promise to have fun, help others have fun, and unlitter!"

■ EDINBURG

Edinburg calls itself the Gateway to the Valley, and does serve that purpose, for land travelers at least. Coming down U.S. 281 every November and returning north every March are the Valley's some 90,000 winter Texans, mainly Midwestern retirees. U.S. 281 looks like a trailer caravan in November and March, as 85 percent of these Texans spend their winters in motor or trailer homes, which they park in about 500 RV and trailer parks. Since winter residents return to the same park every year, a small-town atmosphere prevails. Most stage shuffleboard and bridge tournaments for their guests, and the residents themselves often organize square dance teams, exercise classes, bingo games, even yoga and quilting sessions.

■ SAN JUAN TO BROWNSVILLE

U.S. 281 brings travelers southward into the Valley, but U.S. 83 is its belt line, connecting the most important Valley towns, east to west: **Mission,** on the western edge of the region, and **McAllen,** less than 10 miles (16 km) east. Nearly shoulder to shoulder east of McAllen are **Pharr, San Juan, Donna, Alamo, Weslaco, Mercedes**—named for a Mexican First Lady, not for the car—**La Feria,** and **Harlingen.** Most of the towns have an all-American, Main Street look, with only nominal attractions for the traveler—except for San Juan. On the south side of U.S. 83 stands a rounded brick church built to honor the Virgin of San Juan, a statue of whom was inspired by a similar statue in the Mexican state of Jalisco. Today's shrine was built in 1980, after the image—a copy of the Mexican original—survived a fire that broke out when an enraged Protestant crashed his plane into the original Texas church. The shrine is a destination of pilgrims, and is adjoined by a church-operated hostel. It is an especially important stop for the Valley's migrant workers, who seek benediction there before and after their forays to harvests in the American Northwest and Midwest.

U.S. 83 runs 10 miles (16 km) north of U.S. 281, which takes an east-west route at the tip of the Valley, paralleling the Rio Grande. The settlements along U.S. 281 are much smaller than those on U.S. 283, and include a half-dozen of what Valley residents—often with a wince—call *las colonias,* or in Spanish, "the neighborhoods." *Las colonias* aren't ordinary neighborhoods, and explaining what they are requires an understanding of events that occurred in Mexico between 1917 and 1992.

The Mexican Constitution at that time guaranteed all Mexican citizens the right to own a plot of land. Newcomers to the cities used that right to claim plots of unused land. Ordinarily, a hundred or more homeless families would pick out a tract on the outskirts of a town and—following another Mexican tradition—begin building their homes on it, with their own hands. While occupying the land and building on it, they often kept the legitimate owners and policemen away with armed force. Invariably, the developments were not provided with water, sewer, and utility lines at their onset. Yet with the passage of time, the squatter-residents legalized their stay and regularized services. Recent immigrants to the Valley from Mexico have tried to recreate a similar pattern in Texas. Landowners have cooperated by offering tracts for sale—without sewer lines and other common services. Some of the tracts offered have been as small as 60 by 100 feet (20x30 m), at prices that everyone could afford: signs still advertise lots for $100—with $10 down payments!—and one of the *colonias,* about five miles (8 km) north of Brownsville, came to have 5,000 residents. Because city and county governments weren't able to fund the laying of lines across the Valley—and it's not their legal responsibility, anyway—during the immigration crush of the 1980s, Texas voters approved a $100-million referendum to provide vital services to the shantytown camps. In the wake of that grand disbursement, various legislative measures were passed in an attempt to prevent the rise of new *colonias*. If the border's history is an indication of what might happen in the future, the new regulations are not likely to succeed.

■ SANTA ANA NATIONAL WILDLIFE REFUGE

On the south side of U.S. 281, just east of Hidalgo, a border-crossing town, is the 2,000-acre Santa Ana National Wildlife Refuge. The park preserves the natural habitat that existed before the Valley was developed. Despite its small size, the refuge is rife with birders and botanists. Some 370 bird species live here, and some, like the chicken-like chachalaca, are Mexican denizens rarely seen north of the Rio Grande. Texas ebony grows in the preserve, and even the endangered ocelot and jaguarundi—tropical cats—survive in its thick growth.

Brownsville, at the terminus of U.S. 283/77, and U.S. 281, is the largest city in the Valley, the southernmost city in Texas. It is a deep-water port, through a 25-mile (40-km) channel to the Gulf, and home of the nation's largest shrimp fishing fleet, a fact that enhances menus all over town.

The first gunfire of the Mexican War was heard here in 1846 when the United States, having acquired Texas, decided to test its contention that the state's border was the Rio Grande, not the Nueces River. It did this by establishing an army post, originally called Fort Taylor, on the north bank of the Rio Grande. But not before a fight. In April 1846, Mexican troops lobbed shells at the fort, killing its commander, Maj. Jacob Brown, after whom today's **Fort Brown**, the former Fort Taylor, and the city itself are named.

In May of 1846, conflict between the armies was renewed at **Palo Alto**, some 15 miles (24 km) northeast of Brownsville, at the intersection of FM 1847 and FM 511—where Gen. Zachary Taylor won an artillery duel against Mexican soldiers. The outbreak of the Mexican War is dated by some accounts to the shelling of Fort Taylor/Brown, and by others, to the artillery match at Palo Alto. The Palo Alto site has been granted status as a National Historical Landmark, but its unpaved parking lot gives it a neglected look.

Twelve miles (20 km) east on TX 4 is a sole historical marker, noting the May 12–13, 1865, **Battle of Palmito Ranch**—the last land battle of the Civil War—fought a month after the Confederacy's surrender at Appomattox. On May 11, a Union force on the Gulf Coast sent 300 mostly African-American troops to take Brownsville. The Union commanders presumed that the Confederates holding Fort Brown, knowing of the surrender, would promptly turn over their command. But Fort Brown's defenders didn't know. They met and routed the Union forces at Palmito Ranch. Some 30 Union soldiers were killed, and 113 prisoners captured. From the survivors the Confederates learned that the Civil War was over, arranged a cease-fire and promptly laid down their arms.

The drive down TX 4 is hardly worth the trouble to read a single historical marker, but about a dozen miles beyond it lies **Boca Chica**, one of the loneliest spots in Texas. Boca Chica is an uninhabited, unfrequented beach, just yards from the spot where the Rio Grande meets the Gulf. Its isolation is unmatched outside the Trans-Pecos. But it hasn't always been that way. During the Civil War, the south side of the river was a bustling port called Bagdad because of the frantic commerce carried on there. Nothing remains of it, not even a trace. After the war, Bagdad was swept away by hurricanes. Everything that was once in view of Boca Chica is literally gone with the wind.

A rainbow graces this tropical scene at the headquarters of the King Ranch in South Texas.

■ VISITING MEXICO

If you're visiting South Texas, you'll probably want to set aside a morning or afternoon—probably not more—to visit one of the cities on the Mexican side of the Rio Grande. Access is easy, language and currency are no barriers, and some are well-stocked with merchandise that is hard to find elsewhere.

But the international day-tripper should be forewarned that Mexican border towns are to Mexico what Texas towns are to Western civilization. They were established late in Mexican history, for entirely commercial reasons. Their traditions and history are young, and their connections to the mother country—the Mexican south—are tenuous.

Entering Mexican border towns couldn't be easier. You pay a nominal toll or turnstile fee on the American side of an international bridge, and walk or drive across.

No entry documents are needed, no customs search is conducted, no Mexican auto insurance is required. Travelers who are not American citizens, however, will

Master accordionist Tony de la Rosa has attracted a following on both sides of the border as one of the originators of conjunto music.

(left) Margarita Sames claims to have been the inventor of the popular Mexican cocktail of the same name.

need to take with them entry documents to show U.S. immigration agents upon returning north across the Rio Grande, and drivers should check their policies: some American insurers don't cover border town accidents.

Though it takes less than 10 minutes to enter Mexico from Texas, if you don't plan to bring back any bulky or heavy items, it's probably best to walk. U.S. customs inspections are sometimes thorough, and motorists often find themselves waiting 30 minutes to an hour to re-enter the United States.

Most Texans visit Mexican border towns to buy liquor and cigarettes. Vodkas and tequilas are cheaper there, and American-brand cigarettes sell for less than half of their north-of-the-river price. Each adult returning from Mexico is permitted to bring one liter of liquor and one carton of cigarettes. On the north side of the international bridge, the state of Texas collects a $1 tax on each liter of liquor brought into the state from Mexico. One carton of cigarettes is permitted, tax-free.

Another popular item among Texans is vanilla extract; most Mexican brands are more concentrated than the extracts sold in the United States.

Non-Texans visiting the border towns are usually more interested in sampling the works of Mexican artisans. To serve the day-trip traffic, most Mexican border towns have a street that is lined with arts and crafts shops. These shops price their goods in dollars, and rarely haggle over pricing. English is their language of trade.

Straw and leather goods, and cotton dresses are, after liquor and cigarettes, the most popular items in the bridge commerce. Boots, billfolds, purses, sandals, hammocks, and household decorations are sold on the border by the gross. Many Americans also visit Mexican pharmacies, where antibiotics are sold more freely than in the states. But the visitor should be forewarned: in Mexico narcotic drugs are restricted, just as in the United States, and black market sales are more severely punished there than in this country.

The border's best values are ceramic, papier-mâché, and woolen goods brought to its stores from the Mexican South, not because they are cheaper than their American counterparts but because nothing much like them exists in the United States. The handmade masks, woolen blankets—a little too small for a double bed, but great for wall hangings—and dishes made by Mexico's artisans are prized around the globe, and are sometimes sold by galleries in the United States. Because these items are costly, quality samples are rare even in border towns, while second-grade imitations proliferate. The most trustworthy source on the Texas border is Marti's, a store two blocks south of the "old bridge" in Nuevo Laredo.

NORTH TEXAS

TEXANS WILL TELL YOU THAT NORTH TEXAS, the area west of I-35 and north of U.S. 180, is the plainest, most commonplace region of the state. It's almost entirely rural, without an anchor city, like other regions on the map. Its story is not the story of cities, but of farms and small towns. It is too far away from any big city to be a getaway for urban weekenders, and therefore does not have the subterranean fame that counters even the dismal reputation of East Texas. Most Texans have never been to North Texas, and if those who have been don't rave about the place, it is probably because urban and woodlands Texans don't know how to see: in North Texas, where the earth is monotonous and flat, the sky accounts for most of the landscape.

In North Texas, the sky is continually changing. Nothing on television screens is as fleeting or dramatic as the action in the air above North Texas: snow, hail, tornadoes, dust storms, or strong winds are almost always stirring. The land and skies of North Texas are so foreboding to the uninitiated that a military captain who evaluated the region in 1849 concluded that, "This country is, and must remain, forever uninhabited."

There are variations and exceptions inside the region, but as a whole, it's treeless and nearly flat. Place names derived from vegetation are a rarity, and so is any vegetation not under the plow. In strictly geographic terms, North Texas is part of the semidesert of West Texas, and many of the people who live there say that they live in West Texas. But the North differs from the rest of West Texas in several respects.

North Texas is as much a farming as a ranching region, and its ranches are exclusively devoted to cattle: no sheep or goats here. Ranches tend to be located in rougher terrain, unsuitable for farming. A patient observer is likely to spot antelope, and even a few deer, in the area's canyons or "breaks" (though deer are far more common in South and Central Texas). Rough spots are also home to furtive coyotes, which ranchers have always regarded as pests. Some landowners trap or shoot them—poisoning them is now illegal—and hang their carcasses on fence posts, as if to warn newcomer coyotes to pick a different spread.

There's oil and gas in North Texas, but there's never been a big boom town like Midland or Odessa. Snow is practically unknown in West Texas, below Trans-

Pecos mountain ranges, anyway. But snowfalls come to North Texas almost every year—sometimes in May! North Texas "has weather," locals note. Dust storms turn the sky black, and strong winds can cause temperatures to drop by as much as 40 degrees in two hours. By comparison, weather conditions in West Texas are stable.

El Paso and Fort Worth, the cities of West Texas, were founded in 1827 and 1849, respectively, but the biggest towns in North Texas, Amarillo and Lubbock, didn't exist until a half-century later. Because frontiersmen were cowed by its weather and by the Comanche, who controlled the area until 1874, North Texas was the last area of Texas to be settled.

North Texas is also near to Oklahoma, and parts of it border New Mexico. Texans regard New Mexico as a mostly uninhabited terrain, worthy of mention only during skiing and racetrack seasons. What's important, in regional mythology, is the nearness of North Texas to Oklahoma, a demythologized and downscale place, in the ideology of Texans. Oklahoma's proximity is especially important in those areas west of I-35 where the United States was once a sovereign threat; also, Oklahoma was once the nearest source of beer.

The rivalry between Texas and Oklahoma shows itself in the North Texas expression, "That blew in from Oklahoma," to refer to bad weather, and in a spirited football rivalry between the two states' leading universities.

Massive cattle drives were organized in the 1870s and '80s to herd the stock from grazing lands in North Texas to railheads in Kansas, where they were shipped to the stockyards of Chicago. (Union Pacific Railroad Museum, Omaha)

NORTH TEXAS

Miles
0 20 40 60 80

Elevation
8,751
5,000
4,000
3,000
2,000
1,000
500
250
feet

N E S W

New Mex.co

OKLAHOMA CITY

El Reno

Clinton

Lawton

Altus

OKLAHOMA

Red River

Lake Texoma

Ray Roberts Lake

Lake Lewisville

DALLAS

Fort Worth

Weatherford

Mineral Wells

Caddo

Lyndon B. Johnson Nat'l Grassland

Nocona

Lake Arrowhead State Park

Lake Arrowhead

Olney

Fort Richardson State Park

Possum Kingdom Lake

Possum Kingdom State Park

Breckenridge

Wichita Falls

Electra

Vernon

Crowell

Seymour

Throckmorton

Fort Belknap

Fort Griffin State Park

Albany

Anson

Fort Phantom Hill

Quanah

Paducah

Cooper Breaks State Park

Benjamin

Guthrie

Spur

Dickens

Aspermont

Roby

To Abilene

Childress

Turkey

Matador

Caprock Canyon State Park

Clarendon

Lela

Pampa

Lake McClellan Park

White Deer

Borger

Canadian

The Buried City

Site of Battle of Adobe Walls

Perryton

Stratford

Cactus

Dumas

Lake Meredith Nat'l Rec. Area

Alibates Flint Quarries Nat'l Monument

Lake Meredith

Amarillo

Canyon

Palo Duro Canyon State Park

Plainview

Lockney

Mackenzie State Park

Lubbock

Reese Air Force Base

World's Tallest Windmill

Muleshoe

Littlefield

Lehman

Levelland

Seminole

Brownfield

Lamesa

Post

Snyder

LLANO ESTACADO

CAPROCK ESCARPMENT

Prairie Dog Town Fork

Pease River

Brazos River

Salt Fork

Double Mountain Fork

Clear Fork

HIGH PLAINS

Rita Blanca Nat'l Grassland

Black Kettle Nat'l Grassland

Dalhart

Adrian

Vega

Hereford

Nara Vista

Clovis

Hobbs

To Odessa

To Albuquerque

To Tulsa

Canadian River

Washita River

Hereford

Wichita River

IN LOVE

*D*ear Mama and Daddy—
I know this is going to be a shock to you but I guess it can't be helped. Sonny and I have gone to Oklahoma to get married—I guess it will be in Altus. Even if he is poor we are in love. I don't know what to say about college, I guess we'll just have to talk about that when we get back. We are going to Lake Texoma on our honeymoon and will be home Monday. I guess I will live at the poolhall until we find someplace else to live. Even if you don't like Sonny now I know you will love him someday.

Jacy

She left the note on the cabinet, propped up against a box of crackers. Gene found it when he came in from work three hours later. Lois was in Wichita that day and returned late. When she came in, Gene was pacing the kitchen floor, obviously distressed. He handed her the note.

"Oh goddamn her," Lois said. "I can't believe it."

"Well, we got to get going," Gene said. "I want to catch 'em. Even if we can't get 'em before they marry we can sure as hell get 'em before they go to bed. That way we can get it annulled with no trouble."

"Why bother?" Lois said. "I suppose we could get it annulled anytime—that's what money's for."

—Larry McMurtry, *The Last Picture Show,* 1966

■ TOWNS ALONG U.S. 180

Among the towns in North Texas that lie along U.S. 180, the region's boundary with West Texas, is **Weatherford,** located about 30 miles (48 km) west of Fort Worth on U.S. 180. The town seat of Parker County has a classic Texas courthouse built in 1886 of quarried limestone, topped by a high belfry with clocks on each of its four sides, all of them keeping the correct time. Weatherford was the home town of actress Mary Martin, and a bronze statue of Peter Pan, the role Ms. Martin created in the Broadway show, stands before the city's library. Jim Wright, the former speaker of the U.S. House of Representatives who retired in disgrace during a financial scandal, was elected to Congress from Weatherford: no statue of him!

Architectural buffs come to town to see the Pythian Home, a rambling structure built by the Knights of Pythias lodge in 1907 to look like a castle.

Mineral Wells, further west on U.S. 180, about 50 miles (80 km) from Fort Worth, today derives most of its income from the cattle industry, but in the rough countryside surrounding it, oil, gas, sand, and clay are commercially extracted—and 50 years ago it was a prime site for tourism. Mineral Wells was founded when medicinal properties were ascribed to the waters of what became known as the Crazy Well, dug in 1881. Tourists came from across the Southwest to take cures for maladies as dissimilar as insanity and venereal disease. By the 1920s, some 400 wells were producing water for health-seekers in Mineral Wells, and Crazy Water crystals, produced by evaporating the water, were promoted by NBC radio in broadcasts from the lobby of the Crazy Water Hotel, a seven-story showplace completed in 1927. As many as 150,000 overnight guests were registered annually during the town's Depression-era peak, and two of its spa hotels remain, the Crazy Water, now a retirement hotel, and the once famous but now empty Baker—which still dominates the town's skyline. Contemporary science has validated some

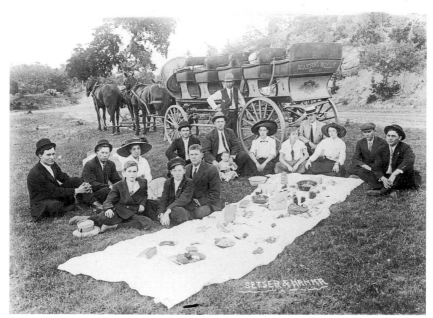

Mineral Wells was a popular spa and picnic area for Dallas and Fort Worth residents, as this bucolic turn-of-the-century photo illustrates. (Center for American History, University of Texas)

of the claims once made for Mineral Wells waters. One study of six wells showed that the waters of four had traces of lithium, a mood regulator, and two of the wells contained potent amounts of the natural drug.

Breckenridge, about 75 miles (120 km) west of Fort Worth on U.S. 180, is one of the North Texas oil-and-cattle towns that was blessed or cursed—and certainly got dizzy—during an early-days drilling boom. The 1952 *Handbook of Texas* tells the story in these lines:

> *By* 1920 a boom was in full sway. In 1921 the crash occurred and within three months the price of oil dropped from a high of $3.00 to $1.00 per barrel. The oil boom brought a full quota of economic and social problems. The population increased rapidly. In January, 1920, it was estimated at 1,500 but one year later the population had reached a total of 30,000. This expansion produced an acute housing shortage, and even water sold for $1.00 a barrel.

The boom left behind an impressive '20s-era courthouse, and a museum with a dozen vintage aircraft, including a British Spitfire, key weapon in the 1940 Battle of Britain.

■ LAKES IN THE LANDSCAPE

Possum Kingdom is a fine clearwater lake with a large park; picnic and swimming areas; canoe and paddleboard rentals; and a fishing pier. Because it is a deep lake, scuba divers have explored it and reached depths of up to 150 feet (46 m). To reach it, turn off U.S. 180 at Caddo and drive north on Park Road 33 for 17 miles (27 km).

Lake Arrowhead State Park, about 18 miles (29 km) southeast of Wichita Falls off U.S. 281 and north on FM 1954, then east, offers swimmers the novel experience of paddling in a lake that has oil derricks in it.

■ WICHITA FALLS AREA

Wichita Falls, 112 miles (180 km) northwest of Fort Worth on U.S. 287, is marked in the minds of many contemporary Texans as the site of one of the state's worst tornadoes. On April 10, 1979, the twister—tornadoes are not named, as hurricanes are—came through, killing 42 people, injuring 1,700, destroying some

3,000 homes, and causing some $400 million in damages. It wasn't the first April that tornadoes had visited the city, either. In April 1964, seven people were killed and 111 injured by another twister. People who live in North Texas, especially in the Red River Valley, learn to live with the threat as much as possible. One hunkers down in a bathtub—bathtubs, being heavy, aren't easily swept into the air—and waits for the danger to pass.

About 50 miles (80 km) west of Wichita Falls on U.S. 287 is **Vernon,** headquarters town of the Zacaweista Ranch, owned by the descendants of a father/son team, Daniel and W. T. Waggoner, who turned their profits from cattle drives into a spread that became 30 miles (48 km) wide and 25 miles (40 km) deep—in all over a million acres, spanning six counties. The discovery of oil at **Electra**—named for a daughter of W. T.—in 1911 led to greater wealth and expansion of the family's brand, three Ds, reversed. Refinery and railcars bore the brand, as well as a race track at Arlington, just east of Fort Worth. The Waggoner estate, set up in 1932, became substantial enough that its manager in the 1950s, Robert Anderson, became Treasury Secretary to Dwight D. Eisenhower, and was reportedly the President's choice as the Republican nominee of 1960, a designation instead won by Richard Nixon.

Electra Waggoner Biggs, named for her aunt, after whom the town of Electra was named by oil and cattle tycoons W. T. and Daniel Waggoner. The Buick Electra and the Lockheed Electra were named for the Electra pictured here.

Vernon's role as the DDD headquarters is today the town's second rung of fame—or infamy, as is actually the case. A local institution, Vernon Savings & Loan was one of the high-profile operations in the S&L banking scandals of the '80s, which cost American taxpayers an estimated $1 to $1.3 billion in bailout expenses.

Quanah, some 30 miles (48 km) west of Vernon on U.S. 287, was at its founding in 1881 named after Quanah Parker, a Comanche whose Texas fame is exceeded only by the heroes of Independence. (See the essay "Last Comanche," below, for more on Parker's life.) Though Quanah never lived in Quanah, apparently the town wanted to connect itself to its Comanche past. Ten miles (16 km) east on U.S. 287 and then five miles (8 km) south on FM 283 are the Comanche Mounds, three cone-shaped hills that rise some 350 feet (106 m) above the surrounding plain and are said to have been a ceremonial site.

LAST COMANCHE

Quanah Parker first became a household name in Texas because he was the son of Cynthia Ann Parker, probably the best-known woman in Texas during the latter half of the nineteenth century. In 1836, at the age of nine, Cynthia Ann had been captured by the Comanche during an East Texas raid in which her father was killed. Parties of whites who traded along the Canadian River in far North Texas spotted her five years later, and again seven years after her kidnapping. She told them that she had married Peta Nocona, a Comanche notable, that she was the mother of two sons, including young Quanah, and that she had no desire to return to the remnants of her birth family. (Nocona, pop. 2,870, about 50 miles east of Wichita Falls on U.S. 82, is named for Cynthia Ann's husband.)

Nevertheless, white Texans continued to keep an eye out for her, and to report sightings. In 1860, at the Battle of Pease River, she was recaptured. As if to repeat the tragedy of her childhood, her infant daughter, Topsanah, was also captured, and Topsanah's father Peta was killed. The following year, the Texas legislature voted a league of land and a pension to Cynthia Ann, who had been returned to her Texas relatives. But she could not adjust to the life she found with them, and her attempts to escape were foiled. In 1864, her daughter died, and a few weeks later, 37-year-old Cynthia Ann was laid in her grave, too. It was said that she died of a broken heart.

Quanah Parker's age at the time he was orphaned has not been accurately established. By some accounts, he was eight; by others, 13. By the early 1870s, he was a leader among his band, the Quahadi Comanche, a people who did not accept treaties with the United States. Parker was reported as a participant and sometimes as a leader of horseback raids on settlements as far south and west as Fort Stockton. In 1874, he joined with leaders of the Kiowa and Cheyenne in one of the last Indian battles in Texas, at Adobe Walls, near today's Amarillo. The Indians were vanquished, and surrendered the following year. Quanah Parker afterwards took up residence on an Oklahoma reservation, and in his last years, became a reluctant celebrity of the region. He died in 1911.

Quanah Parker. (Center for American History, University of Texas)

■ ALONG THE TOP OF TEXAS

North Texas west of the 100th meridian and north of U.S. 180 is a land that can't be discussed without resorting to geographic terms. It includes the Texas Panhandle, which, by some accounts, is the whole area north of about U.S. 180, and west of the 100th meridian. But by other reckonings, the Panhandle includes only the topmost Texas counties between both the New Mexico and Oklahoma state lines. People who live north of U.S. 180 and west of the 100th meridian are apt to say that they live on the High Plains, or in the South Plains or North Plains, descriptions confounding to outsiders. The South Plains are the southern end of the area that lies west of the 100th meridian and north of U.S. 180. The North Plains are above the South Plains, a.k.a. the Panhandle. The High Plains are the North and South Plains, taken together. They're called High Plains rather than Low Plains because they're above something called the Caprock, a sudden 50- to 100-foot (15- to 30-m) shift in elevation. The earth is flat above the Caprock, as flat as a tabletop. Plainview and Levelland are among its towns' names.

The chief difference between the South Plains, whose capital is Lubbock, and the North Plains, whose capital is Amarillo, is that on the North Plains, freezes

Harvesting cotton, one of the major crops of the South Plains.

come too soon, and thaws too late, to make cultivation of cotton possible. The South Plains is cotton country; the North Plains, wheat territory. South Plains cotton is usually planted in May or June and is harvested as late as Christmas, after the first hard freeze kills the greenery of the plant, making defoliants unnecessary.

■ CAPROCK

Looking from space something like the Great Wall of China, its younger, weaker and world-famous imitator, the Caprock, a 175-mile-long (280-km) elevation in the Texas landscape, separates a higher ground from a lower one. It shields the High Plains from everyplace else—or to be more accurate, from all of those cities and regions that think they're someplace.

Human wisdom could not have envisioned a barrier so virtuous and necessary, and indeed, men didn't build the Caprock: God did, and it took eons for Him to make. The Caprock arose, geologists say, through erosion—i.e., when the Lord made Colorado's once-towering Rockies flow toward the sea, lowering their pretentious peaks so that man could meet Him on solid, level Caprock ground. Drive out U.S. 180 east from the town of Lamesa, go north at the little town of Gail,

Local men relax in Archer City, where the movie version of Larry McMurtry's novel The Last Picture Show *was filmed.*

CEREAL KING POST

C. W. Post, the cereal king who founded the town of Post, was not from Texas, but came to know the area during hunting trips in the 1890s. On one of those trips he'd been introduced to "chicory coffee," a beverage made from chicory and wheat berries. Chicory coffee had come into use in the South during the Civil War, when ports were blockaded and importing real coffee wasn't possible. Post tinkered with the formula and produced from it a new non-caffeinated beverage, known today as Postum. In 1897, he concocted the breakfast cereal now called Grape-Nuts, and in 1906, he introduced a brand of corn flakes under the name Elijah's Manna. The following year, he brought his fortune to Texas and set up an experimental community of yeomen. As part of the plan, Texas writer Jan Reid notes, "He clustered four houses at crossroads to ease the rural isolation. Despite Post's good intentions, dogs bit the neighbors' children, and the hens' eggs got all mixed up."

Post established the Algerita Hotel, today an art center for the town. Always an experimenter, after reading about downpours that followed Napoleonic and Civil War cannon battles, he decided to give his colonist-farmers what they needed most: rain. At intervals for three years, residents of Post set off explosions, mainly from the Caprock rim, succeeding, Post claimed, in causing rainfalls in seven of 13 attempts. But on April 12, 1912, one of the experiments brought hail, and crops were ruined. Post left Texas not long afterwards.

Before leaving, however, he helped give to North Texas a part of its plain-spoken character. While reviewing a menu for the Algerita, Reid says, Post commented, "When you have roast beef with juice, say so, and don't say 'aux jus' . . . don't try to make the cowpunchers . . . think we are a lot of frog-eating French."

then northeast from Post to Spur, then north up TX 70 to Matador, Turkey, and Clarendon. Along most of the route, in front and to the left, you'll see the Caprock's rise, forming a one-sided canyon. Drive up onto the Caprock's crest and look back over your shoulder: you'll see the world at the Caprock's feet, a land of tiny tractors and dryland farming.

The world beyond the Caprock, including New York and Paris and Tokyo, is from the point of view of Caprockers a pretty sordid place. Industry, big-time politicians, and commerce have made a mess of things. Yet, beneath the Caprock, agriculture, mankind's authentic and most appropriate pursuit, is undertaken with fervor. The superiority of life on the Caprock shows itself in statistics: its per capita income and educational levels are matched nowhere else in Texas. Highly mechanized, irrigated family farms, plus a few oil and gas discoveries, have made it that way.

Above the Caprock, flatness and the sky overwhelm the senses. Windmills are the tallest structures in sight. The contrast between heaven and earth is nowhere more clearly defined than on these plains. In other locales, people look up to God; on the Caprock, the horizon line is at your feet. The Mexican dictator Porfirio Díaz once remarked that his country's chief problem was that it was "too far from God, and too close to the United States." The Caprock's setting is close to the reverse: the heavens are at one's shoulder, and you've got to fly to Dallas before you feel you're back on terra firma.

During the oil boom of the 1970s and early '80s, when most of Texas succumbed to money fever, the country above the Caprock kept its balance. It felt no flush of capital, it experienced no rush of immigration from the United States; it remained as truly Texan as it ever was. Up on the Caprock, nobody ever wore cowboy boots for show. Caprock dwellers never told Texas jokes, because they've always known that nothing is as hilarious as Oklahoma.

So what if tornadoes, dust storms, and blizzards whip its plains? So what if its homes are made of stucco? So what if the region's newspapers are unreadable, and the Cowboys are in Dallas? Airports in Lubbock and Amarillo aren't crowded, even with football fans. People who live on the High Plains rarely go elsewhere. They've discovered that travel is pointless: when you leave Amarillo, you ain't going nowhere.

The region of North Texas around Wichita Falls reports more tornadoes than does anyplace else in the world. This one, photographed near White Deer, Texas in 1947, killed 167 people across the border in Woodward, Oklahoma.(Western History Collection, University of Oklahoma Library)

■ LUBBOCK

Lubbock, capital city of the South Plains, is laid out in numbered and lettered streets as straight and square as the fields that run up to its limits. Its older homes are mainly of the Prairie and Victorian styles; its business buildings of red or yellow brick reflecting a staid mid-century taste. Lubbock is home to Texas Tech University ("Tech" is not an abbreviation), which enrolls some 26,000 students. The university lies on the north side of town, with a campus so sprawled that students use cars and bicycles to change classes.

Cotton is Lubbock's mainstay. The United States produces about a quarter of the world's supply of cotton; Texas produces more than any state, and about half of the Texas yield comes from the South Plains. So does most of its export crop. Some of the cotton exported from Lubbock goes by truck and train to Galveston, and from Galveston into the Gulf, the traditional route that Texas produce takes overseas. But most of it goes on railcars to the Los Angeles area, from where it is sent over the Pacific to looms and factories in Asia.

Cotton is today harvested by machines that pull the whole boll in which the fibers rest, rather than picking the fibers away, as when the crop was gathered by hand. Harvested cotton is packed into modules about 10 feet (3 m) high and as long as 50 feet (16 m), and left in the fields until processing plants, called gins, can accommodate them. At the gins—some 750 are scattered across the South Plains—the fiber is separated from bolls and seed, and packed into bales; bales bound for export are reduced in size at facilities called compresses.

Besides fiber, cotton provides cottonseed oil, the raw material for products as diverse as cellophane and explosives. Several cottonseed-pressing mills are located on the south side of Lubbock. For years, South Plains cotton was of little use in textile manufacture because its short staples could not be woven into fabrics. Japanese inventors solved the problem during the 1970s, and today, the South Plains has a half-dozen denim mills and factories that make blue jeans.

Besides cotton, Lubbock is known for music. From the South Plains have come rock 'n' rollers Buddy Holly, Ritchie Valens, and country stars Waylon Jennings, Mac Davis, and Jimmy Dean, all of whom are memorialized in bronze in the Walk of Fame, a downtown Lubbock attraction.

Lubbock's reputation among Texans, though somewhat dated, is that it's an all-American town, and that reputation has become part of the stock-in-trade of Bill

(previous pages) Palo Duro Canyon is part of the geological formation known as the Caprock, an escarpment running 175 miles through North Texas, separating the "low country" to the east from the High Plains to the west.

Clement, who operates a very specialized junkyard just a stone's throw from the city's chief all-American shrine, Buddy Holly's grave. In Clement's eyes, Holly wasn't just a musician. He was a soldier who fell in the defense of American civilization, a battle in which Clement considers himself a resistance fighter. In Clement's view of things, the retreat of American civilization began in 1963, when the Beatles displaced American rockers on the music scene. National defeat came, he says, in 1977, when Chevrolet adopted the metric standard.

Clement began his one-man crusade to save America from creeping globalism and mediocrity—the two are the same, as far he's concerned—in 1962, when he bought a five-year-old Chevy. "It started in the morning, it ran good, and it paid for itself. Gasoline was cheap and you could get parts at the TG&Y," he says in reference to a chain of dime stores—and with his usual hyperbole. Outlandish claims like that are a part of him: the telephone answering machine at his company, Chevy Craft, warns callers that "Bargain-hunters need not apply, ever!"

Chevy Craft has on its lot several hundred 1955–57 classic Chevys, the kind of cars that Buddy Holly drove. Clement restores them at prices beginning above $20,000. The company also sells parts by mail, to car collectors and other restorationists, and some simply to "old boys who want to keep their cars running." In nearly 25 years of business, he and his crew have helped save thousands of classic Chevys, keeping their drivers, Clement proclaims, out of "metric jellybean computermobiles." Lubbock is an appropriate place for his operation, not only because its

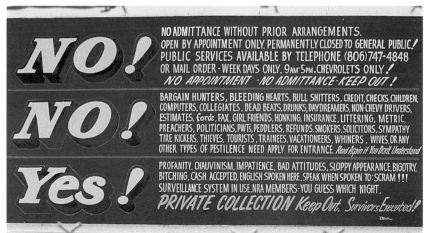

Chevy Craft makes it clear that curiosity seekers are not welcome.

dry climate discourages rust, but also because, on the South Plains, there are hardly any curves in the roads. The Lubbock area was invented for the touring cars that, much to Clement's dismay, are no longer an American standard.

■ IRRIGATION AND PUMPS

Anyone who drives across the South Plains is sure to notice V-8 engines—eight-cylinder engines with four cylinders on each side of a V configuration—standing at the edges of fields, sometimes housed in tin shacks. These turn water pumps hundreds of feet below the surface that bring water from the Ogallala aquifer up to farms.

Unfortunately, the water is about to run out. The Ogallala water aquifer is being pumped dry. Farmers have brought water out of the ground faster than it's being replaced, and whole counties in the High Plains have gone back to dryland farming as their water tables have dropped. The problem has several layers. One of them is that as the water table drops, it costs more money to pump water to the surface. When gasoline prices skyrocketed during the 1970s, about half of the region's farmers converted their motors to cheaper and cleaner-burning natural gas. But no fuel is free, and dropping water levels are catching up with economy measures.

A right-angle pump (above) used to tap the waters of the Ogallala aquifer. (right) Cooling off in the muddy waters of the Canadian River, which traverses the Texas Panhandle.

BUDDY HOLLY

Buddy Holly was born in Lubbock on September 7, 1936, and in the five or so years he recorded (1954–59) he changed the face of rock and roll. A musician who wrote and performed all of his own material and did so with his own band, the Crickets, Holly created the rock band prototype: guitar, bass, drums, vocals.

Until he heard Elvis Presley, Holly played typical country shuffle to no one; Holly and pal Bob Montgomery were dyed-in-the-straw hicks, playing bluegrass and country music even as the music was transforming into something more raw, more exciting.

Holly and Montgomery's earliest recordings in Wichita Falls in 1954–55 featured Sonny Curtis on fiddle and such songs as "Down the Line" (a rockabilly rave-up written by Montgomery, Holly and Norman Petty) and Montgomery's own "Soft Place in My Heart" (straight-ahead country right from the Hank Williams school of heartbreak). The effort showcased two musicians torn between two worlds, those of Elvis and Hank. By the time Holly headed to Nashville and began recording for Decca Records—with the likes of legendary producer Owen Bradley—he chose the rock and roll path, without Montgomery. Decca Records just didn't want another country boy, and Holly was forced to choose between his pal and a record deal.

On January 26, 1956, Holly recorded "Blue Days," "Love Me," and the Jimmy Ainsworth-Earl Lee cut "Midnight Shift" at Bradley's Nashville studio; the first two cuts would be released in April of that year, though the harder rockabilly cut "Midnight Shift" wouldn't see daylight till two years later. But a year before rockabilly became "common currency," as Texas critic Ed Ward wrote in *Rock of Ages,* Holly was performing his own distillation of country and blues and top-of-the-pops that made Elvis a star and would do the same thing for Gene Vincent when "Be-Bop-A-Lula" hit the charts. Nashville didn't know what to make of Holly: Owen Bradley continued to record Holly throughout 1956, and their last work together—the lethargic "Modern Don Juan," featuring the cheesy tenor sax work of Boots Randolph—was among the worst songs Holly ever cut. Shortly after that, Decca released him from his contract, and Buddy figured that was it.

Of course, it was the best thing that could have happened. Without a label, a producer, and Sonny Curtis on guitar (the friends had a falling out), Holly was forced to put together his own band, and found in Lubbock such musicians as drummer Jerry Allison, bassist Larry Welborn, and rhythm guitarist Niki Sullivan. He also headed to pal Norman Petty's place in Clovis, New Mexico, where he knew he'd find a sympathetic ear. On February 25, 1957, the quartet set to wax "That'll Be the Day" and

"I'm Lookin' for Someone to Love"—both of which were released May 27, 1957, on the Brunswick label, then controlled by the Coral Records label—which, ironically enough, was a subsidiary of Decca. Perhaps the most key arrangement of the deal was that Holly and his band, now named the Crickets, would be allowed total artistic freedom over the works; the label would keep its hands off the final masters when the band turned them in, and they would be released as-is.

Holly was a perfectionist both as a songwriter (he often wrote under the name Charles Hardin) and in the studio; the results were heard on the subsequent singles "Peggy Sue," "Not Fade Away," "Everyday," and "Oh Boy!"—all released in short succession from September to November 1957. Thirty-seven years later, each track is a rock classic—simple, clear, powerful. "Maybe Baby" and "Rave On" would follow in early 1958.

By the middle of that year, the Crickets were superstars with number-one, million-selling records, European tours, a couple of guest shots on the Ed Sullivan show. But in June 1958, at the insistence of Coral's Dick Jacobs, Holly went to New York City to record without the Crickets. The result was a giddy cover of Bobby Darin's "Early in the Morning" that sounded like a gospel number, right down to the Helen Way Singers providing the background vocals. While in New York, Buddy met Maria Elena Santiago, and they were married August 15, 1958. Shortly afterward, Holly recorded "Heartbeat" and "It's So Easy"—the latter of which became a hit for Linda Ronstadt in the '70s, though it never reached the charts in the U.S. After its release, Petty and Holly severed their relationship.

In January, 1959, Holly headed out on a package tour with Ritchie Valens, the Big Bopper, and the Belmonts; among those in Holly's new backup band were guitarist Tommy Allsup and a young bass player named Waylon Jennings. The plane carrying Holly, Valens, and the Big Bopper went down on February 2 near Mason City, Iowa, in a snowstorm, killing all aboard. In March, 1980, a statue of Lubbock's favorite son was finally erected in front of the Lubbock Civic Center.

—Robert Wilonsky

In Hale County, where Plainview lies, irrigated acres dropped from 468,000 to 310,000 between 1980 and 1990, and in neighboring Floyd County irrigation has declined from 340,000 to 246,000 acres over the same period. Much of the region's cotton crop is now being grown under dryland conditions, as it was in the early part of the century, and today, there's even speculation that sometime in the next century, if the Ogallala goes completely dry, the South Plains may revert to the grassland prairie that it was a century ago.

■ CANYON AND PALO DURO CANYON

The dividing line between the South Plains and the North Plains, a.k.a. the Panhandle, is an imaginary line that runs west-to-east through a point no further north than the town of **Canyon**, a college and tourist town. West Texas State University has some 6,000 students, but its primary attraction for non-residents is **Palo Duro Canyon**, a 120-mile-long (193-km) break in the tabletop-flat monotony of the terrain, located about 10 miles (16 km) east of town. The canyon, which exposes the handiwork of four geological ages, has for centuries been a refuge from the severities of the plains. It had water, it had greenery (its name, "Hard Wood"

A rare white buffalo robe is displayed in this undated photo.
(Scurry County Museum, Snyder, Texas)

A lone buffalo eyes the photographer on the Creekwood Ranch in Canyon,
where Quanah Parker and his band of comanches were defeated by the cavalry.

in English, refers to juniper trees that grow there) and it provided early inhabitants with a shelter from the cold winds that blew on the flatlands above. It was also useful for buffalo hunts: the mounted Comanche, for example, stampeded the animals over its cliffs, some of which are 1,200 feet high (366 m). During one of the last Indian-cavalry battles in Texas, in 1874, American troopers slaughtered some 1,400 Comanche horses in the canyon, forcing their owners to return to Oklahoma on foot. Today, over 15,000 acres of the canyon are organized as a state park, with rides, a museum, and more, including, in summer months, a nightly open-air production of *Texas,* a romantic rendering of the history of the state.

■ AMARILLO

Amarillo is the anchor town of the North Plains, best known for icy weather. "The only thing between Amarillo and the North Pole," a Texas summation goes, "is a barbed wire fence, and it's down." The landscape is flat, its streets laid out in straight north-south and east-west grids. When 40-mph (64-kph) winds blow through Amarillo's streets during "northers," or cold fronts, the barbed wire quip speaks a truth.

Yet if the North Plains climate is hostile to warm-weather crops like cotton, it's not unfriendly to agriculture in general: North Plains farms produce wheat, corn, and sugar beets. Ranching is also a much bigger business on the North than on the South Plains, and the state's largest cattle auction is held in Amarillo.

For years, Amarillo was best known as a way station on old U.S. 66, which ran along the city's north edge, on its way west to Los Angeles. In its heyday, Route 66 fostered dozens of service stations, motels, and restaurants, and at least one description of Amarillo as "the world's biggest truck stop." Interstate 40, built during the 1960s through the center of town, left U.S. 66 a city route. Now the motels with western theme signs have aged, the eateries are second-rate, and there's an on-again, off-again red-light district. Amarillo's informal red-light district is sometimes out of commission because the town has pursued a policy that is avoided elsewhere: it arrests not only prostitutes, but their clients as well.

Perhaps more than any other sizable town in Texas, Amarillo enjoys a reputation as a cowboy town, and it has the look, with jeans-and-Stetson-wearing men on every side. It was undoubtedly a cow town when its population was less than 10,000, and cattle marched on its outskirts on their way to railheads farther

Downtown Amarillo hustling and bustling in the 1920s.
(Center for American History, University of Texas)

north. But today's cowboys are few and far between; most of the men on Amarillo streets are manual laborers, farmers, or lawyers, all dressed in Western garb.

Class differences are evident between cowboys and their bosses, cattlemen. The cowboy still lives in a "line camp" (usually a farmhouse that once belonged to a cattleman's family) and drives his pickup into town once or twice a month to go shopping. Cattlemen—who wear starched jeans—can be found at the **Western Stockyards,** at the corner of South Manhattan and East Third, downtown, on Tuesday mornings. They're buying and selling cattle, usually in lots, at auction on Tuesday, and you're free to join them; there's no admission, and nobody ganders at people dressed like city folk.

Auctions take place in what's called a ring, a dirt-floor area above which the auctioneer sits at a microphone, calling out prices to the audience, which takes its seats around the ring above floor level. Cattlemen bring animals to the stockyards in trailers, where they're routed through a maze of pens and chutes into the ring, one owner's lot at a time. As the cattle are displayed and the auctioneer makes his calls, prospective buyers—who register beforehand—raise their hands or shout assent to a purchase, and after the show is done, load up the cattle they've bought and take them to their new home—or to a slaughterhouse.

The stockyards' auctions no longer run two days a week, or as many hours as before, because even the auction is shrinking before advancing technology. It's much easier for the cattleman to tune into an auction from a satellite dish, making his purchases by phone. But the stockyards area, in addition to the auction ring, has several cattlemen's restaurants where the satellite-dish bidders stop by, even on days when there's no auction, because no technology has yet replaced the rancher's most important associate, the banker, who holds notes on his cattle, and sometimes, his land.

■ NORTH PLAINS AREA

Perhaps one of the more authentic close-in views of traditional ranch life available in Texas today is to be found at the **Bar H Dude Ranch,** just off FM 3257, north of Clarendon, about 55 miles (88 km) southeast of Amarillo. Guests sleep in bunk houses—five bunks to a room—ride horses and help with ranch chores during the day, dine with the hands and other guests. Prices are moderate and, when your venture is over, you can recuperate in one of the saunas at an Amarillo motel.

About 40 miles (64 km) north of Amarillo off U.S. 287, across a break in the

flat terrain, is **Dumas,** the biggest town and seat of Moore County with a population of about 13,000. A statistic from the 1990 county census points to something that is unmatched elsewhere in Texas: in Moore County, Asians outnumber African Americans, 282 to 95. Because the number is small, the statistic isn't greatly significant, but it bears witness to an unusual event in the county's modern history.

Over the past 20 years, Moore County has become a sort of microcosm of population groups, thanks in great part to what happened at **Cactus,** some 15 miles (24 km) north on U.S. 287. The village, a collection of military-style wood frame fourplexes, all painted white, was built during World War II when an ordnance plant was located nearby. After the war, the plant became a fertilizer producer, but as the years passed, Cactus lost its population. It was practically a ghost town, inhabited by less than 650 people during the early 1970s when, among other things, its largely Hispanic population elected a Mexican citizen to its city council. Cactus hung on, never fully closing, only because there were a few jobs available in the area's beef industry.

North Texas is feedlot country. It's the part of Texas where cattle spend their last days. On the feedlots, hundreds, even thousands of cows are fattened for six to eight weeks on a diet of cooked grains, often leavened with growth hormones and

One of the state's largest rodeo events, the XIT Rodeo occurs in Dalhart every August.
(left) Cadillac Ranch is a bizarre monument to the evolution of the tail fin.

Back in the Saddle

The cowboy was underpaid, overworked, poorly fed, often tired, and usually bored and lonely in the American West. Most became cowboys because they were looking for a new beginning, a second chance. After the Civil War, many cowboys were Confederate veterans. Union veterans, particularly from New England, were also drawn to the range.

One in seven cowboys was black; some had been slaves in Texas, while others were fleeing the hardships of Reconstruction. Another one in seven was Mexican, and there was a sprinkling of Indians. The range had its share of prejudice, but usually one cowboy would acknowledge, if sometimes grudgingly, the skills of another, whatever his race or background. A handful of blacks were trail bosses, and a few became well-known rodeo performers. There were British cowboys, some seeking adventure, others exiled by their families in the hope that the outdoor life would change their dissolute ways.

Whatever their backgrounds, cowboys lived in a heavily Spanish culture; the roundup, branding, western saddle, roping, and cowboy clothing—all were adopted from Mexican vaqueros, who had taught the first Texas cowboys their trade. Words like *cincha* (cinch), *catallerango* (wrangler), and *reata* (lariat) reveal the origins of the cowboy's trade.

Life revolved around the long drive to market and the spring and fall roundups. Each cowboy drove back scattered cattle to the roundup site. The foreman would select the calves to be branded, then the cowboy would chase a calf toward the branding fire, rope it, bring it down, and call for the branding iron. Roping was dangerous work; a steer suddenly pulling a rope taut could topple horse and rider, or the rope could cut off fingers misplaced on the saddle horn.

On the drive, which could take three or four months and cover more than a thousand miles, the cowboy had to keep the line of cattle moving along the course set by the trail boss. Cowboys flanked the column, which stretched for several miles. Another cowboy, the *wrangler,* oversaw the *remuda,* or *cavvy,* a group of fresh saddle horses; on the trail a cowboy could easily wear out two horses a day. The cowboy myth romanticizes the relationship between the cowboy and his horse, but most cowboys rode horses owned by their employer.

A working day on the trail could last fourteen hours, almost all of it in the saddle. Part of every night was spent watching the cattle in case they might be "spooked" into stampeding by lightning, noise, or a sudden movement. The only relaxation was around the campfire, gossiping or spinning yarns. The chuck wagon was more than a traveling kitchen; it was "home," and the cook was doctor, barber, seamstress, black-smith, and keeper of the peace.

At the end of the trail, the cowboy let off steam, perhaps squandering the hundred or so dollars he made on the drive on clothes, liquor, gambling, and prostitutes. A certain amount of hell was raised, but violence was comparatively rare.

On the ranch in the summer, cowboys kept busy tending cattle and treating them for diseases, repairing fences, and doing farm chores. The bunkhouse was one single large room that offered little privacy. Meals were better and more varied than on the trail, although bacon and beans were staples. One dish was "sonofabitch stew," made of beef heart, liver, testicles, and other organ meats.

Most cowboys were let go after the fall roundup, working in town at what jobs they could find or "grub-line riding," going from one ranch to another for an odd job or free meal. Those who were kept on performed repairs and maintenance on the ranch. Some were given the loneliest job of all, "line riding," patrolling the bound-aries of the ranch, living in a primitive hut, riding out every day to track down stray cattle, killing wolves and other predators, and rarely seeing another living soul.

Come spring, the cycle would start again, and ranchers would begin hiring for the roundup. Most cowboys were young, generally in their early twenties. On av-erage, a cowboy would spend seven years on the range before looking for a more human and settled life doing something else.

—Chuck Lawliss, *The Old West,* 1994

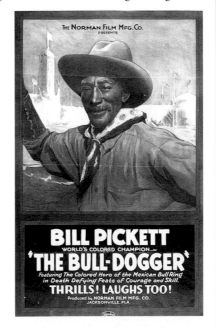

Bill Pickett was one of many rodeo heroes who helped glamorize the life of the cowboy. (Library of Congress)

antibiotics. Cactus is home to a feedlot, and another large operation is based at Sunray, about 10 miles (16 km) east. In the past, when killing time came, Moore County sent its cattle elsewhere in Texas or to the Midwest.

During the late 1960s, as the Johnson administration was enacting programs to aid economically depressed areas, Moore County's wheeler-dealers, some of whom owned property in Cactus, applied for grants to attract a beef-packing house. It opened in 1974 and work in the beef plant paid well. In a chilly atmosphere, workers cut and sliced and sawed beef carcasses in standing positions, hour after hour, usually becoming quite bloodied during the course of a day. Repetitive motion injuries were common, and the turnover rate was high.

Within months of its opening, the beef industry found that Cactus and the immediate area couldn't supply enough labor to keep its 1,000-worker plant staffed. Efforts to recruit elsewhere failed. Authorities of the Catholic Refugee Service in Amarillo caught wind of the situation, and began resettling in Moore County people who had fled to the United States from several troubled nations: Chile, Vietnam, and Cambodia. Within a few years, Moore County, whose population in 1960 included only a handful of Mexican Americans and two African-American

(left and above) Horses and High Plains sunsets are enduring images of this region of Texas.

families, became a relatively cosmopolitan place. Most of the newcomers found jobs at the beef plant, and Cactus, just across the road, filled up overnight.

About 115 miles (185 km) northeast of Amarillo, at **Perryton,** slogans from the past have become present-day icons. Painted on the bricks of the second story of an empty Main Street store is an aerial battle with a B-17 Flying Fortress as its centerpiece. The sign's message, "Buy War Bonds," and its huge backdrop, a giant 48-star flag, isn't flaking or faded, it's practically new, as war bonds were still being sold in the town's banks.

Insurance and real estate agent Joe R. LaMaster is the reason why. LaMaster's father, seven uncles, and an aunt served in the war, and he was named after an uncle who was killed in the conflict: the faded war is almost in his genes. In 1974 LaMaster, just back from college, began collecting one-dollar donations to have the sign, then nearly invisible, restored to its former glory. The restoration was accomplished by the end of 1976. But the south side of Perryton's towering Equity grain elevator bore the ghost of another wartime ad, "Remember Pearl Harbor. Buy War Bonds." About 1986, LaMaster began soliciting one-dollar donations to restore that sign, too. Money for the work came quickly, but the sign's features were so paled that LaMaster had to wait, and hunt, until he could find a trustworthy photo to aid in the repainting job. In 1993, he found a 50-year-old picture showing Main Street in snowdrifts, the Equity war bonds sign clearly in view. Now he's had it restored, too. Old soldiers may die, but in North Texas, mementos of their battles don't fade away.

PRACTICAL INFORMATION

Note: Compass American Guides makes every effort to ensure the accuracy of its information; however, as conditions and prices change frequently, we recommend that readers also contact the regional chambers of commerce for the most up-to-date information. See "Information" beginning on page 316.

■ AREA CODES AND TIME ZONES

All of Texas lies in the Central Standard Time Zone except the El Paso area, whose clocks run an hour earlier, on Mountain Time. Nine area codes for the state—three more than a decade ago—have thoroughly confused its telephone users.

Area codes for major cities:

Austin 512	Galveston 409
Dallas 214	Houston 713
El Paso 915	San Antonio. . . 210
Fort Worth . . 817	

■ CLIMATE

In Texas there's a saying, especially applicable to North Texas, that if you don't like the weather, you should hang around a couple of hours. Texas weather varies with the state's geography, but almost everywhere it is subject to rapid changes as "northers," or cold fronts, blow in.

| CITY | FAHRENHEIT TEMPERATURE | | | ANNUAL PRECIPITATION | |
	Jan. Avg. High/Low	July Avg. High/Low	Record High/Low	Average Rain	Average Snow
Abilene	56 33	95 72	111 -9	24"	4"
Amarillo	49 24	90 66	108 -16	20"	15"
Austin	60 40	95 74	109 -2	33"	1"
Brownsville	69 51	92 75	104 12	27"	0"
Corpus Christi	64 48	90 76	105 11	27"	0"
Dallas	56 35	95 74	112 -8	32"	3"
El Paso	57 32	94 70	114 -8	8"	5"
Houston	61 40	93 72	108 5	47"	0"
Midland	57 30	94 69	116 -11	15"	4"
San Antonio	62 41	94 74	107 0	28"	1"

However, it's safe to trust in a few general rules, governing the more dramatic forms of weather, anyway. Texas is not a state where people expect snow, except in North Texas and on the mountaintops of the Trans-Pecos. It can come in those places from October to May. Heavy snowfalls are rare and visitors from snowy states are sometimes displeased to learn that, in Texas, roads are rarely salted, and snowplows are few: severe winter weather catches most of the state unprepared.

Rain falls east of I-35 almost year-round, so often that it is not a dramatic event. West of that divide, rain sometimes comes in spring and summer, and sometimes doesn't come for years. Hail can blanket the northern part of the state anytime rain falls. Tornadoes mainly affect North Texas, usually in the spring; hurricanes ordinarily affect only the coast in late summer, once or twice in a decade. Strong winds are a feature only of the coast and the Panhandle.

Because much of the state is subtropical, visitors to Texas tend to be more aware of its heat, rather than its cold spells, and heat in Texas is a function of humidity as much as of the thermometer. The 80 percent mean annual relative humidity of Texas coastal areas becomes suffocating in July and August, when temperatures average in the nineties. 100-degree (38° C) July and August days in Dallas are scorchers, despite a humidity of about 65 percent. In Presidio, statistically the hottest spot in Texas, July-August temperatures frequently pass 105 degrees F (41° C), but the Big Bend area's dryness, about 50 percent relative humidity, makes the extra heat nearly tolerable. Alpine, Marfa, Fort Davis, and Amarillo, because of their clear skies and elevations, are pleasant places even when temperatures surpass 90 degrees F (33° C).

Cold months in Texas are mild by comparison to those of the northern reaches of the United States. Very few homes in Texas have basements, for example, because there's no need to protect pipes from extreme freezes. On southern stretches of the coast and in the Rio Grande Valley, freezing temperatures come only two or three times in a decade. Citrus and palm trees can't survive in North Texas, but despite periodic freezes, they have held on in the South.

The best months for travel, anywhere in the state, are October and November, April, May, and June, jean-jacket and sleeveless weather in Texas.

■ TRANSPORTATION

The chief factor influencing travel in Texas is the state's size: 262,017 square miles (678,624 sq km), some 50,000 square miles (129,500 sq km) bigger than France, the largest country in Europe. Though it is served by the same air, bus, and rail lines as other states, the expansiveness of Texas gives rise to travel considerations that are not universal in the United States.

The Texas Fruitmobile provides weary road travelers with some important advice.

■ BY AUTO

It is not sensible to think about travel in Texas without an auto. No city in Texas has a subway, and because Texas cities are sprawling, taxi service is expensive and inner-city bus transportation is poor. Even visitors to Texas cities who arrive by air are well-advised to rent a car.

■ TEXAS HIGHWAYS

There are more than 2,000 cities, towns, and settlements in Texas, and some 72,000 miles (116,000 km) of state-maintained highways, designated on maps as interstate highways, federal highways, Texas highways, farm-to-market roads, ranch roads, and park roads. Locating small towns can be a task, since most maps do not include farm-to-market roads; many overlook all but a few state highways as well. Only one map is a reliable guide to rural Texas, the official map produced annually by the Texas Department of Transportation. In addition to highways, park roads, and farm-to-market and ranch roads, these cartographers' masterworks show topographic features, state and federal park locations, and population figures for towns, even mere villages. The maps are free, but are not easy to come by. The Highway Department gives them to visitors at a dozen Travel Information Centers, located on highways leading into the state, and also by mail. To obtain a copy, call (800) 452-9292.

■ BY AIR

Since Texas is big, air travel is important. The state is served by the usual national and international air transport lines, but for intra-state travel, most Texans fly on a Dallas-based carrier, Southwest Airlines. A product of the 1970s, Southwest developed travel codes peculiarly suited to the state's social atmosphere: there are no class divisions in seating, and since flights are brief, no meals are served in the air. Southwest flights are also based out of inner-city airports that are more convenient to business travelers than the far-flung international mega-ports that serve Houston and Dallas. But even with Southwest, you can't fly to some Texas towns—Tyler, Waco, and Laredo among them.

■ ABOUT TEXAS LODGING AND FOOD

There are 18 million people in Texas, more than five times as many as in Colorado, one-and-a-half times as many as in Illinois—more than in any state except California. What this means to the traveler is that an affordable hotel or motel is rarely far away. America's major hotel and motel chains are well-represented in Texas as are numerous historic and unique hostelries.

As for food, in Texas, the first (or most common) line of fare is simply American: meat-and-potatoes standards, nouvelle cuisine, and fast foods. The state's second line is Mexican food, including Tex-Mex (a variant of the cuisine of northern Mexico) and New Mexican which features the generous use of chiles.

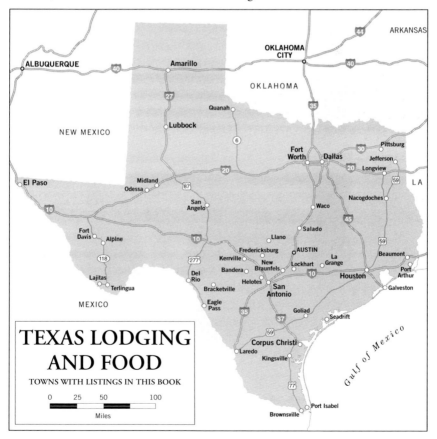

TEXAS LODGING AND FOOD

TOWNS WITH LISTINGS IN THIS BOOK

0   25   50   100

Miles

There is a third line of cuisine in Texas, perhaps called frontier or pioneer food, consisting of fried okra, fried squash, boiled greens, cornbread, and fried chicken. As there are some 50,000 eateries in Texas we had to be selective. We recommend the *Mobil Travel Guide to the Southwest* for its Star Quality Ratings, the Zagat restaurant surveys, or the *Texas Monthly* travel guides for more extensive recommendations. Eating out in Texas is relatively inexpensive, by national standards.

■ HOTEL AND MOTEL CHAINS

To find out what major chains have available, where, and for what price, it's best to use the following toll-free numbers:

Best Western. (800) 528-1234	ITT Sheraton. (800) 325-3535
Days Inn. (800) 329-7466	Marriott Hotels. (800) 228-9290
Doubletree. (800) 222-TREE	Radisson. (800) 333-3333
Hilton Hotels. (800) HILTONS	Ramada Inn. (800) 2RAMADA
Holiday Inn. (800) HOLIDAY	Stouffers. (800) HOTELS-1
Hyatt Hotels & Resorts. (800) 233-1234	Westin Hotels & Resorts. (800) 228-3000

*The tostadas at Dos Amigos Cafe in Pasa Lajitas (above)
and the chicken-fried steak at the Paris Cafe in Fort Worth
(right) are some of the best in Texas.*

■ LODGING AND FOOD BY TOWN

Room rates

Prices based on double occupancy, per night, are indicated as follows.

$ = under $50 $$ = $50–75 $$$ = $75–100 $$$$ = over $100

Restaurant prices

Entree, without drinks or tip.

$ = under $10 $$ = $10–15 $$$ = $15–25 $$$$ = above $25

ALPINE (WEST TEXAS)

✗ **Gallego's.** 1102 E. Holland; (915) 837-2416.
Flat, stacked enchiladas, Big Bend style. $

AMARILLO (NORTH TEXAS)

⌂ **Bar H Dude Ranch.** Off FM 3257, 55 miles (89 km) southeast of town; (806) 874-2634
Bunkhouses, horseback riding. Dine with ranch hands. $$-$$$

⌂ **Best Western Amarillo Inn.** 1610 Coulter; (800) 528-1234 or (806) 358-7861
103 units, heated indoor pool. $-$$

⌂ **Ramada Inn West.** 6801 I-40 W.; (800) 858-2223 or (806) 358-7881
242 standard units, indoor pool. $-$$

⌂ **Westar Suites.** 6800 I-40 W.; (800) 255-1755 or (806) 358-7943
Two-story motel, suites, pool and hot tub. $-$$

✗ **Big Texan Steak Ranch.** 7701 I-40 E.; (806) 372-6000
The place that travelers remember most, probably because it is widely advertised on billboards. Offers a free 72-oz. steak dinner free to patrons who can eat it in an hour, stages an annual steak-eating contest. Also serves buffalo, calf fries, even rattlesnake. $-$$

✗ **Stockyard Cafe.** 100 S. Manhattan; (806) 374-6024
Pioneer, with breakfast and lunch only on weekdays, supper on weekends. $-$$

ARANSAS NATIONAL WILDLIFE REFUGE AREA (SOUTH TEXAS)

⌂ **Hotel Lafitte.** 302 Bay Ave., Seadrift, off TX 185; (512) 785-2319
25 miles (40 km) northeast of Aransas. Rumor has it Bonnie and Clyde spent the night here. Ocean views. $$-$$$

AUSTIN (CENTRAL TEXAS)

The Driskill Hotel. 604 Brazos; (512) 474-5911
Circa 1886, Romanesque with cattle heads replacing gargoyles, saved from the
wrecking ball by a citizens' movement in 1970, restored 1989. Lyndon Johnson kept a
suite here. $$$-$$$$

Four Seasons Hotel. 98 San Jacinto; (800) 332-3442 or (512) 478-4500
On the southeastern edge of downtown, facing town lake, 292 units, Southwestern
decor. Health club facilities and an outdoor pool. $$$$

Omni Austin Hotel. 700 San Jacinto; (800) 843-6664 or (512) 476-3700
Atrium hotel, 315 rooms, rooftop pool, red granite and chrome decor. $$$-$$$$

Radisson Hotel on Town Lake. 111 E. First; (800) 333-3333 or (512) 478-9611
281 units on lake, jogging track, south side of downtown. $$$-$$$$

Basil's. 900 W. 10th at Lamar; (512) 477-5576
Fresh pasta, seafood, veal, and chicken; close quarters. $$$

Fonda San Miguel. 2330 W. North Loop; (512) 459-4121
Austin's longtime, upscale source for authentic Mexican food. $$-$$$

Iron Works Barbecue. 100 Red River; (512) 478-4855
Located in a one-time blacksmith's shed. Roomy and rustic. $

Jeffrey's. 1204 W. Lynn; 477-5584.
Ambitious and original dishes in a quiet cottage setting. A longtime local favorite. $$-$$$

Kerbey Lane Cafe. 3704 Kerbey; (512) 451-1436
Standard American, some vegetarian dishes, a late-night and breakfast stop. Ginger-
bread cakes. $-$$

Las Manitas Avenue Cafe. 211 Congress; (512) 472-9357
New Mexico style food. Choice of downtown office workers and breakfast fanatics. $

Ruta Maya Coffeehouse. 218 W. Fourth St.; (512) 472-9637
Chock-full of folk art from Chiapas; it even gets its beans there. Sit outside on the
raised sidewalk and watch the Texas thunderclouds roll by.
Second location: 2222 Rio Grande St.; (512) 322-0922. $

Scholz Garten. 1607 San Jacinto; (512) 477-4171
Since 1866, beer garden, indoors dining, too. Standard American and Tex-Mex, a venerable hangout for pols. Attached bowling alley belongs to a German-language music
society, not open to the public. $

Threadgill's. 6416 N. Lamar; (512) 451-5440
A former gas station that became famous as the hangout of '60s rock star Janis Joplin.
Traditional fare, rustic decor a bit cute. $-$$

BANDERA (CENTRAL TEXAS)

Dixie Dude Ranch. On FM 1077; (210) 796-7771 or (800) 375-9255
Nine miles (15 km) southwest of Bandera. A working ranch since the turn of the century, with horseback riding, cookouts, hayrides, and swimming. $$$$

Mayan Ranch. Off Pecan St., one and a half miles (2.4 km) west of Main St.; (210) 796-3312
Swimming and tubing, horseback riding, hiking, country dance lessons. $$$$

BEAUMONT (EAST TEXAS)

Beaumont Hilton. 2355 I-10 S.; (800) 445-8667 or (409) 842-3600
Nine-story building, two restaurants, bar, fitness center. $$-$$$

La Quinta Motor Inn. 220 I-10 N.; (800) 531-5900 or (409) 838-9991
Comfortable and convenient. $-$$

David's Upstairs. 745 N. 11th; (409) 898-0214
Seafood, New Orleans-style; some continental and American, extensive wine list. $$-$$$

Partizi's Other Place. 2050 I-10 S.; (409) 842-5151
Big portions of Italian and local seafood. $$

Sartin's. 6725 Eastex Freeway; (409) 892-6771
Cajun cooking. Excellent seafood. The Golden Triangle's most revered restaurant. $-$$

Johnny Boutin (above) is served a formidable platter of onion rings accompanied by spicy habanero catsup at Restaurant Biga in San Antonio. A cool beer on tap from the Shiner Brewery (right) a hundred miles east of town in Shiner will make his job easier.

BIG BEND NATIONAL PARK AREA (WEST TEXAS)

Chisos Mountains Lodge. Chisos Basin; (915) 477-2291
Neither historic nor fancy, but there's no other lodging for miles around. Operated by the National Park Service. Reservations advised. $

Lajitas on the Rio Grande. Lajitas; (915) 424-3471
A resort complex with some 80 rooms, most in mock cavalry outpost style. $-$$$

The Badlands. Lajitas; (915) 424-3471
Standard American, regional Mexican. $-$$

La Kiva Restaurant & Bar. Terlingua; (915) 371-2250
Barbecue, showers, and night life! $-$$

Starlight Dinner Theatre. Terlingua; (915) 371-2326
Supper only, standard American, regional Mexican. Not a dinner theatre but a diner located in the old Terlingua Theatre. $-$$

BRACKETVILLE (SOUTH TEXAS)

Fort Clark Springs. Off U.S. 90, east of downtown; (210) 563-2493
The restored Fort Clark cavalry post, circa 1872. No telephones in rooms. $

BROWNSVILLE (SOUTH TEXAS)

Ft. Brown Hotel. 1900 E. Elizabeth; (800) 582-3333 or (210) 546-2201
17 acres, more motel than hotel, walking distance of the international bridge. $-$$$

The Drive-In. Sixth and Hidalgo in Matamoros; 011-52-88-2-0022
A dining room that looks like a set for the Lawrence Welk Show, continental and Mexican food. Not a drive-in, but the American hang-out in Matamoros. $-$$

CORPUS CHRISTI (SOUTH TEXAS)

Corpus Christi Marriott Bayfront. 900 N. Shoreline; (800) 874-4585 or (512) 887-1600
On the bayfront, 20-story, 474-unit hotel, two restaurants, racquetball. $$$-$$$$

Holiday Inn North Padre Island Resort. 15202 Windward Dr., North Padre Island; (800) 465-4329 or (512) 949-8041
Standard service, weekly rates off-season. $$-$$$

Howard Johnson Hotel. 300 N. Shoreline; (800) 446-4656 or (512) 883-5111
On the bayfront, rafts, bicycles for rent; formerly the Radisson Marina. View from top-floor restaurant. $$-$$$

Puente Vista Condominium Apartments. 14300 Aloha St.; (800) 234-0117
Two-night minimum, 2- and 3-bedroom apartments. $

Harvey's Barn Door. 4135 Alameda; (512) 854-2656
Standard American, a musicians' hang-out, open 24 hours. $-$$

✗ **La Pesca.** 701 N. Water; (512) 887-4558
Mexican-style seafood. $-$$
✗ **Pepe's.** 15 Gaslight Square; (512) 888-7373
Tex-Mex and Mexican, indoors and out. $-$$
✗ **Snoopy's Pier.** 13313 S. Padre Island Dr.; (512) 949-8815
A famously informal seafood and sandwich shop, outdoor deck, view. $
✗ **Water Street Seafood Company.** 309 N. Water; (512) 882-8684
Wide selection of seafood and shellfish. Try the ceviche and deep-fried crab cakes. $$

DALLAS (EAST TEXAS)

▲ **Adolphus Hotel.** 1321 Commerce; (800) 221-9083 or (214) 742-8200
1912 vintage, restored. Built for Adolphus Busch, the beer king. 435 rooms. $$$-$$$$
▲ **The Mansion on Turtle Creek.** 2821 Turtle Creek Blvd.; (800) 527-5432 or (214) 559-2100
Elegance with a Texas flair. $$$$
▲ **Stoneleigh Hotel.** 2927 Maple; (800) 255-9299 or (214) 871-7111
European-style hotel, circa 1923, restored, 146 rooms. $$$
▲ **Wyndham Garden Hotel.** 110 W. John Carpenter Fwy., Irving; (800) 822-4200 or (214) 650-1600
Pretty and homey, close to the airport. $$$
✗ **Addison Cafe.** 5290 Belt Line Rd. (Monfort Dr.); (214) 991-8824
French and extremely popular. Cramped or cozy, depending on your mood. $$-$$$
✗ **Baby Routh.** 2708 Routh; (214) 871-2345
Ultra-modern decor and ultra-nouvelle cuisine. One of the most celebrated restaurants in the city. $$$
✗ **Campesi's Egyptian.** 5610 Mockingbird; (214) 827-0355
Italian, despite the name. Some assassination buffs believe that Lee Harvey Oswald and Jack Ruby dined there together on the night before the Kennedy assassination. $$
✗ **Dream Cafe.** 2800 Routh St.; between Cedar Springs and McKinny; (214) 954-0486.
Alternate to heavy Texas meals. This health-conscious cafe serves home-cooked light meals, fine coffees; breakfast, lunch, and dinner. $
✗ **Gloria's Salvadoran.** 600 W. Davis; (214) 948-3672
Central American. Delicious chocolate flan. $-$$
✗ **Kobe Steaks.** 5000 Belt Line Rd.; (214) 934-8150
Excellent Japanese in a group setting, ritzy ambience. $$$
✗ **La Calle Doce.** 415 W. 12th St.; (214) 941-4304
Mexican. Splendid seafood. $$
✗ **Mama's Daughter's Diner.** 2014 Irving Blvd.; (214) 742-8646
Down-home, pioneer. $-$$

✗ **The Mansion on Turtle Creek.** 2821 Turtle Creek; (214) 526-2121
In the hotel of the same name. Continental. Romantic and inviting. Sets the standard
for haute cuisine in Dallas. $$$$
✗ **Taquería Pedrito's.** 4910 Capitol; (214) 826-2940
Family fare, Mexico style—but on stage at night, a troupe performs folk dances from
across Latin America. $

DEL RIO (WEST TEXAS)

✗ **Crosby's.** 195 Hidalgo in Ciudad Acuña; 011-52-877-2-2020 (from Del Rio)
In Del Rio, residents and knowledgeable passersby consider this venerable American out-
post, on the Mexican side of the Rio Grande, to be the best spot for supper. Continental
and Mexican cuisine, including quail, and a dish to be found only here and in Piedras
Negras, *tortillas portuguesas*—sliced, fried tortillas, covered with cheese sauce. $-$$
✗ **Memo's.** 804 E. Losoya; (210) 775-8104
Tex-Mex and standard American fare since 1936, the local and celebrity hangout. $

EAGLE PASS (SOUTH TEXAS)

✗ **Club Moderno.** Zaragoza and Allende in Piedras Negras; 011-52-878-2-0098
Claims to be the place where *tortillas portuguesas* and *nachos* were first concocted, is
probably right about the former. The American hang-out in Piedras. $-$$

EL PASO (WEST TEXAS)

▲ **Camino Real Paso del Norte Hotel.** 101 S. El Paso; (800) 769-4300 or (915) 534-3099
Built in 1912, this grand old hotel has been a stopping point for Pancho Villa and
Charles Lindberg, Presidents Taft, Hoover, and Johnson, and Gen. John J. Pershing.
Restored in 1981, listed in the National Register of Historic Places. $$$-$$$$
✗ **Avila's.** 6232 N. Mesa; (915) 584-3621, also 10600 Montana; (915) 598-3333
Mexican, New Mexican. $
✗ **Grigg's.** 9007 Montana; (915) 598-3451
Mexican, New Mexican. $-$$
✗ **La Hacienda.** 1720 W. Paisano; (915) 532-5094
Mexican, New Mexican. $
✗ **Leo's.** Four locations: 2285 Trawood; (915) 591-2511
5315 Hondo Pass; (915) 757-0505
5103 Montana; (915) 566-4972
7872 N. Loop; (915) 593-9025
Mexican, New Mexican. $
✗ **Wyng's 'n Spirit.** 100 block of S. Pueblo; (915) 859-3916
Next door to the Tigua arts and crafts center. New Mexican, Tigua bread. $-$$

FORT DAVIS (WEST TEXAS)

Indian Lodge. About one mile (1.6 km) north on TX 17, then three miles (5 km) west on TX 118, then onto Park Rd. 3; (915) 426-3254
Built by the Civilian Conservation Corps, operated by the state of Texas as a part of the David Mountains State Park. 39 rooms, 15 of adobe, Pueblo style, circa 1933. Reservations advised. $

Limpia Hotel. On the town square; (800) 662-5517
Built of native pink limestone in 1912, last restored in 1990, 14 rooms furnished in period reproductions. Rockers and Chinese checkers on its porches. Smoking is not permitted. $$-$$$

The Drugstore. On Main St.; (915) 426-3118
Fountain soft drinks, floats and malts, sandwiches. Breakfast and lunch only. $

Limpia Hotel Dining Room. On the town square; (915) 426-3237
Home cooking, bookstore and souvenir shop. $$

FORT WORTH (WEST TEXAS).

Radisson Plaza Hotel. 815 Main; (800) 333-3333 or (817) 870-2100
As the Texas Hotel, opened in 1921. New interior, red-brick exterior with terra-cotta steer head adornments. This is the last place where President Kennedy slept. $$$$

Stockyards Hotel. 109 E. Exchange, at Stockyards; (800) 423-8471 or (817) 625-6427
52-room restored 1907 hotel, "Cattle baron baroque," cowhide chairs, bleached skulls, etc. $$$-$$$$

Angelo's. 2533 White Settlement; (817) 332-0357
A favorite among barbecue lovers. $

Cattlemen's Steak House. 2458 N. Main; (817) 624-3945
Steakhouse with some seafood, also lamb testicles, a.k.a. "mountain oysters." $$-$$$

Joe T. Garcia's. 2201 N. Commerce; (817) 626-4356
Tex-Mex, mariachis, patio and indoor dining since 1935. $-$$

Mac's House. 4255 Camp Bowie Blvd.; (817) 377-3744
Steakhouse with a full bar. $-$$

Michaels. 3413 W. Seventh; (817) 877-3413
Southwestern or "contemporary ranch" cuisine with an emphasis on fruits and chiles. Rustic decor. $$-$$$

Paris Coffee Shop. 700 W. Magnolia; (817) 335-2041
Down-home breakfasts, chicken and dumplings, other Texas pioneer plate lunches. $

Riscky's Sirloin Inn. 120 E. Exchange, in the Stockyards; (817) 624-4800
Steakhouse. $

✗ **Saint-Emilion.** 3617 W. Seventh; (817) 737-2781
French country theme in former residence, four-course dinners. Reservations recommended. $$$-$$$$

FREDERICKSBURG (CENTRAL TEXAS)

⌂ **Be My Guest Lodging Service.** 402 W. Main; (210) 997-7227
A clearing house for numerous bed and breakfast houses in the area, including ranch locations. $-$$

⌂ **Comfort Inn.** 908 S. Adams; (800) 221-2222 or (210) 997-9811
46 standard units, pool. $-$$

✗ **Altdorf Restaurant.** 301 W. Main; (210) 997-7774
American, German, and Tex-Mex cuisine. In a limestone house, circa 1846, with a beer garden. $-$$

✗ **George's Old German Bakery and Restaurant.** 225 W. Main; (210) 997-9084
Pastries, breakfasts, and light fare. Also serving lunch and dinner. $-$$

GALVESTON (EAST TEXAS)

⌂ **Hotel Galvez.** 2024 Seawall; (800) 392-4285 or (409) 765-7721
1911 vintage, 228 restored rooms, the city's grand old hotel, quarters for Presidents Roosevelt, Eisenhower, and Nixon and the Dorsey Brothers band. $$$-$$$$

⌂ **The Tremont House.** 2300 Ship's Mechanic Row; (800) 874-2300 or (409) 763-0300
Century-old hotel, restored, more than 100 rooms. Free shoe shines, newspapers. $$$$

✗ **Clary's.** 8509 Teichman, Teichman exit off I-45; (409) 740-0771
Located on Offats Bayou, serving seafood and steak. $$-$$$

✗ **DiBella's Italian.** 1902 31st St.; (409) 763-9036
Meat, veal, and seafood specialties. $-$$

✗ **Gaido's.** 3828 Seawall; (409) 762-9625
The standard in seafood since 1911, in a pleasant beachfront setting. $$-$$$

✗ **La Palmita.** 1424 Strand; (409) 763-8276
Even if you don't stop to dine, drive by: the multi-colored masonry, adorned with figureheads, is pleasingly eccentric. *Enchiladas suizas,* the specialty. $

✗ **Mario's Flying Pizza.** 2202 61st St. (at Q 1/2); (409) 744-2975
Islanders rave about this pizzeria. $

✗ **Yaga's.** 2314 Strand; (409) 762-6676
More dancing than dining goes on here, but the soups, salads, and sandwiches are tasty. Seafood entrees as well. $-$$

GOLIAD (SOUTH TEXAS)

✚ **The Dial House.** 306 W. Oak St.; (512) 645-3366
60 miles (97 km) northwest of Aransas National Wildlife Area. A charming B&B,
hearty breakfast. $$

HELOTES (CENTRAL TEXAS)

✕ **Chaparral.** 15103 Bandera Hwy.; (210) 695-8302
Reliable Tex-Mex. $

HOUSTON (EAST TEXAS)

✚ **Embassy Suites Hotel.** 9090 Southwest Fwy.; (713) 995-0123
Two-room suites with kitchenettes. Indoor pool, sauna. $$$
✚ **La Colombe D'Or.** 3410 Montrose Blvd.; (713) 524-7999
Six rooms in a European-style mansion. $$$$
✚ **Lancaster Hotel.** 701 Texas Ave.; (800) 231-0336 or (713) 228-9500
Circa 1926, European style, 93 rooms. $$$$
✚ **Wyndham Warwick.** 5701 S. Main; (800) 822-4200 or (713) 526-1991
310 rooms, circa 1926, restored in 1989. Frank Sinatra slept here. $$$
✕ **Americas.** 1800 Post Oak Blvd; (713) 961-1492
Fred Flintstone might have had a hand in the decor. Features Central and South
American cuisine. $$-$$$
✕ **Berryhill Hot Tamales.** 2639 Revere; (713) 526-8080
A popular diner that serves—unheard of—fish tacos. People swear by them. $
✕ **Brennan's.** 3300 Smith; (713) 522-9711
New Orleans, Cajun cuisine. $$$-$$$$
✕ **Cafe Annie.** 1728 Post Oak; (713) 840-1111
Nouvelle, standard American, some pioneer. $$$$
✕ **Empire Cafe.** 1732 Westheimer; (713) 528-5282
Italian coffees, free newspapers and magazines, light fare. A hang-out. $
✕ **Goode Company Barbecue.** 5109 Kirby; (713) 522-2530
Ribs, brisket, hot links, chicken. $-$$
✕ **Hunan.** The Pavilion, 1800 Post Oak Blvd. (San Felipe); (713) 965-0808
Touted as the best Chinese restaurant in the city. George Bush loves this place. $$-$$$
✕ **Kim Son.** 2001 Jefferson; (713) 222-2461
More than 200 Vietnamese dishes—most of them are sensational. $$-$$$
✕ **Pico's Mex-Mex.** 5941 Bellaire; (713) 662-8383
Even the cuisine of Yucatán! $$

JEFFERSON (EAST TEXAS)

Excelsior Hotel. 211 W. Austin; (903) 665-2513
Second oldest operating hotel in Texas, 13 rooms. $$-$$$

Hotel Jefferson. 124 W. Austin St.; (903) 665-2631
1861 Cotton warehouse converted to hotel in 1900, restored 1977, interior mostly new. 23 rooms. $$-$$$

The Black Swan. 210 W. Austin St.; (903) 665-8922
Cajun and Louisiana dishes. $$

KERRVILLE (CENTRAL TEXAS)

Best Western Sunday Inn. 2124 Sidney Baker St.; (800) 528-1234
97 standard units, pool, restaurant. $$-$$$

Inn of the Hills River Resort. 1001 Junction Hwy.; (210) 895-5000
217 units, some condo and suites, four pools, fishing, tennis, racquetball, bowling, canoe and boat rentals. $$-$$$

Lazy Hills Guest Ranch. About 10 miles (16 km) west of Kerrville; (210) 367-5600
Three-day minimum at this dude ranch, family-style meals included in fee. $$$$

Y.O. Ranch Holiday Inn. 2033 Sidney Baker; (800) 531-2800 or (210) 257-4440
Not a dude ranch. Decorated in a Wild West theme, with 200 rooms. Near I-10, next to a golf course. $$$-$$$$

Bill's Barbeque. 1909 Junction Hwy.; (210) 895-5733
Like many barbecue joints with a steady local trade, this one can run out of meat and close in mid-afternoon. $

Sam Houston's. 2033 Sidney Baker St.; (210) 257-4440
Standard American, Old West decor. $$

KINGSVILLE (SOUTH TEXAS)

King's Inn. Eleven miles (17 km) south on U.S. 77, nine miles (14 km) east on FM 628; (512) 297-5265
Wide variety of seafood, sold by the pound, served family style. $$-$$$

LA GRANGE (EAST TEXAS)

Cottonwood Restaurant. At Cottonwood Inn, on TX 71; (409) 968-3175
Standard American and pioneer. On the western edge of town, the traditional stop for Texans driving between Austin and Houston. $-$$

LAREDO (SOUTH TEXAS)

La Posada. 1000 Zaragoza; (800) 444-2099 or (210) 722-1701
Former schoolhouse. 1920s vintage, with 227 rooms and two internal courtyards.
Located next to international bridge and across from San Augustin Plaza. $$$

El Dorado. Beldén and Ocampo, in Nuevo Laredo; 011-52-87-2-0015
The former Cadillac Bar, where the Ramos Gin Fizz was invented. Change of owner-
ship has improved both Mexican and standard American fare. The American locale in
Nuevo Laredo. $-$$

LLANO (CENTRAL TEXAS)

Cooper's Old Time Pit Barbecue. TX 29 W.; (915) 247-5713
Just what the name says. Pick your meat on the grill outside. $

LOCKHART (CENTRAL TEXAS)

Kreuz Market. 208 S. Commerce; (512) 398-2361.
Probably the best barbecue in the state, served in unpretentious style. $

LONGVIEW (EAST TEXAS)

Bodacious Bar-B-Q. 1402 W. Marshall (U.S. 80); (903) 236-3215
Known for its chopped beef, place has mural of a famous print, with a revision: beer
boxes in the scene have been changed for boxes of soft drinks. But beer is served. $

LUBBOCK (NORTH TEXAS)

The Depot. Ave. G and 19th; (806) 747-1646
Standard American, broiled mesquite dishes, beer garden. $$-$$$

Jimenez Bakery and Restaurant. 1219 Ave. G; (806) 744-2685
Breakfast and lunch only, pastries and lighter fare. $

Josie's. 212 University; (806) 747-8546
Mexican and northwest Mexican, busy at breakfast. $

MIDLAND (WEST TEXAS)

Luigi's. 111 N. Big Spring; (915) 683-6363
Small trattoria serving good Italian food for over 20 years. $

Wall Street Bar & Grill. 115 E. Wall St.; (915) 684-8686
Features a great 1867 bar; specializes in seafood and steaks. $-$$$

NACOGDOCHES (EAST TEXAS)

✖ **La Hacienda.** 1411 North; (409) 564-6450
Tex-Mex, standard American, in former residence, circa 1913. $-$$

NEW BRAUNFELS (CENTRAL TEXAS)

⌂ **Hotel Faust.** 240 S. Seguin; (210) 625-7791
Circa 1928, restored, 62 rooms. $-$$
⌂ **Rodeway Inn.** (800) 967-1168 or (210) 629-6991
130 rooms, 18 efficiencies, restaurant adjacent. $-$$

ODESSA (WEST TEXAS)

⌂ **Holiday Inn Centre.** 6201 E. Business I-20; (800) 465-4329 or (915) 362-2311
274 units, with heated indoor-outdoor pool, miniature golf, wet and dry saunas. $$
⌂ **Odessa Radisson.** 5200 E. University; (800) 533-0214 or (915) 368-5885
194 units, guest membership in health club. Close to University of Texas at the
Permian Basin. $$$-$$$$
✖ **The Barn Door.** 2140 Andrews Hwy.; (915) 337-4142
Adjoins the Pecos Depot Lounge, built in railroad depot, circa 1892. Standard
American, Tex-Mex. Steaks are their specialty. $$
✖ **Manuel's.** 1404 E. 2nd; (915) 333-2751
Fajitas are the specialty of this former tortilla factory. $-$$

PITTSBURG (EAST TEXAS)

✖ **Pittsburg Hot Links Restaurant.** 136 Marshall; (903) 856-5765
The beef sausages that put this village on the map. $

PORT ARTHUR (EAST TEXAS)

✖ **Esther's Cajun Seafood and Oyster Bar.** TX 87, at Rainbow Bridge; (409) 962-6268
Just what the name says. $$

PORT ISABEL (SOUTH TEXAS)

✖ **The Yacht Club.** 700 Yturria; (210) 943-1301
Seafood and 150 wines, at what was once a yacht club. $$$

QUANAH (NORTH TEXAS)

⌂ **Casa Royale Inn.** 1400 W. 11th; (817) 663-6341
40 rooms, pool. $-$$
✖ **Medicine Mound Depot.** U.S. 287 E.; (817) 663-5619
Steaks and Mexican food in depot building, circa 1910. $$

SALADO (CENTRAL TEXAS)

🛏 **Inn at Salado.** N. Main at Pace Park; (817) 947-5999
Seven rooms in circa 1870 style, bed-and-breakfast with private baths. $$$-$$$$

🛏 **Stagecoach Inn.** 1 Main; (817) 947-5111
82 units, motel style, golf, tennis, fishing. The place for family reunions and business gatherings. $-$$

🍴 **Stagecoach Inn Dining Room.** 1 Main; (817) 947-5111
A Texas waystation for 150 years. Traditional American and pioneer food. When it was an inn—an operating motel still adjoins—Sam Houston and General Custer passed through. $$-$$$

SAN ANGELO (WEST TEXAS)

🛏 **Holiday Inn Convention Center Hotel.** 441 Rio Concho; (800) 465-4329 or (915) 658-2828
Six-story hotel with 149 rooms, indoor pool. $-$$

🍴 **Mejor Que Nada.** *Better than Nothing.* 1911 S. Bryant; (915) 655-3553
Tex-Mex, located in a former gas station. $

🍴 **Zentner's Daughter.** 1901 Knickerbocker; (915) 949-2821
Steaks and pioneer cuisine. $$

SAN ANTONIO (SOUTH TEXAS)

🛏 **Best Western Crockett Hotel.** 320 Bonham; (800) 292-1050 or (210) 225-6500
Circa 1905, cheery rooms, across the alley from the Alamo. $$$

🛏 **Fairmount Hotel.** 401 S. Alamo St., (800) 642-3363 or (210) 224-8800
First class. Victorian style. $$$

🛏 **Menger Hotel.** 204 Alamo Plaza; (800) 345-9285 or (210) 223-4361
Circa 1859, limestone, 320 rooms. Teddy Roosevelt recruited Rough Riders here. $$$

🛏 **St. Anthony Park Lane.** 300 E. Travis; (800) 338-1338 or (210) 227-4392
Circa 1909, 350 rooms, quiet. $$$

🛏 **Sheraton Gunter Hotel.** 205 E. Houston; (800) 222-4276 or (210) 227-3241
Circa 1909, traditional cattlemen's hang-out, 325 rooms. $$$

🍴 **The Bayous.** 517 N. Presa; (210) 223-6403
A popular and well-situated restaurant on the River Walk. Tasty blackened redfish, among other cajun fare.

🍴 **Earl Abel's.** 4200 Broadway; (210) 822-3358
Nothing special about its standard American fare, but location and late-night hours have made it a favorite meeting place for locals. $

🍴 **El Mirador.** 722 S. St. Mary's; (210) 225-9444
Azteca soup, other Mexican dishes, a chatty lunch stop for downtown professionals. $

✗ **Jailhouse Cafe.** 1126 W. Commerce; (210) 224-5001
Tex-Mex, pioneer, standard American, as informal as its name. Just a stone's throw away from the hoosegow. $

✗ **Marta's.** Loop 410 at Blanco Rd.; (210) 340-1441
Large, 300-seat Mexican restaurant. Green enchiladas a specialty. Renowned chef Mario Cantu in charge. $$

✗ **La Louisiane.** 2632 Broadway; (210) 225-7984
French Creole and Continental, the city's long-time source for haute cuisine. $$$

✗ **The Landing.** 123 Losoya; (210) 223-7266
In the Hyatt Regency Hotel on the River Walk. A restaurant and club featuring traditional jazz. $$

✗ **Mi Tierra.** 218 Produce Row, Market Square; (210) 225-1262
Mariachis and Mexican atmosphere and food (best at breakfast). Usually crammed because it's big, easy to find, and open 24 hours. $-$$

✗ **Pig Stand.** 1508 Broadway; (210) 222-2794
One of two remaining units of a once far-flung southern chain of '50s-style diners, featuring a pork sandwich. Open 24 hours. $

✗ **Restaurant Biga.** 206 E. Locust St.; (210) 225-0722
An eclectic menu in a 100-year-old mansion. $-$$$

SAN MARCOS (CENTRAL TEXAS)

⌂ **Aquarena Springs Inn.** Above the springs, just east of I-35 Exit 206; (512) 396-8901
This modern-day hostelry also has 25 rooms that have been restored from a 1920s-era inn. $$-$$$

⌂ **Homeplace Inn.** 1429 I-35 N.; (512) 396-0400
Standard, 40 units, pool. $-$$

SONORA (CENTRAL TEXAS)

⌂ **Devil's River Inn.** I-10 and Golf Course Rd.; (915) 387-3516
Standard units, restaurant. $-$$

✗ **Commercial Restaurant.** 154 SW Plum; (915) 387-9928
Tex-Mex for three generations. $

TAYLOR (CENTRAL TEXAS)

✗ **Louie Muller's Barbecue.** 206 W. 2nd; (512) 352-6206
The best barbecue north of Austin and east of I-35, since 1948, in a joint with smoked ceilings and walls. Warning: iced tea is made with Taylor's high-sodium water, has an off taste. $

TYLER (EAST TEXAS)

✕ **Cace's Seafood.** 7011 S. Broadway; (903) 581-0744
Oysters Rockefeller, redfish, Cajun seafood. $$

WACO (EAST TEXAS)

✕ **Elite Cafe.** 2132 S. Valley Mills, on the traffic circle; (817) 754-4941
Circa 1920, refurbished interior. Pioneer, standard America. Sells t-shirts that say,
"I survived the Circle." $-$$

WAXAHACHIE (EAST TEXAS)

✕ **The 1897 Townhouse.** 111 S. College; (214) 937-7261
Standard American, pioneer, favorite of the locals. $-$$

WICHITA FALLS (NORTH TEXAS)

▲ **La Quinta Motor Inn.** 1128 Central Fwy.; (800) 531-5900 or (817) 322-6971
139 standard units, two-story. $$
✕ **McBride Land and Cattle Company.** 501 Scott; (817) 322-2516
Steaks, mesquite grilled, other pioneer and standard American. $$

■ MUSEUMS AND PLACES OF HISTORICAL INTEREST

For more detailed descriptions of the major museums and sites note the region
and refer back to the individual chapters.

■ ALBANY (NORTH TEXAS)

Old Jail Art Center. S. Second St., one block east of courthouse; (915) 762-2669. Works
by Umlauf, Modigliani, Picasso, Klée, other contemporary artists. 34 Chinese terra-
cotta tomb figures, more than a thousand years old. The only fine arts museum in
Texas located in a penal building.

■ ALPINE (WEST TEXAS)

Mural Post Office. 107 W. Ave. E; (915) 837-2524. WPA mural inside shows cowboys and
cowgirls in mountain desert settings, with red Herefords behind. The cowpokes are
reading, not riding!
Museum of the Big Bend. On the Sul Ross campus, U.S. 90, eastern edge of town;
(915) 837-8143. Natural and social history of the Trans-Pecos region.

■ ALTO (EAST TEXAS)

Caddoan Mounds State Historic Site. On TX 21, about six miles (10 km) SW of Alto, U.S. 69; (409) 858-3218. Weekends only. The closest Texas gets to having pyramids. Two temple mounds and a burial mound, believed to be 800 to 1,000 years old.

■ AUSTIN (CENTRAL TEXAS)

Elisabet Ney Museum. 304 E. 44th; (512) 458-2255. The studio of the nineteenth-century German sculptor, a resident of Texas during the last 30 years of her life.

French Legation. 802 San Marcos St.; (512) 472-8180. The oldest house in Austin and one of the last surviving houses from the Republic of Texas era.

George Washington Carver Museum. 1165 Angelina St.; (512) 472-4809. The first museum to concentrate on Texas black history.

Governor's Mansion. 1010 Colorado; (512) 463-5516. Greek Revival, circa 1856, with six first floor rooms, furnished with period antiques, open to public.

Harry Ransom Humanities Research Center. On the campus of the University of Texas, W. 21st and Guadalupe; (512) 471-8944. A treasure house of rare and sometimes expensive items, some of them of academic value. Includes the world's first photograph, circa 1826, and the Burl Ives collection of folk music recordings. Several exhibits for public enjoyment, but rules for viewing some materials are restrictive.

Laguna Gloria Art Museum. 3809 W. 35th; (512) 458-8191. Regional and national art and photo shows, special attention to Mexican-related subjects, no Western art. Located on 28 acres between Mt. Bonnell and Lake Austin. The grounds are themselves a pleasure to behold.

Lyndon B. Johnson Library. On the campus of the University of Texas, 2313 Red River; (512) 482-5136. Memorabilia of the President from Texas.

O. Henry Museum. 409 E. Fifth; (512) 472-1903. The short-story writer lived in this cottage during his ten years in Austin.

State Capitol. 11th and Congress; (512) 463-0063. Eight and a half acres of floor space, topped with a dome taller than the U.S. Capitol's. Tours begin at a Visitors Desk, where you can also obtain a copy of the Texas Transportation Department's highway map of Texas.

State Cemetery. E. Seventh and Comal; (512) 463-8930. Stephen F. Austin, and other notable Texans are buried here.

Texas Memorial Museum. 2400 Trinity St.; (512) 471-1604. Devoted to anthropology and natural history. Gemstones, minerals, Texas wildlife, Native American artifacts.

■ BANDERA (CENTRAL TEXAS)

Frontier Times Museum. 506 13th St.; 796-3864. A 1927 small-town museum. Regional artifacts from the frontier days.

■ BEAUMONT (EAST TEXAS)

Babe Didrikson Zaharias Memorial Museum. I-10 at Gulf Exit; (409) 833-4622. Mementos from the career of this 1930s–'50s women's track, field, basketball, and golf champion.

Gladys City Lucas Gusher Monument. University Dr. and U.S. 69/287, on the campus of Lamar University; (409) 880-8896. Re-creation of oil camp that was built in 1901 when the Spindletop gusher blew in. Oil derricks, clapboard buildings.

■ BROWNWOOD (WEST TEXAS)

Douglas MacArthur Academy of Freedom. On the campus of Howard Payne University, Austin Ave., FM 2524 at Coggin; (915) 646-2502. Memorabilia from General MacArthur, Pacific commander of U.S. forces during World War II. Includes his corn-cob pipe. Three-story mural depicting "man's relationship to God," replica of room where the Declaration of Independence was signed, other right-thinking exhibits.

■ COMFORT (CENTRAL TEXAS)

Cascade Caverns. 15 miles northeast of Comfort, off Hwy. 473 on old Hwy. 9. An old railroad tunnel summer home to over a million Mexican free-tailed bats. Their nightly flight can be spied from the park at the tunnel's south entrance. Closed Oct.–May.

Treue Der Union Monument. High, between Third and Fourth. Commemorates a group of Comfort's German citizens killed by Confederate soldiers in 1862. About 70 Germans, opposed to slavery and secession, fled Comfort to join Union forces but were followed and ambushed by a Confederate cavalry.

■ CORPUS CHRISTI (SOUTH TEXAS)

Corpus Christi Museum. 1900 Chaparral; (512) 883-2862. Naval and aircraft exhibits. Artifacts from three Spanish galleons that sank off Padre Island in 1554 and a repro-duction of one of them.

International Kite Museum. 3200 Sandy Shores, inside the Best Western Sandy Shores Hotel; (512) 883-7456. Unencumbered coastal skies and a Gulf breeze make Corpus Christi a good place for kiting. Museum tells the story of the kite's ancestry, with special emphasis on scientific uses of the device. Gift shop, with kites.

U.S.S. **Lexington Aircraft Carrier Museum.** Corpus Christi Beach; (512) 888-4873. Tours of vintage World War II carrier, naval exhibits.

■ DALLAS

Dallas Arboretum. 8525 Garland Rd.; (214) 327-8263. A 66-acre botanical garden, 200,000 flowering bulbs bloom in the fall.

Dallas City Hall. 1500 Marilla; (214) 744-3600. Building in Brutalist style, by I. M. Pei; courtyard sculpture by Henry Moore.

Dallas Museum of Art. 1717 N. Harwood; (214) 922-1200. Pre-Columbian Art, moderns, colonial American furniture, restaurant.

Mary Kay Museum. Off I-35, Regal Row exit; (214) 630-8787. Advertising memorabilia.

Museum of African-American Life and Culture. 1515 First Ave.; (214) 565-9026. Both African and African-American exhibits.

The Sixth Floor. 411 Elm; (214) 653-6666. Located in the former Texas School Book Depository, at the spot from which Lee Harvey Oswald is supposed to have shot President John F. Kennedy. Visual and video exhibits of Warren Commission findings, tributes to JFK.

■ EASTLAND (WEST TEXAS)

Kendrick Religious Museum. Four miles (6 km) west of town on U.S. 80; (817) 629-8672. Wax museum with 16 dioramas from the life of Jesus, an Easter pageant, and twice-a-week biblical plays with live animals on a 325-foot (99-m) outdoor stage.

Old Rip, The Horned Toad. County courthouse on Main St. When original Eastland County courthouse was built in 1897, a live "horny toad"—now an endangered Texas species—was placed inside a time capsule in the cornerstone. When the courthouse was rebuilt in 1927, the toad was still alive. Old Rip, as he was called, then traveled to the White House, where he met Calvin Coolidge. His embalmed remains are preserved in a glass exhibit case.

■ EL PASO (WEST TEXAS)

Border Patrol Museum. North-South Freeway to 4315 Woodrow Bean Transmountain Rd.; (915) 759-6060. La Migra sets the record straight. Uniform, canine, weapon displays. Gift shop.

Concordia Cemetery. Just north of the I-10/Gateway North interchange. Old burial grounds with the remains of nineteenth-century Chinese laborers and famous Texas outlaws, among others.

El Paso Centennial Museum. On the UTEP campus, Shuster/UTEP exit from I-10, University Ave. and Wisconsin; (915) 747-5565. Opened during the Texas Centennial in 1936, exhibits of human and natural history of the region; dinosaur remains, stone tools, shell jewelry.

El Paso Museum of Art. 1211 Montana Ave.; (915) 541-4040. European classic paintings and sculptures, local photography, Mexican folk art.

El Paso Museum of History. I-10 E. at the Avenue of the Americas, about 15 miles (25 km) from town; (915) 858-1928. Indians, Spanish explorers, cowboys, cavalrymen.

Fort Bliss. Northeast of town on U.S. 54. Built shortly after the Mexican War ended, the fort encompasses four historical museums: Air Defense Artillery Museum, Cavalry Museum, Fort Bliss Museum, and Museum of the Non-Commissioned Officer.

Magoffin Homestead. 1120 Magoffin Ave.; (915) 533-5147. Exemplary of Southwestern residential architecture between 1865 and 1880. Greek Revival style, with walls of adobe.

Socorro Mission. FM 258 (Socorro Rd.) at Nevarez; (915) 859-7718. This church, still in use, is said to be the oldest continually active parish in the United States. Completed in 1681 by the now-extinct Piro Indians, the present structure dates to the 1840s.

Tigua Indian Reservation. 100 block of Old Pueblo Rd., exit I-10 at Zaragosa; (915) 859-7913. Includes arts and crafts center, ceremonial dances, bread baked in adobe ovens. The Tigua, a part of the Pueblo civilization, came to Texas in 1680, but were not federally recognized as a tribe until the 1960s.

Wilderness Park Museum. 2000 Transmountain Rd. and Gateway South, about 15 minutes from downtown; (915) 755-4332. A 17-acre, indoor-outdoor museum with a walking trail and dioramas depicting Tigua Indian life.

Ysleta Mission. 100 block of Old Pueblo Dr., exit I-10 at Zaragosa; (915) 859-9848. The oldest mission in Texas, established for the Tigua Indians in 1681. Present structure dates mainly to 1908 restoration.

■ FORT DAVIS (WEST TEXAS)

Chihuahuan Desert Research Institute. Some three miles (5 km) south on TX 118; (915) 837-8370. Operated by Alpine's Sul Ross State University. About 2.5 miles (4 km) of nature trails, more than 500 species of plants, some potted, for sale to the public.

Fort Davis National Historical Site. On TX 17, at the north edge of town; (915) 426-3225. Cavalry outpost for the fabled African-American "buffalo soldiers" and also for camels, during the period of war with the Apache, 1867–1881. Half of the 50 original buildings have been restored.

■ FORT WORTH (WEST TEXAS)

Amon Carter Art Center. 3501 Camp Bowie Blvd.; (817) 738-1933. Canvases by Western realists Frederic Remington and Charles M. Russell, works by Winslow Homer, Grant Wood, Georgia O'Keeffe, and photographer Ansel Adams.

Fort Worth Museum of Science and History. 1501 Montgomery; (817) 732-1631. Fossils, geography, history of medicine, computers, planetarium, many exhibits with an eye to children's interests.

Kimbell Art Museum. 3333 Camp Bowie Blvd.; (817) 332-8451. Works by El Greco, Velázquez, Rembrandt, Cézanne, Picasso; restaurant and bookstore.

Modern Art Museum of Fort Worth. 1309 Montgomery; (817) 738-9215. Picasso, Rothko, Pollock, Warhol.

Sid Richardson Collection of Western Art. 309 Main; (817) 332-6554. Western paintings by Frederic Remington and Charles M. Russell.

■ FREDERICKSBURG (CENTRAL TEXAS)

Admiral Nimitz State Historical Park. 340 E. Main; (210) 997-4379. A restored hotel and residence of the family of Fleet Admiral Chester Nimitz, a native of the town who was commander of Pacific forces during World War II.

Vereins Kirche Museum. Market Square, off 100 block of W. Main. A reconstruction of the original octagonal Vereins Kirche, or "People's Church," built by early settlers in 1847. Pioneer relics and historical photographs.

■ GALVESTON (EAST TEXAS)

Bishop's Palace. Broadway; (409) 762-2475. Former home of the Catholic bishop. Located in the East End Historic District, 40 blocks of vintage, mainly plutocratic, homes.

***Elissa* and Texas Seaport Museum.** Pier 21 at 22nd; (409) 763-1877. Third oldest operating ship in the world, dating from 1877.

Moody Mansion and Museum. 2628 Broadway; (409) 762-7668. Enormous limestone and brick mansion, circa 1895, built by one of the state's wealthiest families.

The Railroad Museum. 123 Rosenberg; (409) 765-5700. The state's largest collection of retired railroad cars. Life-size plaster sculptures of passengers, H-O scale model of the Port of Galveston, restaurant.

■ GOLIAD (SOUTH TEXAS)

Goliad State Historical Park. About a mile (1.6 km) south of town on U.S. 183; (512) 645-3405. Mission Nuestra Señora del Espiritu Santo de Zuñiga, circa 1749, restored by the Civilian Conservation Corps during the Great Depression. Period furniture, museum, Indian artifacts.

Grave of Goliad Martyrs. Two miles (3 km) south of town, off U.S. 183. Monument and burial grounds of the 342 Texas revolutionaries executed by Mexican troops on Palm Sunday, 1836.

Presidio de La Bahia. About two miles (3 km) south of town off U.S. 183; (512) 645-3752. The Spanish fort that was established to guard the nearby mission, circa 1749, and during the Texas Revolution, the site of the execution of the Goliad martyrs.

■ GONZALES (SOUTH TEXAS)

Gonzales Memorial Museum. 414 Smith; (210) 672-6350. A museum focused on the town's role as the "Lexington of Texas." Includes the small cannon that local Texans refused to return to the Mexican army, precipitating the first skirmish of the Revolution.

■ HEREFORD (NORTH TEXAS)

National Cowgirl Hall of Fame and Western Heritage Center. 515 Ave. B; (806) 364-5252. Exhibits of riding gear and costumes of famous rodeo cowgirls, Western movie stars, other distaff contributors to the mythical and real culture of the West.

■ HOUSTON (EAST TEXAS)

Contemporary Arts Museum. 5216 Montrose; (713) 526-3129. Modern, emerging artists. Across the street from Museum of Fine Arts.

Menil Collection. 1515 Sul Ross; (713) 525-9400. African, Surrealist Modern, Paleolithic, some 10,000 items in hall of cypress.

Museum of Fine Arts. 1001 Bissonnet; (713) 639-7300. Frederic Remington, decorative, Pre-Columbian, Indian, almost everything else.

Museum of Natural Science. One Hermann Circle Dr.; (713) 639-4600. Dinosaurs, medicine, space travel artifacts, petroleum industry exhibits.

San Jacinto Monument and Museum. 3800 Park Rd. on TX 134, in suburb of La Porte, about 25 minutes from downtown Houston. Commemorates the victory of the Texas Revolution.

■ HUNTSVILLE (EAST TEXAS)

Sam Houston Memorial Museum Complex. 1836 Sam Houston Ave.; (409) 294-1832. Two homes where the Texas Independence leader lived, a restored blacksmith shop, memorabilia, including items captured from Mexican general Santa Anna. Souvenir shop.

Texas Prison Museum. 1113 12th St.; (409) 295-2155. Exhibits from penal history, including the electric chair formerly used in Texas; sales of convict craft items.

■ JEFFERSON (EAST TEXAS)

Freeman Plantation House. TX 49, about one mile (1.6 km) west of town; (903) 665-2320. Restored Greek Revival residence, circa 1850, once the center of cotton and sugar cane plantation. The oldest of a half-dozen antebellum mansions that offer public tours.

■ JOHNSON CITY (CENTRAL TEXAS)

Lyndon B. Johnson National Historic Park. Ninth and G; (210) 868-7128. The federal government operates two LBJ park sites out of its Johnson City office. One, in Johnson City, features the home where the future President spent his boyhood; the other, at the LBJ Ranch, west of town, shows the lifestyle he chose. The ranch, still a working operation, is accessible only by means of 90-minute bus tours that leave from the Johnson City site.

■ KERRVILLE (CENTRAL TEXAS)

Cowboy Artists of America Museum. 1550 Bandera Hwy.; (210) 896-2553. Run by an association of some two dozen sculptors and painters of the Western art school. Revolving exhibits.

■ KILGORE (EAST TEXAS)

East Texas Oil Museum. On Kilgore College Campus, U.S. 259 at Ross; (903) 983-8295. Reconstructed boom town from the East Texas oil field of the 1930s, movie with kinetic effects (the floor rattles and shakes as a gusher blows in).

Rangerette Showcase. On Kilgore College Campus, Broadway at Ross; (903) 983-8531. Precision dancing was brought to the gridiron in 1940 by this 53-member team, today drawn from across the country. Museum contains props and costumes, and shows a film about the group, which today makes guest appearances at professional games.

World's Richest Acre. Main at Commerce. Preserved oil rig, one of 24 that sat on the block during the 1930s oil boom, when a thousand wells were drilled in downtown Kilgore alone.

■ KILLEEN (CENTRAL TEXAS)

Fort Hood. Entrance on U.S. 190, just west of town; (817) 287-1110. Most areas of this 339-square mile (878-sq km) army base are open to the public. Two museums, of the First Cavalry Division and the Second Armored Division, recount the history of the base and its troops.

■ LUBBOCK (NORTH TEXAS)

Ranching Heritage Center. Fourth and Indiana; (806) 742-2498. 14-acre display of some 33 restored ranch buildings from across the state, including dugout, bunkhouse, schoolhouse, barn, four types of windmill. Indoor museum of ranching tools.

■ LUFKIN (EAST TEXAS)

Texas Forestry Museum. 1905 Atkinson Dr.; (409) 632-8733. Operated by the Texas Forestry Association, exhibits show the history of logging, sawmills, and the paper industry.

■ MIDLAND (WEST TEXAS)

Confederate Air Force. Midland International Airport, on Business U.S. 20, between Odessa and Midland; (915) 563-1000. More than 140 vintage World War II Allied and Axis aircraft, displays of nose art, uniforms, small arms.

Haley Memorial Library. 1805 W. Indiana at K St.; (915) 682-5785. Western and range life exhibits, the papers of historian J. Evetts Haley, author of *A Texan Looks at Lyndon*, important to the 1964 Republican Presidential campaign.

Permian Basin Petroleum Museum. 1500 I-20 W. at TX 349; (915) 683-4403. Exhibits covering almost everything that is known about geological formation, drilling, and refining.

■ NACOGDOCHES (EAST TEXAS)

Old Stone Fort Museum. On the campus of Stephen F. Austin University, Griffith and Clark; (409) 568-2408. Replica of 1779 fort, rebuilt with the same stones. Site was the headquarters of four premature revolutionary uprisings, and of the first newspaper published in Texas. Museum, period rooms, gun collection.

Sterne-Hoya Museum. Early pioneer house built in 1830 by German-Jewish immigrant Adolphus Sterne, known as the "financier of the Texas Revolution."

■ NEW BRAUNFELS (CENTRAL TEXAS)

Hummel Musuem. 199 Main Plaza; (800) 456-4866 or (210) 625-5636. An $8 million collection of drawings and paintings by Sister Maria Innocentia Hummel, after whose work the famous Hummel figurines are patterned.

Sophienburg Museum. 401 W. Coll; (210) 629-1572. The headquarters of the nineteenth-century Adelsverein, a German immigrant society, during the period when Prince Carl Von Solms-Braunfels was its Texas chief. Exhibits tell the story of German immigrants in the state.

■ ODESSA (WEST TEXAS)

Art Institute for the Permian Basin. On the campus of the University of Texas at the Permian Basin, 4909 E. University between E. Loop 338 and Parkway; (915) 368-7222. Regional and international exhibits.

Presidential Museum. 622 N. Lee at Seventh St.; (915) 332-7123. Campaign memorabilia, cartoons, and First Lady dolls in inaugural dresses.

■ PALESTINE (EAST TEXAS)

Museum for East Texas Culture. Crockett and Park; (903) 723-1914. A restored caboose, rooms devoted to railroading, home life, education. Located in a school building, circa 1914. Some rooms still empty.

Texas State Railroad Historical Park. Four miles (6 km) east of town on U.S. 84; (903) 683-2561. Operated by the Texas Department of Parks and Wildlife, restored steam locomotives pull passanger cars along a 26-mile (42-km) ride through pastures, pine, and hardwood forests. The outing takes just under three hours.

■ PECOS (WEST TEXAS)

West of the Pecos Museum. In the Old Orient Hotel, 20 E. First, at Cedar St.; (915) 445-5076. Artifacts from the Old West. Horse-drawn buggies, a gunfighter's grave.

■ PITTSBURG (EAST TEXAS)

Ezekial Airship Display. At Warwick's Restaurant, 142 Marshall; (903) 856-7881. Mock-up of pre-Wright Brothers-era aircraft built on suggestions from the Bible. The basis of state's claim to have invented flight.

■ PORT ISABEL (SOUTH TEXAS)

Port Isabel Lighthouse. TX 100 on mainland side of causeway; (210) 943-1172. From 1853 to 1905, a working lighthouse, restored in 1970 by the state of Texas. View of the coast from 53-foot observation tower.

■ QUANAH (NORTH TEXAS)

Medicine Mounds. About 10 miles (16 km) east of town on U.S. 287. Four cone-shaped hills that rise about 350 feet (106 m), with sacred significance to former Indian inhabitants of the region. On private property.

■ RIO HONDO (SOUTH TEXAS)

Texas Air Museum. One mile east of Rio Hondo; (210) 748-2112. Displays World War II fighter planes, including a Soviet YAK and two German Focke Wulf 190s.

■ SAN ANGELO (WEST TEXAS)

Fort Concho National Historic Landmark. 213 E Ave. D; (915) 657-2221. A military outpost during the era of wars with Texas Indians, opened 1867–1889. Sandstone and limestone construction, hewn by German immigrant craftsmen from Frederickburg. Many buildings restored, reconstructed, exhibits of Wild West and cavalry history.

Miss Hattie's Museum. 18 1/2 E. Concho; (915) 655-1166. A bordello from 1896 to 1946, when it was closed by the Texas Rangers. Restored, with original furnishings in its 10 bedrooms. Nominal fee for adults, but admission for children is free.

Producer's Livestock and Auction Company and Stockyards. 1131 N. Bell; (915) 653-3371. The nation's leading auction market for sheep, Tuesdays and Wednesdays; cattle sales on Thursdays and Fridays. Cafe.

■ SAN ANTONIO (SOUTH TEXAS)

Alamo. Alamo and Houston Sts.; (210) 225-1391. The shrine of Texas Independence, and the most-visited tourist stop in the state. The 1718-era main building was restored and remodeled by its operators, the Daughters of the Republic of Texas.

Hertzberg Circus Collection. 210 W. Market; (210) 299-7810. Circus memorabilia, miniature models, posters, costumes.

Institute of Texan Cultures. Durango at Bowie; (210) 558-2300. Permanent and revolving exhibits about nationality and cultural groups that make up Texas; gift shop, bookstore.

La Villita. Bounded by Alamo, Nueva and S. Presa, along the River; (210) 299-8610. Restored neighborhood of humble limestone and clapboard residences, today occupied by restaurants, gift shops, art galleries.

McNay Art Museum. 6000 N. New Braunfels; (210) 824-5368. El Greco, Gaugin, Dufy, Cézanne, Picasso, Van Gogh.

Mission Concepción. 807 Mission Rd.; (210) 229-5732.

Mission San José. 6539 San Jose; (210) 229-4770.

Mission San Juan. 9101 Graf; (210) 229-4770.

Mission San Francisco de la Espada. 10040 Espada; (210) 627-2021.

San Antonio Museum of Art. 200 W. Jones; (210) 829-7262. Pre-Columbian and modern Mexican folk art in a former brewery building, circa 1883. Includes Nelson Rockefeller's collection of Mexican toys.

Spanish Governor's Palace. 105 Military Plaza; (210) 224-0601. Built in 1749 for the Spanish governor of Texas. Period furnishings, garden patio.

Witte Memorial Museum. 3801 Broadway; (210) 829-7262. Natural science, history, anthropology, with an eye to children's fascinations. Located at an entrance to San Antonio Zoo and Brackenridge Park.

■ SNYDER (NORTH TEXAS)

Diamond M Foundation Museum. 907 25th St.; (915) 573-6311. Works by N. C. Wyeth, Peter Hurd, C. M. Russel, Frederic Remington, other modern and Western artists.

■ TEMPLE (CENTRAL TEXAS)

Czech Heritage Museum. 502 N. Main; (817) 773-1575. A museum to the nineteenth-century immigrant experience. Located in the SPJST Insurance Company Building; the SPJST is the Slovanská Podporující Jednota Statu Texas, or Slavonic Benevolent Order of the State of Texas.

■ TYLER (EAST TEXAS)

Battle of Neches Site. About 10 miles (16 km) northwest of Tyler on TX 64, then about 4 miles (6 km) north on County Rd. 4923; (214) 701-0074. These 70 acres, where the Texas Cherokee were massacred, bear only a simple historical marker. The American Indian Heritage Center in Dallas is purchasing the tract by selling $1 titles to square foot sections. Plans call for the construction of a museum and historical center.

■ UVALDE (SOUTH TEXAS)

Garner Museum. 104 W. North St.; (210) 278-5018. Located in the home of "Cactus Jack," John Nance Garner, Speaker of the House of Representatives, and Vice President during the first two terms of Franklin D. Roosevelt. Political memorabilia from the most prominent Texan before LBJ.

■ WACO (EAST TEXAS)

Masonic Grand Lodge Library and Museum. 715 Columbus; (817) 753-7395. Lodge paraphernalia, mementos of the Texas Revolution.
Texas Ranger Hall of Fame and Museum. Fort Fisher Park, Exit 335 B off I-35; (817) 745-1433. Dioramas, Winchesters, Colts, Wild West.

■ WAXAHACHIE (EAST TEXAS)

Walking Tour. Information at Chamber of Commerce, 102 YMCA Dr.; (214) 937-2390. About 200 buildings in downtown Waxahachie—some 20 percent of the Texas total—are listed in the National Register of Historic Places. The Chamber provides a map. The city's stock of Victorian homes and late nineteenth-century business buildings has made it an important filming location—the town appears in *Bonnie & Clyde* and *Places in the Heart,* among others.

■ WOODVILLE (EAST TEXAS)

Alabama-Coushatta Indian Reservation. About 15 miles (25 km) east of Livingston on U.S. 190; (800) 444-3507 or (409) 563-4391. Ceremonial dances every day during summer months, on weekends during spring and fall. Museum, crafts shop, restaurant.

■ PARKS AND WILDLIFE AREAS BY REGION

■ WEST TEXAS

Balmorhea State Recreation Area. About 35 miles (55 km) north of Fort Davis on TX 17; (915) 375-2370. The swimming hole of the desert. The **Solomon Springs** feed chilly, 72–76 degrees F (24–25° C) water into 1 3/4 acres of surface area, 30 feet (10 m) deep at some points. Some scuba diving allowed.

Big Bend National Park. At the southern terminus of U.S. 385 and TX 118, 40 miles (65 km) south of Marathon and 78 miles (125 km) south of Alpine; (915) 477-2251. 1100 squares miles (2800 sq km) of Chihuahuan desert, plains, and mountain areas, Rio Grande River. Camping, hiking, river rafting, birding. Sixty kinds of cactus, total plant inventory of 1,000 species, javelina and some 75 other mammals, 400 bird species. The biggest park in Texas. Never congested.

Guadalupe Mountains National Park. About 110 miles (175 km) east of El Paso on U.S. 62/180. Headquarters at (915) 828-3251. A day trip, because there are no lodging facilities in the park or on the road. The highest point in Texas, Guadalupe Peak, 8,749 feet (2,666 m) is inside its limits. Breezes are often so strong that as a warning, the state of Texas puts wind socks on highway signs. Inside the park, low-impact camping and 80 miles (130 km) of trails. Bring your own water: this is desert country, with no commercial amenities. The Texas madrone, a tree with a smooth, red-colored bark, is found in canyons of the park. Also porcupines, 14 species of bat, and in fall months, changing leaves.

Hueco Tanks State Park. About 30 miles (48 km) east and north of El Paso on U.S. 62/180 and FM 2775; (915) 857-1135. An area of huge boulders whose "huecos," or hollows, served as rain-water reservoirs as long as 10,000 years ago. Today, a jaunt for rock climbers, no pitons or bolts allowed. Among other attractions are some 5,000 Indian pictographs, 190 bird species, and 10 varieties of wildflower.

McDonald Observatory. About one mile (1.6 km) north of Fort Davis on TX 17, then 16 miles (26 km) northwest on TX 118, Spur 78, (915) 426-3640. Operated by the University of Texas, the site offers an absence of light pollution and dust, and cloudless Trans-Pecos nights. The Observatory's 107-inch telescope is open for public viewing one night a month, by reservation, and visitors may tour the facility any weekday. Plans call for a 360-inch reflecting scope in 1998.

Monohans Sandhills State Park. Park Rd. 41, about 25 miles (40 km) southwest of Odessa on I-20; (915) 943-2092. The Texas Sahara, dunes up to 70 feet (21 m) high, sand surfing.

Seminole Canyon State Historical Park. Park Rd. 67, 45 miles (72 km) west of the Del Rio on U.S. 90; (915) 292-4464. Indian pictographs, hiking, camping, and boat tours along the Pecos-Rio Grande rivers.

■ E A S T   T E X A S

Big Thicket National Preserve. Visitor center on FM 420, just off U.S. 69, north of Kountze; (409) 246-2337. Lumbering and other forms of commercial exploitation are forbidden in the Thicket, though hiking and canoeing are allowed, with permits. The Thicket's 140 square miles (360 sq km) are concentrated in a narrow, reverse L shape, in pockets here and there across the map of seven counties.

Caddo Lake. Marshall-Jefferson area; (903) 679-3351. The only natural lake in Texas. Small, 40 square miles (103 sq km), but lined with cypress trees and hanging Spanish moss. Primeval.

East Texas National Forests. The federal government operates four mixed-use forests in East Texas, areas in which both preservation and harvesting are managed. The forests occupy some 1,000 square miles (2,590 sq km). Camping, hiking and boating are permitted in parts of all four. The forests are: **Angelina,** 242 square miles (626 sq km), with offices in Lufkin, (409) 639-8620; **Davy Crockett,** 252 square miles (653 sq km), with offices in Crockett, (409) 831-2246; **Sabine,** 294 square miles (761 sq km), with offices in San Augustine, (409) 275-2632, **Sam Houston,** 251 square miles (650 sq km), with offices in Cleveland, (409) 592-6461.

Lake O' The Pines. TX 49 northwest to FM 729, west to lake; (903) 665-2336. 18,000-acre lake excellent for fishing, swimming, boating, and other water sports.

Lake Sam Rayburn. Nacogdoches-Lufkin area; (409) 634-6644. Boating, skiing, arguably the best bass fishing in Texas, 179 square miles (463 sq km) of water.

McFaddin Marsh National Wildlife Refuge. On TX 87 along the Gulf, about 10 miles (16 km) southwest of Port Arthur; (409) 267-3337. Marshland area is the winter refuge of up to 60,000 geese and 100,000 ducks. Alligators are permanent residents.

■ SOUTH TEXAS

Aransas National Wildlife Refuge. About 25 miles (40 km) north of Rockport on TX 35, then east on FM 774 to FM 2040; headquarters on south end of FM 2040; (512) 286-3559. Created by the Roosevelt administration as a waystation for the endangered whooping crane, whose survivors numbered 14. Today the winter home of the cranes, and some 300 other bird species, plus bats, feral hogs, and alligators.

Laguna Atascosa National Wildlife Refuge. About 25 miles (40 km) east of Raymondville on FM 106; (512) 748-3607, then north about two miles (3 km) to park headquarters. Seventy square miles (180 sq km) of what the Rio Grande Valley was like before agriculture. Hiking trails, armadillo, more than 350 bird species, and resacas, small crescent-shaped lakes formed by the receding of the Rio Grande.

Padre Island National Seashore. The 68-mile (109-km) northern end of a barrier island, about 120 miles (190 km) long, that runs from Brownsville to Corpus Christi, entrances on Park Rd. 22 at Corpus, Park Rd. 100 at Port Isabel; (512) 937-2621. Unspoiled beachfront, only five miles (8 km) of which are easily accessible by auto. Scant facilities. The southern end of Padre Island is developed, as is Mustang Island, to the north. The National Seashore occupies land adjacent to the King Ranch.

Sabal Palm Grove. About five miles (8 km) southeast of Brownsville off of FM 1419; (210) 541-8034. Operated by the National Audubon Society, preserve is home to the only native Texas palm, the *sabal texana,* and other rare fauna, as well as of the green jay and other bird species, plus jaguarundi.

Santa Ana National Wildlife Refuge. About seven and a half miles (12 km) south of Alamo on FM 907; (210) 787-3079. This 2,000-acre refuge receives chachalaca, other south-of-the-border bird species, is a habitat for ocelots and the Texas ebony. Tram rides, hiking trails, photo blinds.

■ N O R T H   T E X A S

Caprock Canyons State Park. Three miles (5 km) north of Quitaque on TX 86; (806) 455-1492. 14,000 acres of multi-colored canyons and breaks, 25 miles (40 km) of hiking/horseback trails, camping, fishing facilities. Views are spectacular.

Lake Arrowhead State Park. About 18 miles (29 km) southeast of Wichita Falls off U.S. 281 and north on FM 1954; (512) 528-2211 Oil derricks in the lake, but it's swimable.

Muleshore National Wildlife Refuge. About 20 miles (32 km) south of Muleshoe on TX 214; (806) 946-3341. Founded in 1935, the oldest national refuge in Texas, a wintering spot for sandhill cranes, permanent habitat of prairie dogs.

Palo Duro Canyon State Park. About 12 miles (19 km) east of Canyon via TX 217 and Park Road 5; (806) 488-2227. Some 25 square miles (65 sq km) of the massive JA Ranch have been turned into a state park, with amenities for visitors. Canyon walls in the area tower to more than 1,200 feet (365 m), in hues of red, pink, orange, and gray, with veins of white. The canyon was a Comanche refuge, and in 1874, the scene of their final Texas defeat. Train ride, horse rentals, camping, hiking.

■ C E N T R A L   T E X A S

Enchanted Rock State Natural Area. About 8 miles (13 km) north of Fredericksburg on Ranch Rd. 965; (210) 247-3903. Protrusion of round-top rock, about a mile (1.6 km) square, 500 feet (150 m) high, a feat for climbers. Spartan facilities, camping.

Garner State Park. Ten miles (16 km) north of Concan on U.S. 83 at Park Rd. 29; (210) 232-6132. Cabins, fishing, paddleboats, hiking, and camping on Frio River in Hill Country setting.

Lost Maples State Natural Area. About four miles (6 km) north of Vanderpool on FM 187; (512) 966-3413. More than 10 miles (16 km) of hiking trails, through Hill Country rich in maple, sycamore, oak, hackberry, and witch hazel trees. Leaves change late October to early November.

■ FESTIVALS AND RODEOS

■ JANUARY

Fort Worth. *Southwestern Exposition and Livestock Show and Rodeo.* Will Rogers Memorial Center, 3301 W. Lancaster; (817) 877-2400. Late January, early February. Judging and exhibitions of farm animals, from pigeons to horses to bulls, about 10 nights of rodeo performances, weekend matinees, country and western celebrity appearances. Nearly a million people attend.

■ FEBRUARY

Brownsville. *Charro Days.* Locations across Brownsville and Matamoros; (210) 546-3721. *Charreadas,* or rodeos on the original Mexican model. Locals wear colonial-era and turn-of-the-century garb; parades, pageants.

El Paso. *Southwestern Livestock Show and Rodeo.* El Paso County Coliseum, 4200 E. Paisano at Boone; (915) 532-1401. Parade, exhibits, country and western acts, competition.

Galveston. *Mardi Gras.* Various locations across the city. Two weeks of celebration, ending the Sunday before Ash Wednesday. Parades, floats, revelry, like New Orleans, not yet as grand.

Houston. *Houston Livestock Show and Rodeo.* At the Astrodome, Kirby and S. Loop 610; (713) 791-9000. Mid-February to mid-March. Parade, country and western acts, cowboys, and horses.

Laredo. *George Washington's Birthday Celebration.* Various locations in Laredo and Nuevo Laredo; (800) 292-2122 or (210) 722-9895. Ten days of parades, pageants, appearances by Mexican entertainers, carnival. In calmer times, for this big civic shindig, Mexicans were permitted to enter the United States without border crossing cards.

Odessa. *Shakespeare Festival.* Globe of the Great Southwest, on campus of Odessa College, 2308 Shakespeare Rd.; (915) 332-1586. Twelve days in mid-February to March. The venue is a replica of the Globe Theatre where the Bard's plays were originally produced. Trail rides to surrounding towns open the events. Carnival, western art exhibits.

■ MARCH

Alpine. *Cowboy Poetry Weekend.* On campus of Sul Ross State University, TX 90, eastern edge of town. Readings by cowboy-poets (some more cowboy, some more poet) from across the U.S. and Canada.

Austin. *South by Southwest Music and Media Conference.* 1000 E. 40th; (512) 467-7979. A privately organized showcase at several Austin nightclubs of mainly upcoming bands, usually some 500 of them—a must-see for music critics, talent recruiters.

Palestine. *Texas Dogwood Trails.* Headquartered in Redlands Bldg., 400 N. Queen; (903) 729-7275. Late March, early April. A tour of areas when dogwood is bloom, centered on the Davey Dogwood Park in Palestine, whose 400 acres include 5.1 miles (8.2 km) of auto and hiking trails.

Sweetwater. *Jaycees Rattlesnake Roundup.* Nolan County Coliseum, north end of Elm St.; (915) 235-5488. Hunters bag snakes on area ranches and bring them to the fairgrounds to milk them for venom (for medicinal uses), skin them, and fry their meat. Weekend-long festivities include Miss Snake Charmer Contest, awards for most and biggest Western diamondbacks caught. The biggest rattlesnake roundup in Texas.

■ **A P R I L**

Corpus Christi. *Buccaneer Days.* Locations across town; (512) 882-3242. Parades, regatta, beauty contest, carnival, balls.

Dallas. *Mesquite Championship Rodeo.* 118 Rodeo Dr., off the Military Parkway exit from I-635, in Mesquite, in the suburb of Mesquite, some 20 minutes from downtown Dallas; (214) 285-8777. Competition Friday and Saturday nights, April-September.

Fredericksburg. *Easter Fires Pageant.* Gillespie County Fairgrounds, three miles (5 km) south of town on TX 16; (210) 997-6523. A cast of 600 presents a story of Fredericksburg's origins, in which a mother convinces her children that signal fires lit by Comanches actually came from the Easter Bunny's kitchen while she was boiling eggs.

San Antonio. *Fiesta.* All over town; (210) 277-5191. The city's biggest blow-out, lasting 10 days. Street and river parades, dress balls, fireworks, mariachi serenades, *charreadas;* most events organized by Mardi Gras-style clubs, in commemoration of Texas independence.

■ **M A Y**

Fort Worth. *Van Cliburn International Piano Competition.* Tarrant County Convention Center, 1111 Houston; (817) 738-6536. In May or June, every four years. Next date: 1997. International competition, in honor of Fort Worth's resident Tchaikovsky competition winner (1958).

Kerrville. *Kerrville Folk Festival.* On TX 16, nine miles (15 km) south of town; (210) 257-3600. Late May, early June. An outdoor concert by up to 100 folk, blues, and folk-country artists, sometimes lasting three weeks; local and national talent. Folk mass on Sundays.

San Antonio. *Cinco de Mayo.* Market Square, 514 W. Commerce; (210) 299-8600. Weekend nearest May 5. Events centered on Market Square, but also spread across the city. Celebrations, parade with Mexican mariachi flair, in commemoration of Mexican independence from France.

■ JUNE

Crockett. *World's Championship Fiddler's Festival.* Crockett Civic Center, off Loop 304 E.; (409) 544-2359. A tradition for more than 50 years, with arts and crafts booths and food.

El Paso. *Viva El Paso!* McKelligon Canyon Amphitheatre, McKelligon Canyon off Alabama, about 20 minutes from downtown; (915) 565-6900. Amphitheatre presentation of regional history pageant, evenings during summer months.

Houston. *Juneteenth Blues Festival.* Location varies. (713) 520-3290. A celebration of June 19, 1865.

■ JULY

Brazosport. *Great Texas Mosquito Festival.* Clute Community Park; (409) 265-8392. A 25-foot-tall (7.6-m) statue of a mosquito, Willy Manchew, presides over a carnival, cookoffs, and among other events, a Mosquito Calling Contest. Bring repellent.

Fort Stockton. *Water Carnival.* At Comanche Springs pool, off Spring Dr.; (915) 336-2264. Synchronized swimming, other festivities around Olympic-sized Comanche Springs pool, in celebration of town's founding and its once-flowing springs.

Jacksonville. *Jacksonville Annual Rodeo.* Jacksonville Rodeo Arena, off College Ave.; (903) 586-2217. One of the larger regional rodeos, with evening events, country and western performers.

Paris. *Tour de Paris Bicycle Rally.* From Paris Junior College, 2400 Clarksville; (903) 784-2501. A part of the city's Bastille Day celebration, though Paris wasn't founded by Frenchmen; its original name was Pinhook. 100K, 70K, and 40K events for men and women.

Pecos. *West of the Pecos Rodeo.* Rodeo Arena. (915) 445-2406. A four-day celebration, surrounding the Fourth of July. A Golden Girl pageant, rodeo parades, and a wild cow milking contest, among other events.

■ AUGUST

Austin. *Aqua Fest.* Riverside and First; (512) 472-5664. Dates vary. Water and land parade, athletic events, nightly music, some name acts. The city's traditional festival.

Dalhart. *XIT Rodeo and Reunion.* Rita Blanca Park on FM 281; (806) 249-5646. Amateur rodeo and big barbecue, some six tons of meat; parade, antique car show, marathons.

Hereford. *All-Girl Rodeo.* Riders Club Arena, U.S. 60 on south side of town; (806) 364-3333. A national event for women, whose contests are ordinarily a sideline in rodeos. Bareback broncs, barrel racing, calf roping, even bull riding.

Port Isabel. *Texas International Fishing Tournament.* At South Point Marina; (210) 943-6452, early August. Competition in both bay and offshore categories, entry fee.

Wichita Falls. *Hotter 'n Hell Bicycle Race.* Memorial Stadium, Southwest Parkway and Burnett; (817) 692-2925. An important national event, with races from 10K (6 miles) to 100 miles (160 km), despite the 100-degree F (38° C) weather.

Wichita Falls. *Texas Ranch Roundup.* Mounted Patrol Arena, FM 369; (817) 692-9011, late August. Rodeos having become the sport of specialists, working cowboys have organized a meet of their own. Events include a race between horses that haven't been saddle broken.

■ SEPTEMBER

Denison. *U.S. National Aerobatic Championships.* Grayson County Airport, U.S. 75 south of town to FM 691, west to airport; (903) 465-1551. Sometimes held the first week of October. Nosedives, loops, and other aerial tricks, performed by about 100 competitors.

Lubbock. *Cowboy Symposium.* Civic Center, 1501 Sixth; (806) 767-2241. Story-telling, poetry, academic presentations, chuck wagon breakfast and barbecue. A gathering of Wild West buffs with a historical emphasis.

Lubbock. *South Plains Fair.* Fair Park, 105 E. Broadway; (806) 763-2833. Late September, early October. Week-long livestock shows, midway, country and western acts; an authentic regional fair.

New Braunfels. *Wurstfest.* Wurstfest Grounds, off Landa St.; (210) 625-9167. A 10-day beer blow-out begun some 30 years ago to celebrate sausage-making. More than 100,000 people two-step and tipple each year.

Tascosa. *Cal Farley's Boys Ranch Rodeo.* On U.S. 385, about 40 miles (65 km) south of Dalhart; (806) 372-2341. Even the younger boys participate in events like racing stick ponies. On the grounds of orphanage established in 1939 by a prize fighter.

■ OCTOBER

Dallas. *State Fair of Texas.* Fair Park, First St. and Parry; (214) 565-9931. Midway, musicals, agricultural and auto exhibits, kitchenware auctions. Permanent buildings, art deco style, erected for 1936 Texas Centennial. Some open year-round.

El Paso. *Sierra Del Cristo Rey Pilgrimage.* On the last Sunday in October, pilgrims visit a statue of Jesus dating from 1938, meant to be identical to the one overlooking Rio de Janeiro. The figure stands on a 4,756-foot (1450-m) peak just west of El Paso, where the boundaries of Texas, New Mexico, and the Mexican state of Chihuahua converge.

Lubbock. *Texas Tech Intercollegiate Rodeo.* Fair Park, 105 E. Broadway; (806) 742-3341. Late October, early November. Since 1950, the big event on the college rodeo circuit, with teams from a dozen Texas and New Mexico universities.

Tyler. *Texas Rose Festival.* Municipal Rose Garden Center Bldg. 1900 W. Front; (903) 592-1661. Usually, third weekend of October. Parade with rose-bearing floats, exhibit of some 120,000 cut roses, arts and craft show, beauty contest, dances.

■ N O V E M B E R

Amarillo. *National Old-Timers Rodeo.* Civic Center, Third and Buchanan; (806) 359-4777. Early November. The top 50 cowboys over the age of 40 square off in an annual meet sure to grow more popular as the national population ages.

Terlingua. *World Championship Chili Cookoff.* First weekend in November.

■ D E C E M B E R

Galveston. *Dickens on the Strand.* The Strand; (409) 765-7834. First weekend in December. Carolers, jugglers, mimes, bellringers, and choristers; locals and visitors in Victorian garb. Afternoon and evening promenade through the 12-block downtown Strand Historical District.

San Antonio. *Fiesta de las Luminarias.* River Walk. At Christmastime, the River Walk is lit up with candles in paper bags (or *luminarias*). Choirs carol from floating barges and trees are decorated with lights.

■ GOODS, SERVICES, AND FUN

■ A L P I N E (W E S T T E X A S)

Big Bend Saddlery. East Hwy. 90; (915) 837-5551. Saddles, cowboy tack, and for the city-bound, briefcases.

Ocotillo Enterprises. 205 N. Fifth St.; (915) 837-5353 or (800) 642-0427. Regional literature, maps, etc.

Woodward Agate Ranch. About 15 miles (25 km) south off TX 118; (915) 364-2271. Gift shop sells specimens of regional rocks, or for a fee, you can gather them on 4,000 acres of ranchland.

■ A M A R I L L O (N O R T H T E X A S)

American Quarter Horse Heritage Center and Museum. 2601 I-40 E.; (806) 376-5181. At the headquarters of the American Quarter Horse Association. Sculpture, videos, art museum, gift shop, arena for warm-weather demonstrations.

Cadillac Ranch. I-40 between Soncy and Hope Rd. exit, about five miles (8 km) west of Amarillo. Artists associated with empresario and reformed eccentric Stanley Marsh 3, who in the early 1970s stuck 10 junkyard-quality Caddies nose-down in the sand, creating a monument to—who knows what? The curious have been gaping ever since.

Western Stockyards. S. Manhattan and E. Third.; (806) 373-7464. Tuesdays are sale days. Ranchers buy and sell some 300,000 head of cattle in this traditional stockyard each year, amidst the hubbub of auctioneers' cries, slamming gates, and lowing. Visitors are welcome, but atmosphere is strictly *eau de vache.*

■ AUSTIN (CENTRAL TEXAS)

Barton Creek Greenbelt. Miles of hiking and biking trails starting at Barton Springs and heading west alongside Barton Creek.

Congress Avenue and Sixth Street. Bounded by Congress Ave., Sixth St., 11th St., and I-35. A district filled with restaurants and live music clubs, geared to pedestrian traffic. Victorian architecture.

Congress Avenue Bridge. (512) 327-9721. Bat spectacle every dusk between March and November.

Esther's Follies. 525 E. Sixth; (512) 320-0553. Austin's favorite comedy troupe plays here, new shows monthly.

Hill Country Flyer Steam Train Excursion. Pick up the train between Cedar Park and Burnet; (512) 477-8468. Tour the flower-covered Hill Country on a restored steam engine.

Zilker Park. 2100 Barton Springs Rd.; (512) 472-4914. This 400-acre park is home to **Barton Springs,** the 69-degree (22° C) water hole that is a symbol of the city.

■ BAY CITY (SOUTH TEXAS)

South Texas Project Visitors Center. About 20 miles (32 km) southwest of town on FM 521; (512) 972-5023. Exhibits concerning the South Texas Nuclear Project and nukes in general; telescope for viewing the nearby STNP plant.

■ BIG BEND AREA (WEST TEXAS)

River rafting tours:

Big Bend River Tours. Lajitas; (800) 545-4240.
Far Flung Adventures. Terlingua; (915) 371-2489.
Outback Expeditions. Terlingua; (915) 371-2490.

Horseback riding:

Lajitas Stables. Lajitas; (915) 424-3238.

SLACKER CITY: THE AUSTIN SCENE

These days Austin is well known for its subculture of "slackers." Since the success of Richard Linklater's 1991 film *Slacker,* made in Austin, the city has gained a reputation as a place where young, jobless people sit around all day and do nothing. This is far from the truth. In fact, the city is bursting with activity. A thriving music scene exists in Austin, and local bands enjoy tremendous support from the community, with large turnouts at shows and frequent airplay on the city's major radio stations. "South by Southwest," Austin's annual music showcase for unsigned bands, is becoming one of the largest of its kind nationally.

Austin has also become a center for alternative filmmaking, sort of an anti-Hollywood, with directors like Richard Linklater and Robert Rodriguez (*El Mariachi*) leading the pack. New shops, cafes, and nightclubs are opening up at such a rate that it can be hard to keep up at times. Finally, Austin is a university town, so while it has a reputation for being laid back that is certainly well deserved, it is far from being a community of dropouts.

Following are some hip Austin spots, for slackers and non-slackers:

Antone's. 2915 Guadalupe Street; (512) 474-5314.
World famous as a classic blues venue, Antone's is credited with playing a major role in Austin's musical boom of the '70s.

The Backyard. 1310 TX 71 West, Bee Cave; (512) 263-9707.
The best outdoor venue for live music in the Hill Country. Watch local and national acts—rock, country, folk, blues—under sheltering live oaks while enjoying gussied-up roadhouse fare.

Continental Club. 1315 South Congress Street; (512) 441-2444.
The place to see country bands with a hip edge, or hip bands with a country edge. Located about a mile south of downtown in a neighborhood packed with funky second hand stores.

Dry Creek Saloon. Mt. Bonnell Road; (512) 453-9244.
A good place to watch the sun set and enjoy longneck beers from an ancient fridge. Make sure to bring the bottles back to the bar, however, or suffer the wrath of the Dry Creek bartender.

Electric Lounge. 302 Bowie; (512) 476-3873.
Ironically, it burned down in an electrical fire in April 1994, but it's back, and cooler than ever. "Alternative" bands play nightly.

Emo's Austin Limited. 603 Red River; (512) 477-3667.

The epicenter of Austin punk. Always free. Some nights local bands like Jesus Christ Superfly or the Daddy Longheads play; other nights Emo's features traveling acts. Pool, pinball, the "best jukebox in Austin" (according to a 1994 readers' poll in the *Austin Chronicle*), and a nice patio area to hit on people with body piercings.

Flight Path Cafe. 5011 Duvall Street; (512) 458-4472.

Near the airport; planes fly directly overhead at intervals as they land, adding to the ambience of this retro, 50s/art deco spot. Attracts a young, artsy crowd.

Hole in the Wall. 2538 Guadalupe; (512) 472-5599.

Located across from the University of Texas on "the Drag," as Guadalupe in the UT area is called. Lives up to its name with a mellow atmosphere and dark, smoky rooms. Bands play in the front and six pool tables are located in the back.

Insomnia Cafe. 2222 Guadalupe Street; (512) 474-5730.

Open 24 hours, hence the name. Futuristic interior, with metal furniture that looks like it was made of recycled public-school desks, and menus on eight-foot tripods.

Les Amis Cafe. 504 West 24th; (512) 472-2746.

Near the university campus, this legendary bohemian cafe attracts a young, diverse crowd. There is outdoor seating available and a round fireplace inside for cold days.

The Little City Cafe. 916 Congress Avenue; (512) 476-2489.

Downtown, it attracts a mixed crowd of professionals and young hip things. On the upscale side, but not pretentious.

LoveJoys. 604 Neches; (512) 477-1268.

Off Sixth Street, this is a young, MTV Alternative Nation scene, gone slightly overboard on hip. Pool tables and almost every beer imaginable on tap, often at only $2 a pint.

Outhouse. 3710 Guadalupe; (512) 448-2336.

With its dirt parking lot, dark interior, and crowded, homey feel, this spot serves up great local music in a classic Austin setting.

Quackenbush's. 2121 Guadalupe; (512) 472-4477.

The cafe in the movie *Slacker,* this spot continues to live up to its reputation.

Waterloo Brewing Co. 401 Guadalupe Street; (512) 477-1836.

Home brew and food downstairs. The upstairs is a bar, with pool tables, darts, shuffleboard, and a jukebox.

—John Geraci, 1994

■ BRACKETVILLE (SOUTH TEXAS)

Alamo Village. Seven miles (11 km) north of town on FM 674; (210) 563-2580. A somewhat smaller-than-life replica of the real thing, built by Mexican artisans for the 1959 filming of the John Wayne film *The Alamo.* Sets for Western movies have been added, creating two downtowns where actors duel with blank ammunition.

■ BRENHAM (EAST TEXAS)

Blue Bell Creameries. Loop FM 377; (800) 327-8135 or (409) 836-7977. The state's most popular ice cream, since 1911. Tours every day except Sunday, gift shop.

St. Claire Monastery Miniature Horse Farm. TX 105 east of town, just past intersection with FM 2193; (409) 836-9652. The nuns raise waist-high horses that may be viewed and petted, afternoons, every day of the week.

■ BROWNSVILLE (SOUTH TEXAS)

Gladys Porter Zoo. Ringgold and Sixth; (210) 546-2177. Small, but reputable, this 31-acre zoo presents animals from five continents in near-natural settings, with no bars or cages. Gift shop.

■ CANTON (EAST TEXAS)

First Monday Trade Days. 1001 N. Trade Days Blvd.; (903) 567-2991. The largest flea market in Texas, 100 acres. The first Monday of every month, and over the weekend preceding it.

■ CANYON (NORTH TEXAS)

Texas! Pioneer Amphitheatre in Palo Duro Canyon State Park, about 12 miles (19 km) east of town on TX 217 and Park Rd. 5; (806) 655-2185, nightly, June through August. A cast of 80 re-enacts life in Texas from the 1880s in this somewhat romantic musical drama.

■ CLAUDE (NORTH TEXAS)

Cowboy Morning and Cowboy Evening. Figure 3 Ranch near Palo Duro Canyon; (800) 658-2613 or (806) 944-5562. A day-trip dining experience, by reservation only. Wagons take patrons from the ranch gates to a hearty, ranch-style breakfast or supper, with a view of the canyon. Roping and branding demonstrations afterwards.

■ COMFORT (CENTRAL TEXAS)

Little People Car Company. On High St.; (210) 995-2905. Manufactures and restores pedal cars—a pricey nostalgia item—in a former blacksmith shop.

■ CORPUS CHRISTI (SOUTH TEXAS)

The Flagship. People's Street T-head and Shoreline Blvd.; (512) 643-7128 and (512) 884-1693. Ninety-minute cruises of the bay and harbor on a mock Mississippi riverboat, evening cruises with live dance band, 400-passenger capacity.

Seawall. Along Corpus Christi beach. Wide top ideal for jogging, skateboarding, or walking. Pedal carts may be rented for a cruise along its 2.5-mile (4-km) course.

Texas State Aquarium. Corpus Christi beach; (800) 477-GULF or (512) 881-1300. A privately-owned 7.3-acre showplace. Marine life feedings, exhibits about aquatic life beneath offshore oil rigs, sharks in safe view.

■ CORSICANA (EAST TEXAS)

Collin Street Bakery. 401 W. Seventh St.; (903) 872-8111. Fruitcakes made from an 1896 recipe that calls for a pecan content of more than 25 percent. Most sales are by mail order, but the bakery welcomes drop-in business.

■ DALLAS (EAST TEXAS)

Country Connection. 2051 W. Northwest Hwy.; (214) 869-9923. A popular country dancing spot for the urban cowboy.

Dallas Farmer's Market. 1010 S. Pearl, east side of downtown; (214) 670-5879. Flowers, fresh produce.

Deep Ellum. North end of downtown, centering on Elm St. An area a dozen blocks square of nightclubs for all tastes. Formerly, a retail and night-life district in the city's African-American ghetto. Blind Lemon Jefferson played here.

Paletas Pinguino. 214 S. Llewellyn; (214) 942-4267. Icicle bars made with liberal quantities of mango, watermelon, papaya, other fruits. This company's vendors sell from push carts in Latino neighborhoods all over town.

Reunion Tower. 300 Reunion Blvd.; (214) 651-1234. Linked to Reunion Arena and Union Station (a former train depot) by tunnels. Restaurant and view from ball that sits atop the 50-story structure.

Six Flags Over Texas. 2201 Road to Six Flags, off I-30, in the suburb of Arlington, about 20 minutes west of Dallas; (817) 640-8900. Warner Bros. theme park.

Southfork Ranch. Off FM 2551, east of suburb of Plano, about 30 minutes from downtown Dallas; (214) 442-4868. Location for the former television serial "Dallas."

West End Historical District. Southwest side of downtown. This 20-block section, once a warehouse and garment district, is now occupied by restaurants, night clubs, souvenir shops.

■ DEL RIO (WEST TEXAS)

Val Verde Winery. On the Loop, 100 Qualia; (210) 775-9714. The oldest winery in Texas, founded in 1883 by an Italian immigrant whose descendants still run the place. Daily tours of winery and vineyards.

■ EL PASO (WEST TEXAS)

Sunland Park Racetrack. About five miles (8 km) west of downtown on I-10, just across the New Mexico line at the Sunland Park Exit; (505) 589-1131. Thoroughbred and quarter horses; afternoons, October through May.

Cowboy Boots. Partly because much of today's craftsmanship comes from Mexico, El Paso is a center of the cowboy boot industry. Outlet stores are: **Justin,** 7100 Gateway East, (915) 779-5465; **Tony Lama,** 7156 Gateway East, (915) 772-4327; **Lucchese,** 6601 Montana, (915) 778-8060; **Dan Post,** 40 Walter Jones, (915) 778-3066.

■ FALFURRIAS (SOUTH TEXAS)

Don Pedrito Jaramillo Shrine. Just north of town, FM 2191 east, then south about 50 yards (45 m) on FM 1418. The spot where the *curandero* lived, healed, and died. Souvenirs, grave.

■ FORT STOCKTON (WEST TEXAS)

Paisano Pete. U.S. 290 at Main St. Billed as "The World's Largest Roadrunner," a replica of the bird for children's amusement and photos.

Squawteat Peak. On I-10 between Fort Stockton and Bakersfield. It's privately owned, camping and hiking aren't allowed—but if you see this big hill while driving on I-10, you'll wonder what it's called.

■ FORT WORTH (WEST TEXAS)

Billy Bob's Texas. 2520 Rodeo Plaza; (817) 624-7117. Calls itself as the "World's Largest Honky-Tonk." Culturally, a successor to the defunct Gilley's Club (of *Saturday Night Fever* fame) in Houston's Pasadena suburb. Country and western acts, 42 bars, live bull riding on weekends.

Football—Fort Worth Cavalry. Tarrant County Convention Center, 1111 Houston; (817) 338-0101. Arena football, professional play on 50-yard field.

Justin Boot Company Factory Outlet. 717 W. Vickery; (817) 654-3101. Company headquarters, bare-bones prices. Boots and other leather goods.

Luskey's Western Wear. 101 Houston; (817) 335-5833. Western wear since 1919.

Stockyards Historic Area. N. Main; (817) 626-7921. Old stockyards, restored with an eye to tourism and a museum presenting the district's history. Restaurants, bars, galleries of

Western art, souvenirs. Parts of the stockyards still operate as always; cattle auctions are held on Mondays, open to the public.

Sundance Square. Bounded by W. 2nd, Houston, W. 4th, Commerce, downtown; (817) 390-8711. Early-twentieth-century district, restored for the tourist and leisure trade. Restaurants, boutiques, antique shops. Named for outlaws Butch Cassidy and the Sundance Kid, late denizens of Cowtown.

■ FREDRICKSBURG (CENTRAL TEXAS)

Haas Custom Handweaving. 242 E. Main St.; (210) 997-3175. Wool rugs, wall hangings, and German table linens.

Opa's Smoked Meats. 410 S. Washington; (210) 997-3358. Hickory-smoked sausages and other cuts of beef, pork, turkey; also by mail order.

■ GALVESTON (EAST TEXAS)

Fishing. Commercial piers at **Seawall Blvd. and 25th, 61st, and 90th streets,** free jetties at **10th, 17th, 30th, 37th, and 61st Sts.**

The Colonel. Pier 22, 22nd St.; (409) 763-4666. Reproduction of a nineteenth-century triple-deck stern-wheeler, 152 feet (46 m) long. Two-hour bay cruises daily during spring and summer months, weekends in fall and winter. Moonlight cruises for adults, 800-passenger capacity. Buffet, Dixieland band.

Colonel Bubbie's Strand and Surplus. 2202 Strand; (409) 762-7397. Genuine military gear from more than 50 nations, including caps, all-wool blankets, cooking kits, and gas masks; no functional firearms. The best source in Texas for non-lethal surplus.

■ HUNTSVILLE (EAST TEXAS)

Texas Berry Farm. Visitors pick blackberries, raspberries, and blueberries and pay by the pound.

■ HOUSTON (EAST TEXAS)

Galleria Shopping Center. 5075 Westheimer; (713) 621-1907.

Houston Ballet. Wortham Theater Center; (713) 227-2787.

Houston Grand Opera. Wortham Theater Center; (713) 227-2787.

Lyndon B. Johnson Space Center. NASA Rd. 1 exit off I-45 S., in suburb of Clear Lake; (713) 244-2100. Tours, audio, video exhibits, moon rocks, restaurant, gift shop.

Memorial Park. (713) 845-1000. Miles of lush trails for biking and hiking along Buffalo Bayou and leading into downtown.

Texas Air Aces. In Spring, 25 miles (40 km) north of downtown Houston; (713) 379-2237. Passengers stage combat in fighter planes. For Saturday missions call months in advance.

■ IRAAN (WEST TEXAS)

Fantasyland. U.S. 90. A block-sized city park with concrete statues of comic strip character Alley Oop, his girlfriend Ooola, and dinosaur Dinny. Illustrator V. T. Hamlin created the strip while living in Iraan, which is pronounced "Ira-Ann," after founders Ira and Ann Yates.

■ JACKSONVILLE (EAST TEXAS)

Love's Look Out. Five miles (8 km) north of Jacksonville on U.S. 69, picnicking and a horizon-to-horizon view of forested rolling hills.

■ JEFFERSON (EAST TEXAS)

Bayou Queen. At east end of Polk St. bridge over U.S. 59; (903) 665-2222. Leisurely boat rides along Big Cypress Bayou, mornings and afternoons.
Jefferson & Cypress Bayou Railroad. North end of Austin St., (903) 665-8400. Steam locomotive ride over century-old tracks along Cypress Bayou. Afternoons.

■ JUNCTION (CENTRAL TEXAS)

Y.O. Ranch. Entrance about 25 miles (40 km) south on U.S. 83; (210) 640-3227. The biggest and best-known of the Hill Country's dozens of dude ranches, also a summer camp. Longhorns and exotic African game, for camera shoots only; restored buildings, restaurant, daily tours as well.

■ KINGSVILLE (SOUTH TEXAS)

King Ranch. 2.5 miles (4 km) west of town on TX 141; (512) 592-8055. 1,300-square-mile (3370-sq-km) ranch offers 90-minute bus tours of the biggest spread in Texas.
King Ranch Saddle Shop. Sixth and Kleberg; (800) 282-5461 or (512) 595-5761. Saddles, tack, briefcases, and other leather goods made by hand in 1904 building.

■ LAREDO (SOUTH TEXAS)

Marti's. Victoria and Guerrero in Nuevo Laredo; 011-52-87-2-3137. Designer clothing, kitchenware, jewelry, the widest selection of quality Mexican artcrafts in northern Mexico.

■ LUBBOCK (NORTH TEXAS)

Llano Estacado Winery. About seven miles (11 km) southeast of Lubbock, on FM 1585; (806) 745-2258. The region's most famous winery, founded in 1976, tastings and tours, seven days a week.
Mackenzie State Park. Fourth and Ave. A; (806) 762-6418. Five hundred acres with picnicking and fishing facilities and a walled prairie dog town.

Walk of Fame. Eighth and Ave. Q. A series of bronze plaques to area musicians, outdoors at the Lubbock Civic Center, encircling a bronze statue of Buddy Holly, the rocker killed in a 1959 plane crash. Holly's grave, about 50 yards (45 m) inside the city cemetery on the east end of 34th St., is another stop for music pilgrims.

■ LUCKENBACH (CENTRAL TEXAS)

Luckenbach Dance Hall, General Store, etc. About six miles (10 km) east of Fredericksburg on U.S. 290, then six miles (10 km) south on FM 1376; (210) 977-3224. There's only one building around, sometimes with live music on weekends. If you remember the name, it's because of a forgettable song.

■ MULESHOE (NORTH TEXAS)

National Monument to Mules. Near juncture of U.S. 70 and 84. In 1965, the town's residents appealed for money to erect this monument, and received contributions even from a mule driver in the former Soviet Union.

■ NAVASOTA (EAST TEXAS)

Peaceable Kingdom School. About eight miles (12 km) west of town on TX 105; (409) 878-2353. An organic farm and commune, with classes in basketry, gardening, cooking; rustic accommodations for students. Tours.

■ NEW BRAUNFELS (CENTRAL TEXAS)

John Newcombe's Tennis Ranch. About three miles (5 km) west of town on TX 46; (210) 625-9105. Tennis camp for both youngsters and adults, 28 courts, mainly Aussie instructors; lodging in motel, condo, or cottage style.
Natural Bridge Caverns. About 17 miles (27 km) southwest of town, on FM 3009; (210) 651-6101. About a mile (1.6 km) of wet caverns, even an underground creek.

■ NEW YORK (EAST TEXAS)

New York (Texas) Cheesecake Outlet. On U.S. 175 some seven (11 km) miles southeast of Athens, at FM 804; (903) 675-2281. New York, which lies another seven miles (11 km) down FM 804, has a population of 12, but the name is enough to support this bakery and its goods.

■ NOCONA (NORTH TEXAS)

Nocona Boot Outlet. E. U.S. 82; (817) 825-3279. Boots made by the Nocona company, western wear.

■ **ODESSA (WEST TEXAS)**

World's Largest Jackrabbit. Eighth St. and Sam Houston. Six-foot-tall (2-m) fiberglass replica, a photo prop.

■ **PORT ARTHUR (EAST TEXAS)**

Queen of Peace Park. 801 9th St. Huge, painted concrete statue to the Virgin Mary, built by Vietnamese immigrants.

Rainbow Bridge. On TX 87 north of the city, connects Port Arthur and Orange. 177-foot clearance provides view of Sabine Lake.

Tex Ritter Park. 1500 Boston, in suburb of Nederland; (409) 722-0279. Mementos from the career of the lawyer who became a country singer. The small park also includes the **Windmill Museum,** a shrine to Dutch heritage, and **La Maison des Acadiens Museum,** concerning Cajun legacy.

■ **PORT ISABEL (SOUTH TEXAS)**

Le Mistral. 1250 Port Rd.; (800) 334-9489; (210) 943-7447. Gambling and the cruise experience on six-hour trips into the Gulf.

■ **POST (NORTH TEXAS)**

Algerita Art Center. 131 E. Main; (806) 495-4000. Works by members of the local artists guild, in a hotel built by C. W. Post, town founder and inventor of breakfast cereals.

■ **SAN ANGELO (WEST TEXAS)**

Bart Mann Originals. 105 S. Irving; (915) 653-2902. Jewelry made from pink pearls found in San Angelo's Concho River, about $50 and up.

■ **SAN ANTONIO (SOUTH TEXAS)**

Brackenridge Park. 3800 Broadway; (210) 821-3000. A 343-acre wooded park, includes Japanese Tea Garden—flowers and goldfish, with concrete fixtures styled to look like wood—aerial skyride, Witte Museum, zoo, miniature railroad. The city's most popular picnic site since 1899.

Buckhorn Hall of Horns, Fish and Feathers. 600 Lone Star Blvd.; (210) 270-9467. A collection of 3,500 stuffed game animals, fish, and fowl; antique firearms; a bar that serves free beer. In the Lone Star brewery.

Paseo del Rio Boats. Near Market Street Bridge, across from Hilton Palacio del Rio; (210) 222-1701. Leisurely rides along the river on 38-passenger motor barges.

River Walk. 35 entrances by stairway at bridges, south side of downtown; (210) 227-4262. Some 2.8 miles (4.5 km) of riverbank that the Depression-era WPA covered with sidewalks, now lined with restaurants and souvenir shops. Nearly five million tourists visit the River Walk each year.

San Antonio Zoo. In Brackenridge Park, 3800 Broadway; (210) 734-7188. Nearly 4,000 creatures from some 700 species in one of the best zoos in the nation, known for its natural and mock-natural settings. Bird collection, monkey island, rocky cliffs, moats, motorized transport for foot-weary walkers on these 70 acres.

Sea World of Texas. 16 miles (26 km) northwest of downtown, at 10500 Sea World Dr.; (210) 523-3611. Whales trained as aquatic acrobats, penguins in an environment with artificial snow, river rapids rides, dolphins, sea otters. 250 acres; gift shops, restaurants, country and western acts.

Segovia Mexican Candy Manufacturer. 1837 Guadalupe; (210) 225-2102. Retail sales of *leche quemada, cocadas,* other Mexican candies produced for the mass market.

Southwest Craft Center. 300 Augusta at Navarro; (210) 224-1848. Offering pottery, workworking, and weaving classes and exhibits in a Gothic-style former convent.

Tower of the Americas. E. Market and Bowie; (210) 299-8615. 750-foot (229-m) needle with revolving restaurant offers views as far away as the Hill Country.

■ SAN JUAN (SOUTH TEXAS)

Shrine of La Virgen de San Juan del Valle. San Juan exit off of U.S. 83; (210) 787-0033. A duplicate of an icon to the Virgin of San Juan, originally from the Guadalajara area, is at the center of this modern shrine, important to the life of migrant workers in the Rio Grande Valley. Holy water dispensed from hydrants.

■ SAN MARCOS (CENTRAL TEXAS)

Aquarena Springs. Just off I-35 at exit 206; (512) 396-8900. Half-hour rides in glass-bottomed boats, view of underwater flora, percolating springs, fish; 45-minute underwater show by divers, swimming pig.

Canoeing and Tubing along the San Marcos River. Three outlets offer canoes/inner tubes, shuttle service: **Amkon Canoe Company,** (512) 396-2894; **T.G. Canoes,** (512) 353-3946; **Lions Club Tube Rental,** (512) 392-8255.

■ SAN SABA (CENTRAL TEXAS)

Oliver Pecan, Inc. 1402 W. Wallace; (915) 372-5771. Native pecans, in the shell or shelled, by mail order.

■ SHELBYVILLE (EAST TEXAS)

The National Hall of Fame Cemetery of Foxhounds. On FM 2694 in Sabine National Forest, about one mile north (1.6 km) of Shelbyville. Granite gravestones with inscriptions like "Died like a Champion."

■ SHINER (SOUTH TEXAS)

Spoetzl Brewery. 603 E. Brewery; (512) 594-3852. This small brewery, established in 1909, produces Texas' most beloved beer. Though the brewery's formula is now similar to that of other beers, the label remains as a symbol of regionality. Tours, free beer.

■ SNYDER (NORTH TEXAS)

White Buffalo Statue. On courthouse square. A nineteenth-century hunter who claimed to have killed more than 20,000 buffalo also claimed to have killed an albino of the species near Snyder, one of two reported in the state; the monument commemorates that kill. Children are fascinated by the statue, despite the story of its origin.

■ SONORA (CENTRAL TEXAS)

Caverns of Sonora. About 15 miles (25 km) southwest of town, Caverns exit off I-10; (915) 387-2880. Nearly eight miles (12 km) of caves, described by a founder of the American Speological Society as "the most indescribably beautiful cavern in the world." Some 1.5 miles (2.4 km) are used for 90-minute tour.

■ TEXARKANA (EAST TEXAS)

Photographer's Island. On State Line Street, in front of the post office. Camera bugs set up here to photograph people straddling the Arkansas-Texas state line, which bifurcates the city's post office. The line is important in a daily life, too: Texarkana, Texas is "dry," while Texarkana, Arkansas is "wet."

■ TURKEY (NORTH TEXAS)

Bob Wills Museum. Sixth and Lyles; (806) 423-1253. Memorabilia from the King of Western Swing, a former barber in town. The museum is also headquarters for Bob Wills Day, the last weekend in April: remnants of his Texas Playboys perform, Old Fiddlers Contest, parade.

■ TYLER (EAST TEXAS)

Municipal Rose Garden. 1900 W. Front; (903) 531-1370. 14-acre park with some 30,000 rosebushes of 500 varieties; most bloom between May and October. Next door, the Rose Museum, with gowns and memorabilia from Rose Festivals.

■ UTOPIA (CENTRAL TEXAS)

Wagon Wheel Riding Stable. Five miles (8 km) north on FM 187; (512) 966-3678. Rents horses and saddles for rides in Lost Maples area.

■ WACO (EAST TEXAS)

Armstrong-Browning Library. On the Baylor University campus. Houses the world's largest collection of works by Robert and Elizabeth Barrett Browning.

Dr. Pepper Museum. 300 S. Fifth; (817) 757-1024. Birthplace of this soft drink, concocted in Waco in 1885. The museum is housed in the original bottling plant, which is listed on the National Register of Historic Places. Memorabilia, souvenirs.

Texas Masonic Grand Lodge. 715 Columbus Ave.; (817) 753-7395. The collection includes Stephen Austin's and Sam Houston's papers, Masonic memorabilia, and an exhibit devoted to U.S. Presidents who were Masons.

Texas Ranger Museum Hall of Fame. Rte. I-35 and University Parks Blvd.; (817) 754-1433. Features an extensive collection of antique pistols and wax figures of the Rangers.

Texas Sports Hall of Champions. Fort Fisher Park, U.S. 84 at 14th St.; (817) 756-6206. Memorabilia from professional as well as Texas high school athletes.

■ SPORTS

■ BASEBALL

Houston Astros. Astrodome, Kirby and S. Loop 610; (713) 799-9555.

Los Tecolotes. 2200 Santa Maria, Laredo; (210) 722-8143. A Mexican pro team, Los Tecolotes de los Dos Laredos, plays on both sides of the Rio Grande.

Midland Angels. A farm team for the California Angels, April through August, evening games, 4500 N. Lamesa Rd., at north end of Hogan Park; (915) 683-4251.

San Antonio Missions. Municipal Stadium, Callahan Exit off of U.S. 90W; (210) 675-7275. A farm club for the Los Angeles Dodgers.

Texas Rangers. The Ballpark In Arlington, Collins St. Exit from I-30, in the suburb of Arlington, about 20 minutes from downtown Dallas; (817) 273-5100.

■ BASKETBALL

Dallas Mavericks. Reunion Arena, 777 Sports St.; (214) 939-2712.

Houston Rockets. The Summit, Southwest Freeway at Edloe; (713) 627-2115.

San Antonio Spurs. Alamodome, I-37 at Market; (210) 207-3663.

■ FOOTBALL

Dallas Cowboys. Texas Stadium, 2401 E. Airport Freeway, in the suburb of Irving, about 15 minutes from downtown Dallas; (214) 438-7676. A NFC team.

Houston Oilers. Astrodome, Kirby and S. Loop 610; (713) 797-1000. An AFC team.

■ HOCKEY

Dallas Stars. Reunion Arena, downtown at 777 Sports St.; (214) 712-2890.

■ POLO

Midland Polo Club. N. Garfield north of Loop 250; (915) 683-2272. Matches on Saturday and Sunday afternoons, some weekday afternoons, April to November.

■ SOCCER

Houston Hotshots. The Summit, 10 Greenway Plaza; (713) 468-5100.
Dallas Sidekicks. Reunion Arena, 777 Sports St.; (214) 653-0200.

■ INFORMATION

■ ANTHONY

Texas Visitor Center. On I-10, about 20 miles (32 km) west of El Paso, at the New Mexico state line; (915) 886-3468.

■ AUSTIN

Austin Convention and Visitor's Bureau. Austin Convention Center, 201 E. Second; (800) 888-8287 or (512) 478-0098.

■ CORPUS CHRISTI

Corpus Christi Area Convention and Tourist Bureau. 1201 N. Shoreline; (800) 678-6232 or (512) 882-5603.

■ DALLAS

Dallas Convention and Visitors Bureau. 1201 Elm St.; (214) 746-6600.
Visitors Information Center, 603 Munger; (214) 880-0405.

■ EL PASO

El Paso Tourist Information Center. Civic Center Plaza, I-10 E. and Avenue of the Americas; (800) 354-6024 or (915) 534-0653.
Mexico Tourist Information Center, also in the Civic Center Plaza; (915) 534-0533.

■ FORT WORTH

Fort Worth Convention and Visitors Bureau. 415 Throckmorton; (800) 433-5747; (817) 336-8791.

Fort Worth Visitor Information Center. E. Exchange, across from the Livestock Exchange Building; (817) 624-4741.

■ GALVESTON

Galveston Island Convention and Visitors Bureau. 2106 Seawall; (800) 351-4236; (409) 763-4311.

The Strand Visitors Center. 2016 Strand; (409) 765-7834. Provides map for a walking tour of historic homes, other sites.

■ HOUSTON

Greater Houston Convention and Visitors Bureau. 801 Congress; (800) 231-7799 or (713) 327-3100.

■ LAREDO

Laredo Convention and Visitors Bureau. 2310 San Bernardo; (800) 292-2122 or (210) 722-9895.

■ RIO GRANDE VALLEY

Rio Grande Valley Chamber of Commerce. U.S. 83 at Airport Dr., Weslaco; (210) 968-3141.

■ SAN ANTONIO

San Antonio Chamber of Commerce. 602 W. Commerce; (210) 229-2100.
San Antonio Convention and Visitors Bureau. 121 Alamo Plaza; (800) 447-3372 or (210) 270-8700.
San Antonio River Association. 211 Broadway; (210) 227-4262.
Visitor Information Center. 317 Alamo Plaza; (210) 299-8155.

■ SOUTH PADRE ISLAND

South Padre Island Tourist Bureau. 600 Padre Blvd.; (800) 343-2368 or (512) 761-6433.

RECOMMENDED READING

■ HISTORY

Acuna, Rodolfo. *Occupied America.* New York: Harper & Row, 1981. A Latino view of Texas and the Southwest. The heroes of the Alamo are not heroes in this book, written in 1972.

Carter, Hodding. *The Doomed Road of Empire—The Spanish Trail of Conquest.* New York: McGraw-Hill Book Company, Inc., 1963. A volume in the American Trails Series, this book covers more than three centuries of conflict and drama of the Camino Real—the Royal Road.

Diaz, Bernal. *The Conquest of New Spain.* New York: Penguin, 1963. It's not possible to understand Texas without understanding Mexico, and this memoir of a soldier who accompanied Hernán Cortés is *the* primer in Mexican history. It is available in many editions by many publishers.

Fehrenbach, T. R. *Lone Star.* New York: Collier, 1985. A patrician and "Anglo" view of Texas history, circa 1968, in which the men at the Alamo really are heroes. Also author of *Fire and Blood.* New York: MacMillan, 1973. The encyclopedic Texas historian gives his pro-Texan take on the history of Mexico.

Horgan, Paul. *Great River: The Rio Grande in North American History.* New York: Rinehart & Company, 1954. In two volumes, the history of the river and the surrounding area (both U.S. and Mexico).

Long, Jeff. *Duel of Eagles.* New York: Wm Morrow, 1973. A history of the Battle of the Alamo.

Machann, Clinton, and James Mendl. *Krasna Amerika.* Austin: Eakin Press, 1983. The history of Czech settlement in Texas.

Montejano, David. *Anglos and Mexicans in the Making of Texas, 1836–1986.* Austin: University of Texas Press, 1987. The title says it all.

Paredes, Américo. *With a Pistol in His Hand.* Austin: University of Texas Press, 1973. The story of Gregorio Cortez, a fabled hero and/or bandit from the borderlands, a mythic figure whenever Anglo-Latino conflict is at hand.

Webb, Walter Prescott. *The Great Frontier.* Austin: University of Texas, 1979. The classic work of the 1951 "Turner thesis." It places Texas and the United States in a European context, compares frontier individualism with corporate culture. Also the author of *The Great Plains.* New York: Grosset & Dunlap, 1978. Written in 1931, this study puts the Plains and Texas in an American context. Water, Indians, and the cattle industry are its pivots.

Williams, John Hoyt. *Sam Houston: A Biography of the Father of Texas.* New York: Simon & Schuster, 1993. The story of one of the most colorful and legendary figures of American history. Houston defeated General Santa Anna at San Jacinto in 1836, winning Texas' independence from Mexico, then served as President of the Republic of Texas for most of its 10-year life. He went on to serve as congressman and governor of the state after its entry into the United States.

■ CULTURE

Eisen, Jonathan and Harold Straughn, eds. *Unknown Texas.* New York: Collier, 1988. A sampler of Texas culture, including fiction, by authors who are anything but unknown: Sam Houston, Davy Crockett, and General Santa Anna on the Texas Revolution. Also contributions by more contemporary famous Texans such as Dan Rather and Larry McMurtry.

Graham, Don. *Cowboys and Cadillacs.* Austin: Texas Monthly Press, 1983. A critical and sometimes funny review of the Texas that Hollywood has made.

Gregory, Joel. *Too Great a Temptation.* Fort Worth: Summit, 1994. Ostensibly the account of how the state's most promising preacher came to turn his back on the Baptist hierarchy, it's really an inside look at urban mega-churches, from the mechanics of deacons' boards to the details of pledge cards. "There are more Baptists in Texas than people," an adage says; Gregory shows how they maneuver.

Hoggart, Simon. *America—A User's Guide.* London: Collins, 1990. Very funny stories and comments about the United States, from the point of view of a Brit.

Richards, Ann, with Peter Knobler. *Straight from the Heart.* New York: Simon & Schuster, 1989. Governor from 1990–1994, Ann Richards became an important player in national politics and one of the most visible women in the Democratic Party. This is her story, from her beginnings in Lakeview, Texas, to her campaign in the 1990 Texas gubernatorial race.

Schutze, Jim. *The Accommodation.* Seaucus, NJ: Citadel, 1986. Forget what you've seen in movies and on the TV serial, this account reveals how Dallas is ruled.

Swindle, Howard. *Deliberate Indifference.* New York: Viking, 1994. An award-winning report on the death of an African-American in the custody of East Texas police. Catalogued in the true crime sections of libraries, it belongs on social commentary shelves.

■ FICTION

Ferber, Edna. *Giant*. Garden City, New York: Doubleday & Company, Inc., 1952. The story of a ranching family and the oil wildcatting that eventually superseded the cattle ranching industry.

Grey, Zane. *West of the Pecos*. New York: Black's Readers Service, 1937. The quintessential Western writer, Grey has written dozens of novels about the West. This one focuses on a young women who must pose as a man to survive in the Trans-Pecos.

McCarthy, Cormac. *All the Pretty Horses*. New York: Alfred A. Knopf, Inc., 1992. A coming-of-age story about a boy who leaves his Texas ranch home on horseback and goes to Mexico.

McMurtry, Larry. *The Last Picture Show*. New York: Penguin Books, 1966. A love story set in a small Texas town. Made into the 1971 Peter Bogdanovich film starring Cybill Shepherd, Beau Bridges, and Cloris Leachman. Also author of *Lonesome Dove*. New York: Simon & Schuster, 1985. Set in the late nineteenth century, this is the story of a cattle drive from Texas to Montana. Part love story, part adventure, part Western. An American epic.

■ GUIDES

Byrne-Dodge, Teresa. *Zagat Houston Restaurant Survey*. New York: Zagat Survey, 1994.

Cummings, Joe. *Texas Handbook*. Chico, CA: Moon Publications, 1992.

Hicks, Michael. *How to Be Texan*. Austin: Texas Monthly Press, 1981. A witty guide to the pop culture of Texas. Pickups, gimme caps, chile peppers explained.

Rafferty, Robert R., ed. *The Texas Monthly Guidebook*. Houston: Gulf, 1993.

Ruggles, Ron, and Susan Safronoff, eds. *Zagat Dallas and Fort Worth Restaurant Survey*. New York: Zagat Survey, 1994.

Simpson, Benny J. *A Field Guide to Texas Trees*. Houston: Gulf, 1988. Classifications, maps, and photos of flora, nonessential in other regions, maybe, but a must for viewing East Texas.

Texas Highways. Austin. Patterned after *Arizona Highways*, this monthly covers civic festivals, is chock-full of bluebonnet, mansion, and mockingbird pix. The postcard as magazine.

The WPA *Guide to Texas.* Austin: Texas Monthly Press, 1986. This tome shows what Texas was in 1940, when it was written. It provides a good gee-whiz view for both contemporary visitors and natives.

Zelade, Richard. *Hill Country.* Houston: Gulf, 1987. An architectural, historical, and dining guide to the area of Texas that presently enjoys the most cachet. No small town or out-of-the-way wonder is overlooked.

I N D E X

COMPASS AMERICAN GUIDES

Comprehensive, literate, and beautifully illustrated guides to the individual cities and states of the United States and Canada, Compass American Guides are unparalleled in their cultural, historical, and informational scope. They are to the 1990s what the WPA guidebook series was to the 1930s — insightful, resourceful, and entertaining.

"Each [Compass American Guide] pairs an accomplished photographer with a writer native to the state. The resulting pictures and words have such an impact I constantly had to remind myself I was reading a travel guide."

— National Geographic Traveler

"You can read [a Compass American Guide] for information and come away entertained. Or you can read it for entertainment and come away informed . . . an informational jackpot."

—Houston Chronicle

"Wickedly stylish writing!"

—Chicago Sun-Times

Compass American Guides are available in general and travel bookstores, or may be ordered directly by calling 1-800-733-3000; or by sending a check or money order, including the cost of shipping and handling, payable to: Random House, Inc. 400 Hahn Road, Westminster, Maryland 21157. Books are shipped by USPS Book Rate (allow 30 days for delivery): $2.00 for the 1st book, $0.50 for each additional book. Applicable sales tax will be charged. All prices are subject to change. Or ask your bookseller to order for you.

"Books can make thoughtful (and sometimes even thought-provoking) gifts for incentive travel winners or convention attendees. A new series of guidebooks published by Compass American Guides is right on the mark." —Successful Meetings magazine

Consider Compass American Guides as gifts or incentives for VIP's, employees, clients, customers, convention and meeting attendees, friends and others. Compass American Guides are available at special discounts for bulk purchases (100 copies or more) for sales promotions or premiums. Special editions, including personalized covers, excerpts of existing guides, and corporate imprints, can be created in large quantities for special needs. For more information, write to Special Marketing, Fodor's Travel Publications, 201 E. 50th St., New York, NY 10022; or call 800/800-3246. Inquiries from the United Kingdom should be sent to Fodor's Travel Publications, 20 Vauxhall Bridge Rd., London, England SW1V 2SA.

COMPASS AMERICAN GUIDES

Critics, Booksellers, and Travelers All Agree You're Lost Without a Compass.

"This splendid series provides exactly the sort of historical and cultural detail about North American destinations that curious minded travelers need... they offer good maps, beautiful color photography and — far more importantly — a strong historical and cultural perspective."
— *Washington Post*

"Use them not only to plan your trip, but to savor the memories once you're back home."
— *Mademoiselle*

"Highly evocative... the chapter on food forced me to stop reading and go eat."
—*New York Times*

"Compass Guides capture the true spirit of a place from its early settler days to modern times."
— *America Online*

Arizona (2nd Edition)
1-878-86732-6
$16.95 ($21.50 Can)

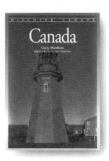

Canada (1st Edition)
1-878-86712-1
$14.95 ($19.95 Can)

Chicago (1st Edition)
1-878-86728-8
$16.95 ($21.50 Can)

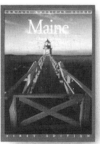

Maine (1st Edition)
1-878-86751-2
$16.95 ($22.95 Can)

Manhattan (1st Edition)
1-878-86737-7
$17.95 ($25.00 Can)

Montana (2nd Edition)
1-878-86743-1
$17.95 ($25.00 Can)

South Carolina (1st Edition)
1-878-86766-0
$16.95 ($23.50 Can)

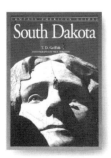

South Dakota (1st Edition)
1-878-86726-1
$16.95 ($22.95 Can)

Utah (2nd Edition)
1-878-86731-8
$16.95 ($22.95 Can)

Colorado (2nd Edition)
1-878-86735-0
$16.95 ($21.50 Can)

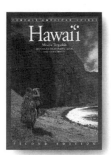

Hawaii (2nd Edition)
1-878-86769-5
$17.95 ($25.00 Can)

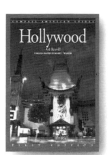

Hollywood (2nd Edition)
1-878-86771-7
$16.95 ($23.50 Can)

Las Vegas (3rd Edition)
1-878-86736-9
$16.95 ($22.50 Can)

New Mexico (1st Edition)
1-878-86706-7
$15.95 ($19.95 Can)

New Orleans (1st Edition)
1-878-86739-3
$16.95 ($21.50 Can)

Oregon (1st Edition)
1-878-86733-4
$16.95 ($21.50 Can)

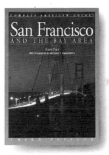

San Francisco (3rd Edition)
1-878-86770-9
$16.95 ($23.50 Can)

Virginia (1st Edition)
1-878-86741-5
$16.95 ($22.95 Can)

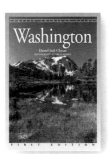

Washington (1st Edition)
1-878-86758-X
$17.95 ($25.00 Can)

Wisconsin (1st Edition)
1-878-86744-X
$16.95 ($22.95 Can)

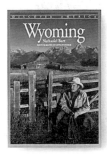

Wyoming (2nd Edition)
1-878-86750-4
$17.95 ($25.00 Can)

ABOUT THE AUTHOR

Dick Reavis is a Texas writer who began his career as a journalist with the *Moore County News* in the Panhandle town of Dumas, where he covered everything from stock shows to the wheat harvest to courthouse news. Between 1977 and 1990 he worked in various capacities as a writer for *Texas Monthly*, and in 1987 he drove every road on the state highway department map of Texas (or 72,000 miles) as the basis of his *Texas Monthly* column, "National Tour of Texas." Reavis is the author of *Conversations with Moctezuma*, published in 1990 by William Morrow, and of an upcoming book to be published with Simon & Schuster describing events that occurred at Mt. Carmel in Waco in 1993.

ABOUT THE PHOTOGRAPHER

Will van Overbeek lives in Austin, Texas. His first major project was a photo documentary book entitled *AGGIES: Life in the Corps of Cadets at Texas A&M*. His photography has been published in numerous magazines, including *Smithsonian, Travel Holiday, Texas Monthly, Forbes, Fortune,* and *Texas Highways*. Mr. van Overbeek's work has won juried competitions and been honored by inclusion in the photo annuals of *Communication Arts, American Photography,* and *Graphis*.